Greg Perry

SAMS
Teach Yourself

D1364357

Microsoft® Office 2000

in 24 Hours

SAMS

A Division of Macmillan Computer Publishing
201 West 103rd St., Indianapolis, Indiana, 46290 USA

Sams Teach Yourself Microsoft® Office 2000 in 24 Hours

Copyright © 1999 by Sams Publishing

International Standard Book Number: 0-672-31439-8

Library of Congress Catalog Card Number: 98-87000

Printed in the United States of America

First Printing: May 1999

01   00   99   4   3   2   1

Trademarks

Warning and Disclaimer

EXECUTIVE EDITOR
Angie Wethington

ACQUISITIONS EDITOR
Stephanie McComb

DEVELOPMENT EDITOR
Ben Milstead

MANAGING EDITOR
Tom Hayes

PROJECT EDITOR
Damon Jordan

Copy Editor
Keith Cline

Proofreader
Debra Neel

Indexer
Chris Wilcox

Technical Editor
Kyle Bryant

PAGE LAYOUT
Cyndi Davis-Hubler

Overview

Contents

About the Author

Greg Perry is a speaker and a writer on both the programming and the application sides of computing. He is known for his skills at bringing advanced computer topics to the novice's level. Perry has been a programmer and a trainer since the early 1980s. He received his first degree in computer science and a master's degree in corporate finance. Perry has sold more than 1.5 million computer books, including such titles as *Sams Teach Yourself Windows 98 in 24 Hours*, *Absolute Beginner's Guide to C*, and *Sams Teach Yourself Visual Basic 6 in 21 Days*. He also writes about rental property management and loves to travel. His favorite place to be when away from home is either at New York's Patsy's or in Italy because he enjoys only the best pasta!

Acknowledgments

Once again, I'm thanking Mr. Dean Miller for providing me with this writing opportunity. Dean, you must have been desperate for an author when you chose me! I now know, however, from firsthand knowledge, that you are a better husband to Fran and father to your kids than you are an editor. That's the best compliment any man can get and it's well-deserved.

The people at Macmillan Computer Publishing all take their jobs seriously. They want readers to have the best books possible. They accomplish that goal. Among the MCP editors and staff who produced this book, I want to send special thanks to Stephanie McComb who nurtured this book. Ben Milstead and Kyle Bryant honed my writing and turned a mediocre manuscript into one we can be proud of. Damon Jordan and Keith Cline also added their excellent editing skills to my work. To each of them I am most grateful.

Although they did not have a direct hand in this book, I must thank MCP's two most outstanding members, Rosemarie Graham and Grace Buechline. Rosemarie and Grace are friends I made when working on previous books, and I want them to know I appreciate the jobs they do.

My lovely and gracious bride stands by my side night and day. Thank you once again. You, precious Jayne, are everything that matters to me on earth. The best parents in the world, Glen and Bettye Perry, continue to encourage and support me in every way. I am who I am because of both of them.

—Greg Perry

Tell Us What You Think!

As the reader of this book, *you* are our most important critic and commentator. We value your opinion and want to know what we're doing right, what we could do better, what areas you'd like to see us publish in, and any other words of wisdom you're willing to pass our way.

As the Executive Editor for the General Desktop Applications team at Macmillan Computer Publishing, I welcome your comments. You can fax, email, or write me directly to let me know what you did or didn't like about this book—as well as what we can do to make our books stronger.

Please note that I cannot help you with technical problems related to the topic of this book, and that due to the high volume of mail I receive, I might not be able to reply to every message.

When you write, please be sure to include this book's title and author, as well as your name and phone or fax number. I will carefully review your comments and share them with the author and editors who worked on the book.

Fax: 317-581-4770
Email: `office_sams@mcp.com`
Mail: Angie Wethington
Executive Editor
General Desktop Applications
Macmillan Computer Publishing
201 West 103rd Street
Indianapolis, IN 46290
USA

Introduction

Microsoft Corporation's Office products have an installed base of more than 20 million licensed users. More than 90 percent of the Fortune 500 companies use Microsoft Office. When developing Office 2000, Microsoft conducted thousands of hours of customer research and beta testing. Based on that research and user feedback, Microsoft designed Office 2000 to be more user friendly as well as more integrated among applications and the Internet. You won't regret your decision to learn and use Office 2000. With the Office 2000 skills that you master in these 24 lessons, you will know the most popular application software on earth.

You probably are anxious to get started with your 24-hour Office 2000 tutorial. Take just a few preliminary moments to acquaint yourself with the design of this book, as described in the next few sections.

Who Should Read This Book?

This book is for both beginning and advanced Office 2000 users. Readers rarely believe that lofty claim (and for good reason), but the design of this book and the nature of Office 2000 make it possible for this book to address such a wide audience. Here is why: Office 2000 is a major improvement over the previous Office products.

Readers unfamiliar with the Windows-style of windowed environments will find plenty of introductory help here that brings them quickly up to speed. This book teaches you how to start and exit Office 2000 as well as how to manage many of the Internet-based Office 2000 elements that you need to use Office 2000 in today's online world. If you are new to the Internet, this book helps you get started and shows how to make the most of the Internet and Office 2000. This book talks to beginners without talking down to them.

This book also addresses those who presently use a Microsoft Office product. Here is how: Step-Up sidebars contained in this book explain how a specific Office 2000 feature improves on or replaces a previous Office feature. With your fundamental Office understanding, you will appreciate the new features and added power of Office 2000. Keep in mind that Office 2000 is similar to previous Office versions but includes plenty of new features, improvements, and Web-based add-ons to keep Office gurus intrigued for a long time. This book teaches the Office 2000 Professional Edition, the edition that includes all the Office 2000 products and the one that sells the best.

What This Book Does for You

Although this book is not a complicated reference book, you learn almost every aspect of Office 2000 from the user's point of view. Office 2000 includes many advanced technical details that most users never need, and this book does not waste your time with those. You want to get up to speed with Office 2000 in 24 hours, and this book helps you fulfill that goal.

Those of you who are tired of the plethora of quick-fix computer titles cluttering today's shelves will find a welcome reprieve here. This book presents both the background and descriptions that a new Office 2000 user needs. In addition to the background, this book is practical and provides more than 100 step-by-step tasks that you can work through to gain practical hands-on experience. The tasks guide you though all the common Office 2000 actions you need to make Office 2000 work for you.

Can This Book Really Teach Office 2000 in 24 Hours?

Yes. You can master each chapter in one hour. (By the way, chapters are referred to as *hours* in the rest of this book.) The material is balanced with mountains of tips, shortcuts, and methods that make your hours productive and hone your Office 2000 skills.

Conventions Used in This Book

Each hour ends with a question-and-answer session that addresses some of the most frequently asked questions about that hour's topic.

This book uses several common conventions to help teach the Office 2000 topics. Here is a summary of those typographical conventions:

- Commands, computer output, and words you type appear in a special monospaced computer font.
- To type a shortcut key, such as Alt+F, press and hold the first key, and then press the second key before releasing both keys.
- If a task requires you to select from a menu, the book separates menu commands with a comma. For example, File, Save As is used to select the Save As option from the File menu. All menus in this book are shown in full even though Office 2000 users can elect to display only menu options they use most.

In addition to typographical conventions, the following special elements are included to set off different types of information to make them easily recognizable:

Special notes augment the material you read in each hour. These notes clarify concepts and procedures.

You find numerous tips that offer shortcuts and solutions to common problems.

The warnings are about pitfalls. Reading them saves you time and trouble.

STEP-UP

Users of previous Office products, such as Office 97, advance quickly by reading the Step-Ups provided for them.

 Each hour contains new term definitions to explain important new terms. New term icons make those definitions easy to find.

PART I

What's New in Office 2000

Hour

HOUR 1

Getting Acquainted with Office 2000

Microsoft Office 2000 improves your work environment by offering integrated software tools that are powerful yet easy to learn and use. Offices large and small can use Office 2000-based applications for many of their day-to-day computer needs, as can home-based businesses and families who want simple but robust writing and analysis tools for their computer.

If you have used previous versions of Office, Office 2000 takes you to the next step by adding more products, automation, and Web-based tools than previous Office versions. Office 2000 automates many of your computing chores and provides products that work in unison by sharing data between them. This hour shows you how Office 2000 tackles many of the standard software requirements of today's offices.

The highlights of this hour include the following:

- What Office 2000 contains
- Which Office 2000 products you use for the various tasks
- When to use an Office 2000 product
- How Office 2000 complies with year 2000 dates
- What the document-centric concept means to all Office 2000 products

What's in Office 2000?

Office 2000 contains Microsoft's most powerful applications, such as Word and Excel, in a single package. The programs work well together now that Microsoft has combined them in the Office 2000 collection of programs. Program collections such as Office 2000 are often called a *suite of programs*. You can still purchase the Office programs individually, building a suite of products, but the Office 2000 package offers the best deal.

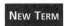 A *suite of programs* is a collection of programs that work well together and have a similar interface. The suite is often less expensive than purchasing each product separately.

The following is a quick overview of each Office 2000 program:

- Word 2000 is a word processor with which you can create notes, memos, letters, school papers, business documents, books, newsletters, and even Internet Web pages.

- Excel 2000 is an electronic worksheet program with which you can create charts, graphs, and worksheets for financial and other numeric data. After you enter your financial data, you can analyze it for forecasts, generate numerous what-if scenarios, and publish worksheets on the Web.

- PowerPoint 2000 is a presentation program with which you can create presentations for seminars, schools, churches, Web pages, and business meetings. Not only can PowerPoint 2000 create the presentation overheads, it can also create the speaker's presentation notes.

- Access 2000 is a database program with which you can organize data collections. No matter what kind or how much data you must organize, Access 2000 can analyze, sort, summarize, and report on that data. Your Web pages can reflect your latest data when you incorporate an Access 2000 database into your site.

- Publisher 2000 takes document publishing past the word processing stage into the publication arena. With Publisher 2000, you can easily combine graphics and text into multi-columned professional publications and put those publications on the Web.

- FrontPage 2000 enables you to create your own Web pages without having to learn tricky coding languages. With FrontPage 2000, you'll combine documents from the other Office 2000 products into a series of Web pages you can be proud of.

- Outlook 2000 is a personal information manager (*PIM*) that organizes your contact addresses, phone numbers, and other information in an address-book format. Use Outlook 2000 to track your appointments, schedule meetings, generate to-do lists, keep notes, manage all your Internet email, and keep a journal of your activities.

All the Office 2000 products share common features and common menu choices. Figure 1.1 shows the Word 2000 screen, for example, and Figure 1.2 shows the Excel 2000

screen. Both screens display the open File menu. As you can see, the two program interfaces look virtually identical even though the programs accomplish entirely different tasks.
Also, information created in one program can be inserted into another program. If you create a financial table with Excel 2000, for instance, you can put that table in a Publisher
2000 publication that you send to your Board of Directors and embed the table in a
PowerPoint 2000 presentation to stockholders. After you learn one program in the Office
2000 suite, you will be comfortable using all the others due to the common interface.

FIGURE 1.1.

The Word 2000 inter-
face behaves like that
of Excel 2000.

One of the most helpful features of Office 2000 is its ability to adjust menus
and toolbars to work the way you do. For example, Word 2000 does not display all menu commands on the File menu when you display the File menu.
Instead, Word 2000 displays only those commands you use most often. The
less often you use a menu option, the more likely Word 2000 will remove
that option from the initial menu that first appears. All of the commands
are there, however, so when you click the arrows at the bottom of a menu,
the menu expands to show all its commands. The Office 2000 products, thus,
attempt to keep your screen as free from clutter as possible. As you use
menus and toolbars, Office 2000 analyzes the menu options and buttons you
use most; those options and buttons you use infrequently will begin to go
away so that only your common choices remain. You can always access these
hidden menu options and toolbar buttons, but Office 2000 puts them out of
the way until you need them.

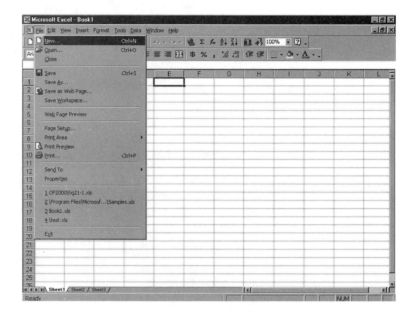

FIGURE 1.2.

The Excel 2000 inter-face behaves like that of Word 2000.

 This book always displays all menu options although your Office 2000 installation will show the shorter menus that reflect the options you use most.
You can show the full set of menu commands by selecting Tools, Customize,
Options and unchecking the option labeled Menus show recently used commands first.

The Office 2000 products are general purpose, meaning that you can customize applications to suit your needs. You can use Excel 2000 as your checkbook-balancing program,
for example, and as your company's interactive balance-sheet system.

You can integrate Office 2000 into your network system. This way, Office 2000 provides
useful features whether you are networked to an intranet, to the Internet, or to both. You
can share Office 2000 information with others across the network. Office 2000 continues
the trend began with Office 97, the previous Office version, by integrating Internet access
throughout the Office 2000 suite.

STEP-UP

If you've mastered some of the advanced programming techniques behind earlier versions of Office products, you will be glad to know that every program in the Office 2000

suite supports Visual Basic for Applications, often called Visual Basic, Microsoft's cross-program application programming language. Word 2000 does not support Word Basic (the programming language that Microsoft included with early versions of Word), however, because Word Basic is incompatible with other applications. Visual Basic for Applications, *VBA*, is fully compatible with Visual Basic 6, Microsoft's newest version of the programming language.

Introducing Word 2000

When you need to write any text-based document, look no further than Word. Word 2000 is a word processor that supports many features, including the following:

- Integrated grammar, spelling, and hyphenation tools (see Hour 5, "Managing Documents and Customizing Word 2000").

- Wizards and templates that create and format documents for you (see Hour 2, "Introducing Office 2000's Powerful Features").

- Automatic corrections for common mistakes as you type (see Hour 3, "Welcome to Word 2000") using special automatic-correcting tools that watch the way you work and adapt to your needs.

- Advanced formatting capabilities (see Hour 4, "Formatting with Word 2000")

- Numbering, bulleting, and shading tools (see Hour 4).

- Multiple document views so that you can see a rough draft of your document or the look of a final printed page as you write (see Hour 4).

- Drawing, border, and shading tools that enable you to emphasize headers, draw lines and shapes around your text, and work with imported art files (see Hour 21, "Office 2000's Synergy").

- Web-page development for Internet users so that they can turn their documents into Web pages (see Hour 23, "Creating Web Pages with Office 2000").

Figure 1.3 shows a Word 2000 editing session. The user is editing a business letter to send to a client.

FIGURE **1.3.**

*Word 2000 helps you
create, edit, and for-
mat letters.*

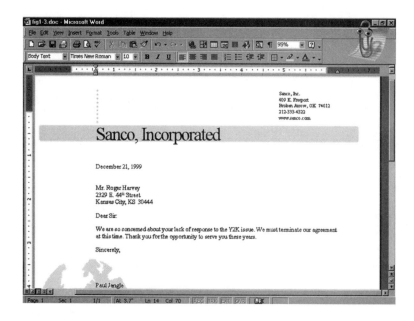

Introducing Excel 2000

Although Excel 2000 can be used for non-numeric worksheets, the primary goal for
Excel 2000 is to help you organize and manage financial information such as income
statements, balance sheets, and forecasts. Excel 2000 is an electronic worksheet program
that supports many features, including the following:

- Automatic cell formatting (see Hour 7, "Excel 2000 Workbooks").
- Worksheet proofing tools, such as spell checking (see Hour 8, "Using Excel 2000").
- Automatic row and column completion of value ranges with AutoFill (see Hour 8).
- Automatic worksheet formatting to turn your worksheets into professionally pro-
  duced reports (see Hour 10, "Formatting Worksheets to Look Great").
- Built-in functions, such as financial formulas, that automate common tasks (see
  Hour 9, "Editing Excel Worksheets").
- Powerful maps, charts, and graphs that can analyze your numbers and turn them
  into simple trends (see Hour 10).
- Automatic worksheet computations that enable you to generate multiple what-if
  scenarios and decide between different courses of action (see Hour 7).

Figure 1.4 shows an Excel 2000 editing session. The user is getting ready to enter
invoice information for a sale. As you can see, Excel 2000 can start with a predesigned
form. If you have worked with other worksheet programs, you might be surprised at how
fancy Excel 2000 can get. The wizards make creating advanced worksheets easy.

FIGURE 1.4.

Excel 2000 helps you create, edit, and format numeric worksheets.

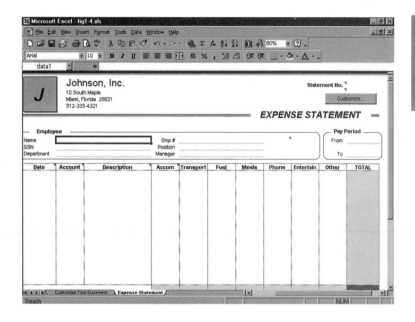

Introducing PowerPoint 2000

Before PowerPoint's original version, users had no way to generate presentations without making a tedious effort to design each color slide using some kind of graphics drawing program. Although presentation products similar to PowerPoint 2000 now exist, PowerPoint 2000 is recognized as a leader. PowerPoint 2000 supports many features, including the following:

- The capability to turn Word 2000 document outlines into presentation notes (see Hour 21).

- Automatic proofing tools such as spelling and hyphenation (see Hour 11, "PowerPoint 2000 Presentations").

- Sample slide and slide collection templates that provide you with a fill-in-the-blank presentation (see Hour 11).

- A slide projector that displays your presentation on your screen (see Hour 12, "Editing and Arranging Your Presentation").

- Complete color and font control of your presentation slides (see Hour 13, "PowerPoint 2000's Advanced Features").

- A collection of clip art files, icons, sounds, and animations that you can embed to make presentations come alive (see Hour 13).

- Numerous transitions and fades between presentation slides to keep your audience's attention (see Hour 13).

- The capability to save presentations as Web pages that you can then present on the Internet (see Hour 23).

Figure 1.5 shows a PowerPoint 2000 editing session. The user is getting ready for a presentation and has only a few minutes to prepare 10 color slides for the meeting. With PowerPoint 2000, a few minutes are more than enough time!

FIGURE 1.5.

PowerPoint 2000 helps you create, edit, and format presentations.

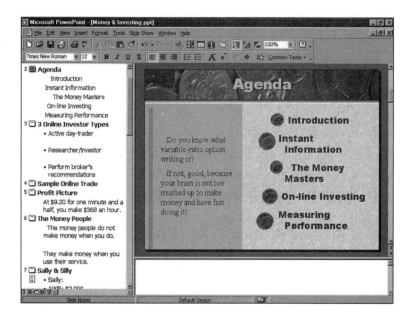

Introducing Access 2000

Access 2000 provides one of the most comprehensive relational database systems available today. If you want to organize large collections of data, such as customer and inventory records, Access 2000 makes your job simple. Access 2000 goes far beyond other databases in power and ease of use by supporting features that include the following:

- Simple table-creation wizards and data-entry tools that enable you to set up and enter database information easily (see Hour 17, "Access 2000 Basics").

- Report-generation that enables you to track and publish your data (see Hour 20, "Advanced Access 2000").

- Information retrieval query tools that enable you to quickly get to the data you need (see Hour 19, "Retrieving Your Data").

- Automatic proofing tools such as spelling and hyphenation of data (see Hour 18, "Entering and Displaying Access 2000 Data").

- The capability to filter data rows and columns so that you see only data you want to see (see Hour 19).

- Sorting of data by any value (see Hour 20).

- The capability to produce custom labels for any printer (see Hour 20).

- Complete relational database support to reduce data redundancies (see Hour 17).

- Automatic summary provisions such as totals, averages, and statistical variances (see Hour 20).

- The capability to save databases in Web pages so that Internet users can view your database's information (see Hour 23).

Figure 1.6 shows an Access 2000 editing session. The user is editing employee records. Notice that Access 2000 accepts and tracks all kinds of data, including numbers, text, and even pictures embedded as objects.

FIGURE 1.6.

Access 2000 manages your database data.

Introducing Publisher 2000

Although you can create professional documents and Web pages with Word 2000, including color pictures and artwork, nothing beats a *desktop publishing program* for high quality publications that get your audience's attention. Today's color printers, color copiers, scanners, and digital cameras give you a complete publishing house on your desktop.

NEW TERM A *desktop publishing program* enables you to efficiently combine text, charts, and graphics in various layout styles that can turn a drab document into an appealing publication.

Despite its power, Publisher 2000 is one of the easiest desktop publishing programs on the market to use, and it sports many features, including:

- Automatic wizards that guide you through one of several publication designs including Web pages and resumes. You can use Publisher 2000's wizard technology to make global changes to a publication after you've created it (see Hour 14, "Introducing Publisher 2000").

- A collection of lines, borders, buttons, fonts, and artwork that you can use to spruce up your publication (see Hour 14).

- A postcard wizard that lets you design and create card-size publications, such as invitations, guest cards, and thank-you notes (see Hour 14).

Figure 1.7 shows a publication being created in Publisher 2000. The placement of objects and columns of text is easy when you use the tools in Publisher 2000.

FIGURE 1.7.

With Publisher 2000, your publications look great.

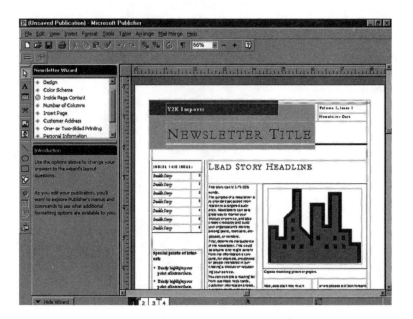

Introducing FrontPage 2000

FrontPage 2000 is a Web page creation tool that helps you design Web pages by clicking and dragging objects and text and other Web page elements to their final location. Before tools such as FrontPage 2000, you would have to master advanced programming commands to create Web pages. With the visual tools available in FrontPage 2000, you can create Web pages as easily as you create documents in Word 2000 and Publisher 2000. In addition, since FrontPage 2000 is integrated into Office 2000, you can combine documents from the other Office 2000 products into your Web pages and manage your complete site's Web pages (many pages that you possibly created in the other Office 2000 products). FrontPage 2000 includes features such as the following:

- The ability to send your Web pages directly to the Internet or an inner-company intranet (see Hour 24, "Introducing FrontPage 2000").

- Menus and toolbars that closely match those of the other Office 2000 products so that you can more quickly begin creating Web pages (see Hour 24).

- Numerous samples of Web pages from which you can add your own elements (see Hour 24).

- A collection of pre-designed themes from which you can select that gives your Web pages design consistency (see Hour 24).

Figure 1.8 shows a Web Page being edited inside FrontPage 2000. Without learning tedious commands, you, too, can create such effective pages.

FIGURE 1.8.

Create your own effective Web pages with FrontPage 2000.

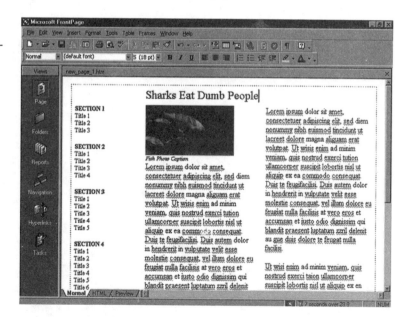

Introducing Outlook 2000

Outlook 2000 is a simple-to-use tool that manages your business and personal meetings, email, to-do lists, contacts, and appointments. Outlook 2000 provides many features, including the following:

- The capability to track your contact information, including multiple phone numbers and computerized email addresses (see Hour 16, "Communicating with Outlook 2000").
- The capability to track your computer activities in a journal (see Hour 16).
- Management of your email, phone calls, and to-do lists (see Hour 16).
- The capability to schedule appointments (see Hour 16).
- The capability to plan people and resources you need for meetings (see Hour 15, "Outlook 2000 Basics").
- The capability to sound an alarm before an important event (see Hour 15).

Figure 1.9 shows an Outlook 2000 calendar screen. The user is getting ready to schedule a meeting on a particular day. As with all the Office 2000 programs, you can modify screen elements in Outlook 2000 so that they appear in the format most helpful to your needs.

FIGURE 1.9.

Outlook 2000 tracks appointments and events.

Unlike previous versions of Office, Office 2000 includes no version of
Bookshelf Basics.

The Office 2000 Shortcut Bar

The Start menu is not the only way to start an Office 2000 product. In fact, you will
probably forsake that menu and select from the Office 2000 *Shortcut Bar*. Figure 1.10
shows a typical Office 2000 Shortcut Bar, which automatically appears at the top of most
Office 2000 user screens.

FIGURE 1.10.

Start Office 2000 pro-
grams quickly with the
Office 2000 Shortcut
Bar.

Depending on your installed options, the Office Shortcut Bar shown in
Figure 1.10 might look different from yours.

The Office 2000 Shortcut Bar offers pushbutton access to any Office 2000 product. You
can open or create an Office 2000 document by clicking the appropriate button. The
Office 2000 Shortcut Bar always stays *active* and appears on your screen even if you
work non-Office 2000 programs. Therefore, you can always access Office 2000 programs and documents from wherever you are.

 The Office 2000 *Shortcut Bar* displays a toolbar on your screen at all times
from which you quickly can start Office 2000 programs and open Office 2000
documents.

 A window is *active* when its title bar is highlighted and its controls are available
for you to use.

If you click the four-colored icon button on your Office 2000 Shortcut Bar (no ToolTip
exists for this button), the Office 2000 Shortcut Bar displays a menu from which you can
modify the Office 2000 Shortcut Bar's appearance or remove it from your screen. This
icon is called the Shortcut Bar *Control icon*.

If you use certain Office 2000 programs more often than others, you might want to select the Shortcut Bar's Customize option and add those specific program icons to the Office 2000 Shortcut Bar. If the Office 2000 Shortcut Bar contains buttons you rarely use, such as the New Journal Entry button, use Customize to remove any of the existing buttons.

To get rid of the Office 2000 Shortcut Bar, perform these steps:

1. Click the Office 2000 Shortcut Bar's colored Control icon to display the drop-down menu.
2. Click Exit. Windows displays the dialog box shown in Figure 1.11.
3. If you want to remove the Office 2000 Shortcut Bar just for this session, click Yes.

If you want to keep the Office 2000 Shortcut bar from appearing in subsequent Windows sessions, click No.

FIGURE 1.11.

You can control when the Office 2000 Shortcut Bar appears.

The Office 2000 Shortcut Bar appears automatically (unless you remove it) because Office 2000 installs the Office 2000 Shortcut Bar Startup command in your Start menu's Startup folder. If you click Yes to keep the Office 2000 Shortcut Bar from reappearing, Windows removes the command from your Startup folder.

You can add the Shortcut Bar Startup command back to your Startup folder by selecting the Start menu's Start, Programs, Office Tools, Microsoft Office Shortcut Bar option and clicking Yes when asked if you want the Shortcut Bar to appear automatically when you start Windows.

You can move your Office Shortcut Bar to another location by dragging the bar to a different place on your Windows desktop.

Year 2000 Compliance

Whether you read this before or after January 1, 2000, you won't have to worry about Office 2000 mishandling dates. Microsoft carefully produced Office 2000 to comply with the Year 2000 Compliance standard, an internal 2000-compliance standard Microsoft developed to ensure that all Microsoft products stringently adhere to date-accurate information.

> Microsoft has set up a year 2000 Web site that you can check for more information on the year 2000 problem and what tools Microsoft offers to help you manage dates that follow January 1, 2000. Check the following Web address to access the Microsoft Year 2000 Resource Center:
> `www.microsoft.com/technet/year2k`

SUPPORT FOR THE EURO

Along the same lines as the year 2000 compliance, Europe is quickly moving toward a single economy and Office 2000 provides support for the single Euro currency. Each individual country's former currency symbols still reside in Office 2000 as well.

Enabling Office 2000 for a specific language is easier than ever before. To activate a specific language, select Start, Programs, Microsoft Office Tools and select the Microsoft Office Language Settings option. Select the language you want to enable from the Enabled Languages tab and click OK to apply that language to the Office 2000 environment.

Getting Acquainted with Document Files

All Office 2000 products use a *document-centric* model. Whether you write a letter or a book (or create an Access 2000 database or an Excel 2000 worksheet), the text you write appears in a document. The term document is just an Office 2000 term for file. Figure 1.12 shows the many kinds of Office 2000 documents with which you will work.

NEW TERM   *Document-centric* refers to the way that all Office 2000 products work with documents rather than traditional and distinct kinds of data files such as database files, worksheet files, and presentation files. The document-centric concept lets Office 2000 products work uniformly with each other's files. Although each Office 2000 product stores its document in a different format from the other Office 2000 programs, document-centricity keeps terms uniform throughout the products.

Figure 1.12.

*All Office 2000 prod-
ucts interact with
documents.*

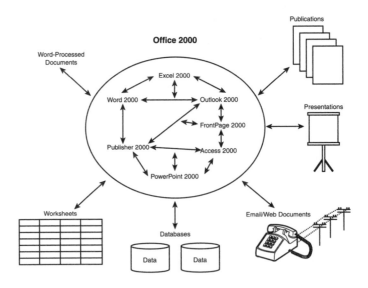

After you create a document, name it just as you label a file folder before you put it in a file cabinet. The document file's extension tells Office 2000 which application (such as Word 2000 or Excel 2000) was used to create that particular document.

You can use either uppercase or lowercase letters for your document names. Although neither Windows nor Office 2000 considers Proposal.doc to be different from PROPOSAL.DOC, the document names are easier to read when you mix the case. If you let Office 2000 add the extension, as you should usually do when you name documents, Office 2000 adds a lowercase extension, such as .doc.

One of the ways that Office 2000 integrates the Web more into its products is by offering a uniform file-saving format that is fully compatible with all Internet browsers. You will be able to view Word 2000 or Excel 2000 documents from Word 2000, Excel 2000, or from any browser that supports the HTML format. You can elect to save specific documents in the HTML format or set up Office 2000 to save all documents in the HTML format.

1

Summary

This hour introduced the Office 2000 programs by showing you a little of what each program can accomplish. Before learning Office 2000 specifics, you need to get the big picture. This hour provided that big picture and introduced the Office 2000 tools that you will use.

All Office 2000 programs share a common interface. After you learn one Office 2000 program, the others are easy to master. Some users find that they can use Office 2000 for all their computer needs.

The next hour begins a tour of Office 2000's features so that you can begin to see what Office 2000 can really do.

Q&A

Q I've used Word and Excel. Do I need the other Office 2000 products?

A Only you can answer that question, because only you know whether you need a program to keep track of your appointments and contacts (Outlook 2000) or your database (Access 2000). Only you know whether you will be called to present a topic in a meeting or at a conference (PowerPoint 2000).

If you need word processing and worksheet computing only, you may not need the other Office 2000 products. In which case, you need to install only those programs that you want to use. If you have truly mastered Word and Excel, however, you will be glad that Microsoft kept the same uniform interface throughout all the Office 2000 products. This enables you to use what you already know.

Q Why don't I see the Office Shortcut Bar?

A Your Office 2000 installer probably failed to install the Office Shortcut Bar. Just rerun the Office 2000 Setup program and install the Office Shortcut Bar. The Setup program acts like most other Windows-based installation programs, but if you feel uncomfortable running the Setup program, ask whoever installed your Office 2000 to help you. If you don't want to see the Office Shortcut Bar every time you start Windows, you can display the Office Shortcut Bar only when you want to see it by selecting Start, Programs, Office Tools, Microsoft Office Shortcut Bar and clicking No when asked whether you want the Shortcut Bar to appear automatically when you start Windows.

Q **Suppose that I want to keep track of names and addresses. Which Office 2000 product would I use?**

A This is actually a trick question. Word 2000, Excel 2000, Access 2000, and Outlook 2000 all track names and addresses! Word 2000 keeps track of names and addresses for mail merging (sending the same letter to many people); Excel 2000 includes a simple database feature that can track items such as names and addresses; Access 2000's primary purpose is to track virtually any data in an organized list; and Outlook 2000 records all your name and address records. Generally, use Outlook 2000 for your names and addresses (all the other Office 2000 products can read Outlook 2000's data) and save the other Office 2000 products for their primary purposes.

Q **Is it true that the Office 2000 programs are simple after I learn one well?**

A The Office 2000 programs share common interfaces, such as uniform menus and dialog boxes. After you learn how to use one Office 2000 program, you already understand the basic interface of the others. Therefore, you can concentrate on the specifics of each product instead of having to learn a new interface in each program.

HOUR 2

Introducing Office 2000's Powerful Features

This hour previews the most impressive Office 2000 features. If you are new to the Office environment, this hour whets your appetite for Office 2000. Once you get the overview, you'll be ready to study the specific Office 2000 programs and learn how they work.

Office 2000 attempts to move beyond the normal Windows-based help system. If you have used Windows programs in the past, you have probably read online documentation, clicked hypertext links to other related topics, and searched for keywords with which you need help. Office 2000 includes all these standard online help tools, but takes that help to a new level of functionality. Office 2000 provides some rather unusual help with the Office Assistant and its support for plain-language help queries. Every product in the suite of Office 2000 programs includes these helpful guides. In a way, Office 2000 looks over your shoulder and offers advice about a better way of doing things.

In addition to improving the Windows online help system, Office 2000 helps disabled users by providing several accessibility options. These options magnify the screen's views and offer keyboard shortcuts that the user can define and control.

The highlights of this hour include the following:

- What Office Assistant is
- When Office Assistant offers help that you didn't even know you needed
- How to use group-related options that Office 2000 supports, such as revision marks
- Where to locate a huge assortment of drawings, photos, sounds, and videos that you can include in your documents
- How to work with templates and wizards

The Office Assistant

When you start any Office 2000 program, the first feature you will notice is the *Office Assistant*, an online cartoon character that hangs around as you work. Figure 2.1 shows the Office Assistant (named Clippit), who appears when you start an Office 2000 product.

FIGURE 2.1.

Clippit, the helpful Assistant, remains faithful as you use Office 2000.

Clippit is here to help you

NEW TERM *Office Assistant*, an animated cartoon character, offers advice as you use Office 2000.

> You may see a different character. The next section, "Customizing Office Assistant," explains how to change the Office Assistant's animated character.

Keep your eyes on the Office Assistant as you work because you will be amused at the contortions it goes through as it provides advice. If you have your speakers turned on, the Office Assistant makes noises to draw your attention.

Move the Office Assistant to a different screen location by dragging the character. If the Office Assistant is about to cover an area in which you are typing, it automatically moves out of the way.

Suppose that you want help italicizing Word 2000 text. You can search through the online help system (via the Help menu), or you can click Office Assistant and type a question, such as How do I italicize text?, and press Enter. Office Assistant analyzes your question and displays a list of related topics (as shown in Figure 2.2). Click the topic that best fits your needs, and Office Assistant locates that help topic and displays the Help dialog box.

FIGURE 2.2.

Office Assistant offers a lot of advice.

If you do something and Office Assistant can provide a better way, a yellow light bulb that you can click for shortcut information displays. If you begin to create a numbered list using menus, for example, Office Assistant displays the light bulb to let you know that you can create a numbered list by clicking a button on the toolbar.

Customizing Office Assistant

If you work on a slow computer, you might want to disable Office Assistant to keep things moving a little faster. When you right-click Office Assistant, a pop-up menu appears with these options:

- *Hide*. Gets rid of Office Assistant. Display Office Assistant again by clicking the toolbar's Office Assistant button.
- *Options*. Displays Figure 2.3's Office Assistant dialog box, from which you can control the behavior of the Office Assistant (such as Office Assistant's response to pressing the F1 key).
- *Choose Assistant*. Enables you to change to a different animated Office Assistant character. As you work with Office 2000, check out all the Office Assistants (they are fun to see). You will learn how to change the Office Assistant character in the steps that follow.
- *Animate!* Causes Office Assistant to dance around its window; Office Assistant likes to show off! Select Animate a few times to see Office Assistant's contortions. As Office Assistant offers advice, it also moves through these animations. If you attempt to exit a program without saving your work, for example, Office Assistant gets your attention. (You will even hear Rocky, the canine assistant, barking!)

FIGURE 2.3.

Control the way that Office Assistant behaves.

Office 2000 includes several Office Assistants to help you do your job. They differ in animation, but not in their advice. Suppose you get tired of Clippit and decide that you want to see a different Office Assistant. Try this:

1. Right-click Office Assistant.

2. Select Choose Assistant. Office Assistant displays an Office Assistant Gallery screen.

3. Click Back and Next to cycle through the Office Assistants. Each Office Assistant goes through a song and dance to convince you that it is the best.

4. When you come to an Office Assistant you like, click the OK button to begin using that Office Assistant.

This book's inside back cover lists all the Office Assistants from which you can choose.

The Office Assistant appears when you press F1, although you can return to the normal content-based help system if you prefer by right-clicking over Assistant and selecting Options and click the option labeled Respond to the F1 key to disconnect the Assistant from the F1 keypress. Office 2000 uses a Web-like *HTML*-based help so that you can navigate the online help as you navigate Web pages. As Figure 2.4 shows, when you display non-Office Assistant help, office 2000 displays two panes with the help text in the left pane and a condensed Office 2000 program screen in the right pane. (You can drag the center bar left and right to adjust the width of the panes.) With the help shown in a second pane, you can keep working in the right pane while referring to helpful instructions in the left pane.

NEW TERM *HTML* stands for Hypertext Markup Language and refers to a formatting language used to display Web pages.

Help stays here...   ...while you work here.

FIGURE 2.4.

Office 2000 products provide a two-pane help view.

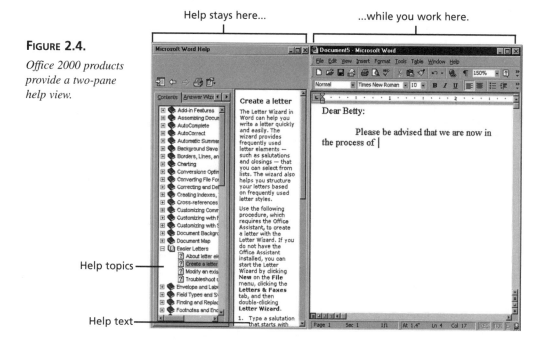

Help topics

Help text

Using Office 2000 to Share Information with Others

Although many people will use Office 2000 on single-user computers, Microsoft understands that today's office worker needs the ability to share information globally. Today's computers are often networked to other computers, either through a *network*, an Internet connection, or an *intranet* connection.

NEW TERM A *network* is a collection of two or more computers linked together to share programs and data. An *intranet* is an internal network system that uses an Internet browser, such as Microsoft's Internet Explorer, to access information from other computers on the local area network.

As long as you use e-mail programs such as Outlook Express, Outlook 2000, Microsoft Exchange, Windows Messaging, Microsoft Mail, or Netscape Messenger, you can create a Word 2000 document and send it to users on your mail system. When you send a document, the receivers can read the document and even make changes to the document using Word 2000. Word 2000 keeps track of revisions, and each reviewer's notes appear separate from the others. Using Word 2000's Tools, Track Changes menu, you can accept or reject any of the reviewer's comments after the document gets back to you.

> Office 2000 enables you to integrate all Office 2000 products. Therefore, if you want to send a report with an Excel 2000 worksheet graph to someone over the network, embed that graph into a Word 2000 document (as explained in Hour 21, "Office 2000's Synergy") and send the Word 2000 document. The graph travels along with the document.

Office 2000 supports several document-routing options such as these:

- *Send a document.* Sends a copy of your document to your list of reviewers. Each reviewer can make changes to his copy, and then return the document to you.

- *Route a document.* Sends a single copy of your document to each reviewer in turn. Every subsequent reviewer can read the preceding reviewers' comments and add his own. The document finally gets back to you after the final reviewer makes revisions.

- *Post a document.* Sends a copy of your document to a public folder that everyone on your receiver list can read. Posting is useful when you have a company-wide policy or message that you want everyone to read. Posting requires that Microsoft Exchange Server, a separate program from those supplied with Office 2000, be run with a Public Folder shortcut. Your network administrator should be able to help set up a public folder.

Word 2000 keeps track of who made each revision. You can have the reviewers make changes to a copy or to the original document. To determine who made a revision, point to the edit and the editor's name appears over the edit, along with the date the edit was made.

> If the reviewers insert sound objects into the routed document, they can review the document with speech as well as with editing marks!

Figure 2.5 shows a screen from Word 2000 with revision marks. The revisions appear on your screen in color—a different color for each editor who made a revision—so that the revisions are easy to distinguish from the original text. Word 2000's accept or reject Tools, Track Changes menu options enable you to quickly incorporate or delete any and all revisions made by the editing team.

FIGURE 2.5.

Revision marks enable a team of editors to revise the same document electronically.

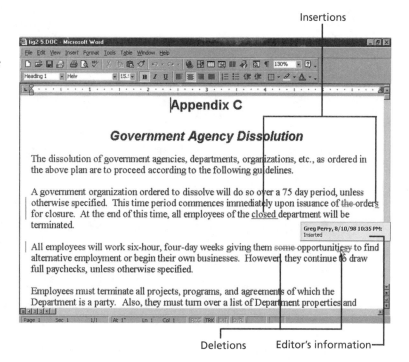

Both Word 2000 and Excel 2000 currently support revision marks. You can use the Tools, Track Changes menu options to see revision marks, hide revision marks (to see what the document will look like if you incorporate all revisions), and accept or reject revision marks.

> You can right-click a revision mark and view a pop-up menu that enables you to easily accept or reject the revision mark.

Working with Multiple Data Types

Office 2000 handles today's massive data needs. In the past, you worked primarily with text in word processors and with numbers in electronic worksheets. Today's multimedia computers require much more data support from programs. A database might hold text, numbers, pictures, sounds, and even Internet *hyperlink* connections, for example. Using OLE, COM, and ActiveX technologies (the advanced data-sharing and linking tools Office 2000 uses to track all kinds of data), your documents really come alive. You are no longer bound by outdated data limitations. You can elect to store all Office 2000 documents in a uniform, HTML format, or you can save each of the Office 2000 products' documents in their own specific formats. No matter how you save documents, all the Office 2000 programs can read each other's data.

Suppose that you are creating a Web page in Word 2000, and you want to insert a hyperlink to another Web site as in Figure 2.6. The Insert menu enables you to do just that because a Web address's hyperlink is just another kind of data—just as text and numbers are two kinds of data—that the Office 2000 products support. Such multiple-data support frees you from the boundaries of yesterday's software and enables you to work from a global computing perspective.

NEW TERM   A *hyperlink* is an underlined word or phrase that you can click to display a different document or document section. Hyperlinks often describe Web page locations, but can also refer to other data and documents on your PC or on a network of computers.

FIGURE 2.6.

The Office 2000 products recognize Web addresses and insert hyperlinks where you need them.

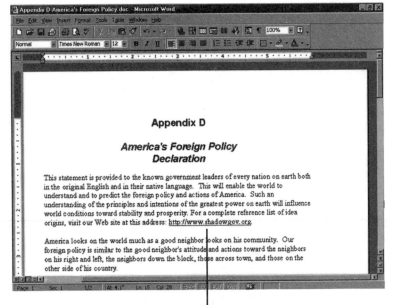

Hyperlink to a Web site

2

 The Office 2000 products automatically turn Web addresses that you type into hyperlinks if the addresses begin with www and end with com. You, therefore, don't have to select from the Insert menu to embed hyperlinks in those sites. You can turn off the automatic conversion of hyperlinks from the Tools I AutoCorrect dialog box. Throughout this 24-hour tutorial, you will learn more ways to work with the multiple data formats that Office 2000 supports.

When you want to insert a hyperlink into any Office 2000 document, you need only to select Insert, Hyperlink from the menu (Ctrl+K is the shortcut key). Office 2000 supports several kinds of hyperlinks, not just links to Web page addresses. When you select Insert, Hyperlink, the Insert Hyperlink dialog box appears, as shown in Figure 2.7.

The Insert Hyperlink dialog box enables you to insert many different kinds of hyperlinks, including the following:

- A Web page that appears when the user clicks the hyperlink.
- A file on your own system or on another computer networked to your computer.
- An email address that opens Outlook 2000 and creates a message to that email address when the user clicks the hyperlink.

- Text that pops up, including a ScreenTip that appears when the user rests the mouse cursor over the hyperlink.
- A bookmark inside the current document so that the user can click the hyperlink to move to the bookmarked location.

Therefore, you can insert a hyperlink to a file on your own PC. When you or another user who uses your document in Excel 2000 or Word 2000, for example, clicks on that file's hyperlink, Office 2000 opens and displays that file in place of the document previously viewed.

FIGURE 2.7.

Insert many different kinds of hyperlinks from the Insert Hyperlink dialog box.

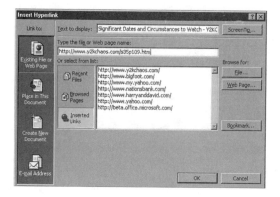

One of the benefits of Office 2000's full support for HTML-based Internet Web pages is that any Office 2000 product can read your existing Web pages and your created Web pages look consistent in any browser or Office 2000 program. In other words, you can open a Web page in Word 2000 and make edits directly to the page even if you did not originally use Word 2000 to create the page.

Making Office 2000 Easier to Use

Several accessibility features make Office 2000 easier to use. You will become familiar with many of these features as you work with Office 2000. Following is a sample of some of these features:

- The Change document option magnifies documents for easier viewing. Even the toolbar buttons are larger to make them easier to find.
- The Office 2000 programs contain many *AutoComplete* features with which you can begin typing items such as dates, times, days of the week or month, names, and any other AutoText entries you set up. Office 2000 completes the entry for you. If you begin typing a month name such as Nov, for example, Word 2000 displays a

small box with November above your month abbreviation. If you press Enter, Word 2000 completes the month name for you! If you type a full month name, such as July, Word 2000 offers to complete your entry with the current date, such as July 7, 1999. You can accept the complete date by pressing Enter or ignore it by typing the rest of the sentence as you want it to appear.

NEW TERM *AutoComplete* is an Office 2000 feature that completes text entries it recognizes as you type them.

- You can rearrange toolbar buttons and customize toolbars so that they contain only the buttons you use most frequently. As you learned in the previous lesson, Office 2000 analyzes how you use the menus and toolbars and begins to hide those options and buttons you use less frequently to reduce screen clutter. You can always see all menu options and toolbars when you want by displaying a menu for a couple of seconds until the hidden options appear. In addition, you can drag a toolbar left or right to see hidden options.

- PowerPoint 2000 presentations provide a special high-contrast viewing mode in which you can more easily see the details of a presentation in virtually any light.

- You can assign shortcut keys to just about any task in any Office 2000 product. Suppose that you often need to color and boldface an Excel 2000 value. Create a shortcut keystroke and press it whenever you want to apply the special formatting.

Clip Art

Not only can Office 2000 work with text, numbers, and even Web hyperlinks, but it can also work with sound, pictures, and moving video.

Office 2000 includes a huge collection of royalty-free *clip art* files for personal use that you can use when you want to embed a special data item—such as a picture or video—into a document, spreadsheet, or Web page. When you need a graphic to spice things up, or when you want to include an attention-getting sound file in an Outlook 2000 email message, select Insert, Picture, Clip Art to access the Office 2000 clip art collection called *Microsoft Clip Art Gallery*. The gallery includes several hundred sounds, pictures, and drawings arranged by category, as Figure 2.8 shows.

NEW TERM *Clip art* is a data file that you can include in your own documents.

Perhaps one of the most impressive features from the Microsoft Clip Art Gallery is that you can click the Clips Online button to link to Microsoft's clip art Web site and search for even more files to use in your documents.

FIGURE 2.8.

You will have no shortage of clip art to use with Office 2000.

Templates

A *template* is nothing more than a formatted outline of a document. Suppose that you follow a monthly budget, and you prepare monthly statements to follow. You like to include your savings account interest calculations, so you determine that Excel 2000 will function well as the creation tool for your statements.

 A *template* is an outline that holds the format of a document, database, or other Office 2000 data file.

When you create your monthly statements, you have three options:

- Create each monthly budget from scratch.
- Modify a saved monthly budget to change the details for each subsequent statement.
- Create a monthly budget template and fill in the details for each statement.

Obviously, the first option requires the most work. Why create a new statement for each budget, adding the titles, date, time, details, summaries, creditors, and new investment information if many of those details remain the same from statement to statement?

The second option is not a bad idea if the statements are fairly uniform in design and require only slight formatting and detail changes. Some people feel more comfortable changing an existing statement's details than creating statements from scratch or using a template. New Office 2000 users might prefer to change an existing statement until they get accustomed to Office 2000's programs.

Although templates are great for Office 2000 newcomers, you do not always want to start with them. Sometimes, it's easier to understand an Office 2000 program if you create your first few data files (documents, databases, electronic worksheets, and so on) from scratch. For example, until you've created an Access 2000 database from scratch and until you've learned all the terminology related to such data, the Access 2000 templates do not make a lot of sense to you. After you master the fundamentals of the Office 2000 programs, you can leverage the power that templates provide.

2

When you get used to Office 2000, however, you discover that the template method makes the most sense for repetitive statement creation. The template literally provides a fill-in-the-blank statement. You don't have to format the same information from statement to statement, and you're guaranteed a uniform appearance.

Using Existing Templates

Office 2000 supplies several common templates, and each Office 2000 product contains templates of its own. For example, when you want to create a new Excel 2000 electronic worksheet, you can select from a blank worksheet or you can click the Spreadsheet Solutions tab to see four icons that represent templates. When you click a template icon, Office 2000 shows you a preview of that template (as shown in Figure 2.9).

FIGURE 2.9.

Office 2000 provides several templates that you can preview.

Selected template   The template's preview area

After you select a template, the Office 2000 program opens it and presents the file. Edit the template and save the details in a new file. The new file becomes your template file that you use for subsequent documents.

If you use the same template for the majority of your work, each Office 2000 program lets you specify a template that you want to be the basis for *all new files you create*. For example, if you create an Excel 2000 template, save the template under the name BOOK.XLT and store it in the XLSTART directory. Excel 2000 automatically loads that template every time you create new worksheets.

Creating New Templates

Although Office 2000 supplies several predesigned templates, you won't find a template for everything, such as a monthly budget you may want to create. You may want specific titles, special formatting, and unusual expense items that don't often appear in routine monthly budgets.

Because your specific monthly budget template does not exist in Office 2000, you have to create your own. Generally, to create a template, follow these steps:

1. Create a properly formatted sample data file, such as a monthly budget, so that you know what design the template is supposed to produce.
2. Print the sample budget so that you can reference it later when designing the template from the sample.
3. Use File, New to create a new Office 2000 Excel 2000 worksheet.
4. Based on the document you created in step 1, add all titles, formatting, and footer information that does not change from statement to statement. Leave blank space for details.
5. Save the template. Select Template option in the Save as type text box to let Office 2000 know you're creating a template file and not a normal data file.

If you are new to Office 2000, creating the initial template may seem like a *lot* of work. (As you learn more about Office 2000, you see that creating a template document gets easier.) After spending the time to create the template, however, subsequent statements become extremely simple. Instead of creating a statement from scratch, you can create the statement from the template; all you need to do is enter the details. The template supplies the proper formatting and the information that doesn't change from statement to statement.

After you create the initial sample document in any Office 2000 product that you want to use as the basis for a template, you can save that file as a template by selecting File, Save As and then selecting Document Template as the document's type.

As you learn more about the Office 2000 products, you learn how to add specialized *fields* to the template to make the creation of your template-based statements even easier.

 NEW TERM   A *field* is an area of a template designed to accept certain information, such as a name or phone number. The field contains all necessary formatting and spacing, so you need only be concerned with the data.

2

Wizards

One reason so many users have switched to Microsoft-based Office products is Microsoft's wizard technology. *Wizards* are step-by-step guides that walk you through the development of a document or through a complicated process such as creating an Internet web page from scratch. (You learn more about Office 2000's Internet integration later this hour and in Hour 22, "Office 2000 and the Internet.")

 NEW TERM   A *wizard* is a step-by-step set of dialog boxes that guides you through the creation of a document or through a complicated selection process (such as a report's design).

Although each wizard differs in its goal, all follow a similar pattern. Wizards display a series of dialog boxes, and each dialog box asks for a set of values. As you fill in the dialog boxes, you answer questions to help the program perform a specific job.

Generally, each dialog box within a wizard contains Next and Back buttons, which you can click to move back and forth through the wizard. If you change your mind after leaving one dialog box, you can back up to that dialog box and change its values.

Microsoft supplies you with several wizards you can use to create Office 2000 documents. For example, if you use Word 2000 to create a résumé, you can select the Résumé Wizard. Figure 2.10 shows the Résumé Wizard's opening dialog box.

When you select File, New, each Office 2000 product offers a list of template and wizard icons. You'll know the difference between them because the wizard icons include a magic wand waving across the icon.

FIGURE 2.10.

The opening Résumé Wizard dialog box.

Many wizards contain opening dialog boxes that display information about the wizard. Figure 2.10 informs you that you selected the Résumé Wizard. If you click the Next button, the wizard asks which of the following kinds of résumés you want to create:

- Entry-level résumé
- Chronological résumé
- Functional résumé
- Professional résumé

Clicking Next again displays a dialog box that requests your name and address information for the top of the résumé. Office 2000 is smart enough to automatically pull your name from the Office 2000 registration information, but you can change the name if you create résumés for other people. Often, wizard dialog boxes present you with a selection of styles, formats, graphic elements, and colors.

Every wizard's final dialog box includes a Finish button that you will click to complete the wizard and generate the document based on the wizard. Generally, wizards create shells of documents, such as Word 2000 template documents or Access 2000 databases, that contain no data. It's your job to enter the details.

After a wizard designs a document, you are free to make whatever additional edits you need.

Some wizards are less complicated than Word 2000's Résumé Wizard. For example, Access 2000's Table Wizard creates a single table of data within a much larger database. The Table Wizard asks you fewer questions than the Résumé Wizard.

The first wizard appeared in Microsoft Publisher's first version. Publisher 2000 continues to set the standard for wizards by offering a huge catalog of publication wizards, sorted by category, as shown in Figure 2.11. These wizards will save you countless hours of formatting and aligning work when creating publications.

FIGURE 2.11.

Publisher 2000 supports a large variety of wizards.

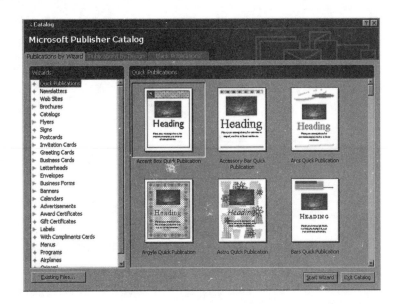

2

Get Ready for the Internet and Office 2000

Microsoft did not make Office 2000's Internet interface really stand out; instead, the Internet interface appears as just one of a long line of Office 2000 features so that you can access the Internet from within the Office 2000 environment. The seamless web integration lets you get to Internet information much easier than before. The Internet interface between the various Office 2000 products differs a little, but the Internet interface is always underneath Office 2000, ready to handle the connection.

The Web Toolbar

All core Office 2000 programs contain a Web toolbar button that you can click to display the Office 2000 Web toolbar shown in Figure 2.12. The buttons give you web access from within an Office 2000 program.

Refresh current | Start | Search | Show only | Web
page | page | the web | web toolbar | address

FIGURE 2.12.

Access the Internet from this Office 2000 Web toolbar.

Back

Forward

Stop current jump

Favorites list

Go list

If you're logged on to the Internet when you click a Web toolbar button, such as the Start Page button, Office 2000 takes you directly to your Start page, substituting your web browser for the current Office 2000 program on your screen. If you're not logged on to the Internet before using the Web toolbar buttons, Office 2000 initiates your logon sequence for you.

> If you use Internet Explorer as your web browser, type the name of any Office 2000 data file in the *URL* Address drop-down list and Internet Explorer displays your properly formatted Office 2000 data file.

NEW TERM *URL*, short for *Uniform Resource Locator*, uniquely identifies an Internet site.

An inserted hyperlink is just one way that you can connect an Office 2000 document to the outside, online world. The Office 2000 products enable you to create web pages from data located inside your documents as the next section demonstrates.

> If you're giving a PowerPoint 2000 presentation and need to reference something on the web, simply insert a hyperlink jump to that web site and click it during the presentation. PowerPoint 2000 jumps to the web and displays the page.

> A web site does not have to exist yet for you to insert a hyperlink to it. For example, you may be creating an in-house reference manual for your company's new web site. You can insert a hyperlink to an address on your company site before the site actually appears on the Internet.

2

You can even use the Internet as your Office 2000 data repository. Not only can you access the Internet web pages from the Web toolbar, but you can also edit web pages as if they were on your own PC. If you want to edit a document located on an FTP or HTTP site, just enter the document's URL when you open the document. You can also save to HTTP and FTP sites by using any of the Office 2000 Save commands.

Summary

This hour introduced some of the more fun features of Office 2000, including the Office Assistant, accessibility features, and clip art files. By routing documents to your co-workers over your network (or over the Internet using Office 2000's built-in Internet support), you can all work on the same documents and track revisions as each of you review Office 2000 material.

This hour explored three of the most powerful features in the suite of Office 2000 products: templates, wizards, and Office 2000's Internet interface.

Hour 3, "Welcome to Word 2000," introduces Word 2000. You'll soon see why Word 2000 is considered to be the most powerful word processor available.

Q&A

Q What if I want to use Office Assistant only when I need help?

A Right-click Office Assistant to display the pop-up menu and select Hide Assistant. The Office Assistant window disappears. When you want to use Office Assistant again, click the toolbar's Office Assistant button. You might want to display the

Office Assistant's Options dialog box (right-click Office Assistant and select Options) to change the way Office Assistant responds to you. The Options dialog box enables you to modify the timing of Office Assistant's responses.

Q Why would I route a document instead of sending a document if co-workers needed to make revisions?

A Use the document routing option when you want to send the same document to multiple co-workers and let each co-worker see the revisions made. When you send a document, Office 2000 sends a copy to each of the recipients, who then make revisions to that single copy and return it to you. Office 2000 users often route when they have more time to wait for revisions and when they want to send a document through a predetermined chain of organizational command.

Q Can I add my own collection of clip art files to the Microsoft Clip Art Gallery?

A Certainly. Not only can you add your own sound, video, graphic, and picture files to the Clip Art Gallery, but you can also add your own categories to organize the gallery in the way that works best for you. If you see a category or clip art image that you will probably never use, you can also remove that category or image from the gallery to make subsequent browsing through the gallery more efficient. Hour 13, "PowerPoint 2000's Advanced Features," explains in detail how to use the Clip Art Gallery.

Q What is the difference between a template and a wizard?

A A *template* is a formatted shell, design, or empty data file. For example, an Excel 2000 accounts-receivable template would contain no data but would contain all the titles, fields, and formatting necessary for an accounts-receivable worksheet. After you load the template, you're able to add specific data easily without having to format titles and totals.

A *wizard* is more than a formatted shell. A wizard is a step-by-step guide that presents a series of dialog boxes. As you fill in each dialog box, the wizard builds a data file for you. You can create complex documents like professional résumés, newsletters, and web pages by answering a few simple questions within the dialog box series.

Part II

Processing with Word 2000

Hour

HOUR 3

Welcome to Word 2000

This hour introduces you to Word 2000. You will soon see why Word is the most popular word processor on the market. With Word 2000, you can create documents of any kind with amazing ease. Word 2000 helps you painlessly create letters, proposals, Web pages, business plans, résumés, novels, and even graphics-based multicolumn publications, such as fliers and newsletters.

The highlights of this hour include the following:

- How to start Word 2000
- How to edit multiple documents at once
- When to use the Find and Replace text features
- How to modify Word 2000's automatic editing tools
- How to quit Word 2000 properly and why this is important

Starting Word 2000

You can start Word 2000 in several ways:

- Click the Office 2000 Shortcut Bar's New Office Document button and double-click the Blank Document icon to create a new document.

- Click the Office 2000 Shortcut Bar's New Office Document button and open a Word 2000 template or start a Word Wizard. Hour 2, "Introducing Office 2000's Powerful Features," explains how to use templates and wizards.

- Click the Office 2000 Shortcut Bar's Open Office Document button and select an existing document you want to edit.

- Use the Windows Start menu to start Word 2000 by selecting Microsoft Word from the Programs menu.

- Select a Word 2000 document from the Windows Start menu's Documents option. Windows recognizes that Word 2000 created the document, starts Word 2000, and loads the document automatically. (The Start menu's Documents option holds a list of your most recent work.)

- Click the Office 2000 Shortcut Bar's Word 2000 button to create a blank document.

FIGURE 3.1.

Word 2000's opening screen.

Figure 3.1 shows the opening Word 2000 screen. (Your screen might differ slightly depending on the options that the installer set.)

> If you forget what a toolbar button does, rest the mouse pointer over any button to learn the toolbar button's name.

Editing with Word 2000

This section reviews fundamental Word 2000 editing skills and brings you up to speed if you are new to word processing. In this section, you learn how to do the following:

- Type text into a document
- Delete text
- Copy, cut, and paste text from one location to another
- Locate and replace text

Entering Text

When you start Word 2000, it displays a blank editing area in which you can type text to create a new document. You can also load an existing Word 2000 document and make changes to that document. If you have started Word 2000 through the Start menu's Documents option, Word 2000 starts with the open document you selected.

> If you want to work with an existing document, you must select File, Open and select that document. When finished, you save the document to long-term disk storage. You can close a document if you want to clear that document from the editing area; if you have not first saved changes, Office 2000 gives you a chance to save your work before closing the document.

The text you write appears in the editing area. The flashing vertical bar (called the *cursor* or *insertion point*) shows where the next character will appear. As you type, remember these basic editing points:

- Don't press Enter at the end of a line. As you type close to the right edge of the screen, Word 2000 automatically wraps the text to the next line for you.
- Press Enter at the end of each paragraph. Each subsequent press of the Enter key adds an extra blank line before the next paragraph.

- If you type a Web address in your document, Word 2000 automatically changes that Web address to a hyperlink that you can click to jump to that page if you (or someone who reads your document file) have Internet access.

NEW TERM The flashing vertical bar that shows where your next typed character will appear is called the *cursor* or *insertion point*.

Insert mode is Word 2000's default startup mode. When in Insert mode, new typing appears at the text cursor, and new text pushes existing characters to the right (and down the page if needed). When in *Overtype mode*, new text replaces existing text.

NEW TERM Word 2000 uses *Overtype mode* when you want typed characters to replace existing characters.

NEW TERM Word 2000 uses *Insert mode* when you want to insert newly typed characters before existing characters.

The Word 2000 status bar indicates Word 2000's Insert mode. If the letters OVR are visible, Word 2000 is in Overtype mode. If OVR is grayed out, Word 2000 is in Insert mode. You can switch between the two modes by pressing Insert.

Not only can you insert text, but Word 2000 also enables you to insert blanks. Suppose you forget a space or want to insert three spaces before the start of a paragraph. Move the cursor to the place you want the blanks (to the left of text that you want to shift right) by pointing and clicking the mouse pointer to anchor the cursor in position. Press the Spacebar as many times as you need to shift the existing text right.

Word 2000 includes a new feature called *click and type* that enables you to double-click anywhere in the blank area of a document and begin typing where you click. If you double-click in the center of a blank line, Word 2000 automatically turns on centering for that line. If you double-click toward the right margin, Word 2000 right-justifies that margin. The next hour, "Formatting with Word 2000," explains more about margins.

NEW TERM *Click and type* enables you to double-click anywhere in a document and begin editing at that location.

 Remember that all menus and toolbars shown in this book's figures display all options but Office 2000 typically displays only the most common options when you display a menu or toolbar.

Navigating Word Documents

When you first type a document, you might enter the rough draft all at once and edit the
text later, or you might be the kind of writer who likes to edit as you go. No matter how
you write, you need to be able to move around a Word 2000 document quickly, locating
text that you want to change or read. Much of the time you navigate through a Word
2000 document using these general practices:

- Use the four arrow keys to move the text cursor around the editing area.

- Click the scrollbars until you locate text you want.

- Click your mouse pointer anywhere inside the editing area to move the text cursor
  to that location.

- If you type more text than fits in the editing area, use the scrollbars, arrow keys,
  PageUp, PageDown, Ctrl+Home, and Ctrl+End keys to scroll to the portions of text
  that you want to see.

If you open an existing document, press Shift+F5 to jump directly to the last
typed letter or edited text that you made. Keep pressing Shift+F5 to jump to
each of your previous edits.

To quickly navigate through a lot of text, press Ctrl+G (the shortcut for Edit, Go To) to
display the Find and Replace dialog box (shown in Figure 3.2) with the Go To page
selected. After you type a page number and press Enter, Word 2000 immediately takes
you to that page.

FIGURE 3.2.

*Quickly jump to any
page.*

The skills you learn here also apply to the other Office 2000 products. Excel
2000, for example, has a similar Find and Replace dialog box.

Selecting Text

Word 2000 is more of a document processor than a word processor; Word 2000 enables you to work with multiple words, paragraphs, pages, and complete documents. Earlier in this hour, you learned how to insert and delete individual characters; you now learn how to select entire sections of text you can move or delete.

When you or Word 2000 highlights (*selects*) text, you can perform tasks on that selection. You might want to select two sentences and underline them for emphasis, for example. Highlighted text that you want to work on as a single block is called a *selection* or *selected text*. Some people call a selected text section a block of text.

You can select text using your keyboard or mouse. Table 3.1 shows the mouse-selection operations.

TABLE 3.1. WORD 2000'S TEXT-SELECTION OPTIONS.

To Select This	Do This
Any text	Click the mouse at the start of the text and drag the mouse to the end of the text. (Figure 3.3 shows a partial paragraph selection.)
Word	Double-click the word.
Sentence	Press Ctrl and click the sentence.
Line	Click to the left of the line.
Paragraph	Double-click to the left of the paragraph or triple-click anywhere inside the paragraph's text.
Entire document	Press Ctrl and click to the left of the document.

To select with your keyboard, move the text cursor to the beginning of the selection, press the Shift key, and move the text cursor (with the arrow keys or other cursor-movement keys you learned about in the section titled "Entering Text") to the final selection character. When you release the Shift key, the selected text appears.

Ctrl+A selects your entire document. When you want to apply global formatting or Clipboard-related tasks (you will learn about the Clipboard in the next section) to the entire document, Ctrl+A makes quick work of selecting the entire document.

FIGURE 3.3.

A partial text selection.

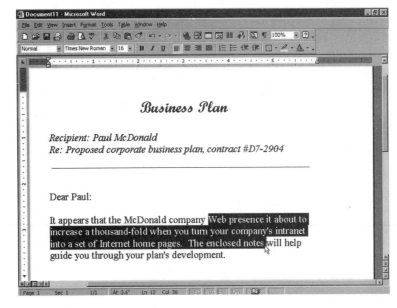

3

Deleting Text

No matter which mode you are in (Insert or Overtype), press Delete to delete any character at the text cursor's position. Delete also deletes selected text. Any characters to the
right of the deleted character shift left to close the gap. Press the Backspace key to
reverse the text cursor and erase the preceding character.

> Here's a tip that even advanced Word 2000 gurus often forget:
> Ctrl+Backspace erases the word to the *left* of your text cursor, and Ctrl+Del
> erases the word to the *right* of your text cursor.

The section found earlier this hour titled "Selecting Text" illustrates how to select multiple
characters. After selecting multiple characters, press Delete to delete the entire selection.

Copying, Cutting, and Pasting

After you select text, you can *copy* or *cut* and move that text to a different location. One
of the most beneficial features that propelled word processors into the spotlight in the
1980s was their capability to copy and move text. In the medieval days (before 1980),
people had to use scissors and glue to cut and paste. Now, your hands stay clean.

NEW TERM   To *copy* is to reproduce selected document text and send it to the *Clipboard*. You then can *paste* that copied text from the Clipboard into another document.

NEW TERM   To *cut* is to send selected document text to the Clipboard and remove that text from the document. You then can paste that cut text from the Clipboard into another document.

Windows uses the Windows Clipboard during the copy, cut, and paste processes.

NEW TERM   The *Clipboard* is an area of Windows where you temporarily store data that you can paste elsewhere.

To copy text from one place to another, select the text, copy the selected text to the Clipboard by selecting Edit, Copy (or by pressing Ctrl+C or clicking the Copy toolbar button), and paste (that's computer lingo for *insert from the Clipboard*) the Clipboard contents in their new location. To paste, select Edit, Paste, press Ctrl+V, or click the Paste toolbar button. You can paste the same text again and again wherever you want it to appear.

NEW TERM   To *paste* is to send the Clipboard contents to a location inside your document.

When you cut text from your document (select Edit, Cut, click the Cut toolbar button, or press Ctrl+X), Word 2000 erases the text from your document and sends it to the Clipboard where you can paste the Clipboard contents elsewhere. In effect, cutting and pasting moves the text.

> You can also move and copy by using your mouse. Select the text you want to move, click the selection, and drag the text to its new location. To copy with your mouse, press Ctrl before you click and drag the selected text. Word 2000 indicates that you are copying by adding a small plus sign to the mouse cursor during the copy.

Beginning with Word 2000, you can paste up to 12 different selections of text on the Clipboard. The Windows Clipboard holds a maximum of one selection, but Office 2000 overrides the Windows Clipboard when you copy or cut more than one item to the Clipboard. You can copy or cut up to 12 items onto the Office Clipboard and paste one or more of those 12 items into an Office document such as a Word 2000 letter or Web page.

As you cut or copy more than one item to the Office Clipboard, you can display the Clipboard toolbar shown in Figure 3.4 that displays a new Windows document icon for each item on the Clipboard. The icon specifies which Office 2000 product you copied from. You can paste all the items into the document, paste one or more items, one at a time, into the document wherever you wish, or erase the entire Office Clipboard by clicking the Clear Clipboard button. To determine which icon represents certain copied text, rest your mouse over any document icon in the Clipboard window and Office 2000 displays a ToolTip that displays the first few characters of that Clipboard item.

FIGURE 3.4.

The Office Clipboard can hold up to 12 items.

Finding and Replacing Text

Word 2000 locates text for you. When searching through extremely long documents, Word 2000's search capabilities come in handy. Suppose that you are writing a political letter, for example, and you want to correct a congressional district's seat name. Ask Word 2000 to find all occurrences of the word *district* by following these steps:

1. Select Edit, Find. Word 2000 displays the Find and Replace dialog box, as shown in Figure 3.5.

Some people prefer to use the Ctrl+F shortcut key; others click the Select Browse Object button on the vertical scrollbar (refer to Figure 3.1) and click the binoculars to display the Find and Replace dialog box. The Select Browse Object button has a round dot to distinguish it from the scrolling arrows. Use whatever method you can remember because you often search for (and replace) text in word processing sessions.

FIGURE 3.5.

Enter text that you want Word 2000 to locate.

2. Type the word or phrase you want to find in the Find What text box. For example, type District to locate that word. By default, Word 2000 searches from the top of the document and does not worry about exactly matching your find text with its occurrences in the document.

3. When Word 2000 locates the first occurrence of the search word, Word 2000 highlights the word (as shown in Figure 3.6). (As you saw in the section titled "Selecting Text," this highlighted text is said to be *selected*.)

FIGURE 3.6.

Word 2000 found a match.

Selected text   Search word

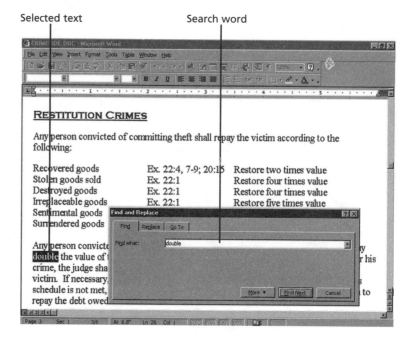

4. If the selected text is the text you wanted to find, click the Cancel button or press Escape to return to your document. Word 2000 keeps the selected text highlighted so that you can identify the found text. To remove the selection, press an arrow key or click anywhere in the editing area. If the selected text is not the text you want, click the Find Next button in the Find and Replace dialog box to search for the next occurrence of the text.

As you probably can guess from the name of the Find and Replace dialog box, Word 2000 not only finds but also replaces text. Suppose that you wrote a lengthy business proposal to an associate you thought was named Paul McDonald. Luckily, before you sent the proposal over your corporate network (using Microsoft Outlook as shown in Hour 15, "Outlook 2000 Basics"), you realized that Paul's last name is spelled *Mac*Donald.

Tell Word 2000 to change all names of *McDonald* to *MacDonald* by following these steps:

1. Select Edit, Replace. Word 2000 displays the Find and Replace dialog box (shown in Figure 3.7) with the Replace tab displayed.

FIGURE 3.7.

*Make Word 2000 find
and replace text for
you.*

2. Type McDonald in the Find What text box. Unless you change the default (you learn how to do this in the next section), you don't need to worry about distinguishing between uppercase and lowercase letters.

3. Press Tab to move the text cursor to the Replace with text box.

4. Type the replacement text (in this case, MacDonald). Use the correct case because Word 2000 replaces the find text with your exact replacement text.

5. If you want Word 2000 to replace all occurrences of the text, click the Replace All button. After Word 2000 finishes replacing all the occurrences, it indicates how many replacements were made.

   If you want to replace only one or a few of the occurrences (for example, there might be another person with the name McDonald in the business plan whose name is spelled that way), click the Find Next button, and Word 2000 locates the next occurrence of the text. Upon finding a match, Word 2000 selects the text and gives you a chance to replace it by clicking Replace. To skip an occurrence, click Find Next rather than Replace after a match is found that you want to ignore.

6. Press Escape or click Cancel when you are finished.

If you want to delete all occurrences of a word or phrase, leave the Replace with text box blank when you click Replace All.

Be careful when using Replace All because it could change more than you expect. To be safe, locate each replacement and click Replace individually so that you can see the context of the found text before you decide to replace it with something else. If you do use Replace All but then realize that Word 2000 replaced too much, use Word 2000's Undo feature to reverse the replacement.

Advanced Find and Replace

Both the Find and the Find and Replace dialog boxes (see the preceding section) contain More buttons. If you want more control over your text searches and replacements, click the More button when you want to find or replace text. The dialog box expands to show more options, as Figure 3.8 shows.

 After you click the More button and the dialog box expands, the More button becomes a Less button that you can click to return to the simpler Find or Replace pages.

FIGURE 3.8.

Advanced options enable you to control your find-and-replace operations.

Table 3.2 describes each of the advanced find-and-replace options.

TABLE 3.2. THE ADVANCED FIND AND REPLACE DIALOG BOX OPTIONS.

Option	Description
Search	Determines the scope of the find and replace. Select All to search the entire document starting from the beginning, Down to search the document from the text cursor's current position down in the document, and Up to search the document from the text cursor's current position up through the document.
Match Case	Finds text only when the text exactly matches the capitalization of your search text.
Find Whole Words Only	Matches only when complete text words match your search phrase. If this box is checked, Word 2000 does not consider McDonald a match for *McD*, for example. If unchecked, *McD* matches *McDonald*, *McDonald's*, and *McDonalds*.

Option	Description
Use Wildcards	Uses an asterisk (*) to indicate zero or more characters, or a question mark (?) to indicate a single character in your search. If you search for *Mc** and click this option, for example, Word 2000 matches on *Mc*, *McDonald*, and *McDonald's*. If you search for *M?cDonald*, Word 2000 considers *MacDonald* a match but not *McDonald*.
Sounds Like	Bases the match on words or phrases that phonetically match the search phrase but are not necessarily spelled the same way as the search phrase. Therefore, Word 2000 would consider both *to* and *two* matches for the search phrase *too*.
Find All Word Forms	Matches on similar parts of speech that match the search phrase. Therefore, Word 2000 would not consider the verb *color* to be a match for the noun *color* when you check this option.

Word 2000 cannot conduct a Word Form search if you have checked either the Use Wildcards or Sounds Like options.

AutoCorrecting and AutoFormatting

Word 2000 is smart. Often, Word 2000 fixes problems without you ever being aware of them, thanks to Word 2000's *AutoCorrect* feature. AutoCorrect uses a Microsoft-created technology called Intellisense to hunt constantly for errors. As you type, Word 2000 analyzes the errors and makes corrections or suggested improvements along the way. If you have selected Tools, AutoCorrect and selected Replace text as you type and Automatically use suggestions from the spelling checker options, Word 2000 makes spelling corrections as you type.

 AutoCorrect is a Word 2000 feature that corrects your document as you type it.

The Office Assistant is always there to guide you, but AutoCorrect is integral to Word 2000 as well as to the other Office 2000 products. If AutoCorrect recognizes a typing mistake, it immediately corrects the mistake.

Following are just a few of the mistakes AutoCorrect recognizes and corrects as you type:

- AutoCorrect corrects two initial capital letters at the beginning of sentences. LAtely, we have been gone becomes Lately, we have been gone.
- AutoCorrect corrects sentences that don't begin with an uppercase letter by capitalizing the first letter for you.

- AutoCorrect capitalizes the names of days and months that you forget to capitalize.
- AutoCorrect corrects a sentence that you accidentally type in the Caps Lock key mode. For example, `lATELY, WE'VE BEEN GONE` becomes `Lately, we've been gone`.
- AutoCorrect replaces common symbols' predefined characters. When you type `(c)`, for example, Word 2000 converts the characters to a single copyright symbol.
- AutoCorrect replaces common spelling transpositions, such as `teh` with `the`.

If AutoCorrect corrects something that you don't want corrected, press Alt+Backspace and AutoCorrect reverses itself.

All the AutoCorrections in this list are preset. You can add your own, as you will want to do when you run across common words and phrases that you often type. You will most certainly want to add your initials to the AutoCorrect table, for example, so that you need only to type your initials when you want to enter your full name in a document.

To add your own AutoCorrect entries, perform these steps:

1. Select Tools, AutoCorrect. Word 2000 displays the AutoCorrect dialog box, as shown in Figure 3.9.

FIGURE 3.9.

*Add your own
AutoCorrect entries.*

2. Type the AutoCorrect shortcut, such as an abbreviation, in the Replace text box.
3. Press Tab.
4. Type the AutoCorrect replacement text in the With text box.

5. Press Enter.

After you enter a new AutoCorrect entry, you can begin using the AutoCorrect feature immediately.

In addition to AutoCorrect entries, Word 2000 also automatically formats special character combinations within your document as you type. Word 2000 converts common typed fractions, such as 1/2, to their single character equivalent. You can control exactly which *AutoFormat* features Word 2000 uses by selecting Tools, AutoCorrect and clicking the AutoFormat As You Type tab. Figure 3.10 shows you what options you can control.

FIGURE 3.10.

Word 2000 formats your text as you type.

3

 AutoFormat is a feature within Word 2000 that changes the format of some text, such as fractions and dates, as you type.

Editing Multiple Documents

With Word 2000, you can work with multiple documents. You could be typing a letter to a friend and composing that memo to your out-of-state office before the mail runs, for example.

> **STEP-UP**
>
> Unlike previous versions of Word, Word 2000 tracks multiple documents in separate Word 2000 windows. Each window has its own taskbar button. Therefore, you can switch between documents by selecting from the Window menu, by pressing Ctrl+F6 to switch between the Word 2000 documents, or by pressing Alt+Tab or clicking a button on the Windows taskbar to activate the window that contains the document you want to see.

Instead of closing your letter, click the toolbar's New button to create a blank document. The new document appears on top of your letter. Switch between the letter and your memo by selecting the filename from the menu bar's Window option. In most instances, only one document is active (visible on the screen) at one time. When you issue a Close or Save command, Word 2000 closes or saves the active document.

Select Window, Arrange All to show both (or as many as you currently have open) documents simultaneously, as shown in Figure 3.11. (The documents must not be maximized before you select Arrange All.) When you display both documents, you can scroll each document individually, rearrange the window sizes to give more or less space to one of the documents, and copy and paste text between the documents. (The section that appeared earlier this hour titled "Copying, Cutting, and Pasting" explained how to copy, cut, and paste text within a document, between windows, and between applications.)

FIGURE 3.11.

Word 2000 enables you to edit two or more documents simultaneously.

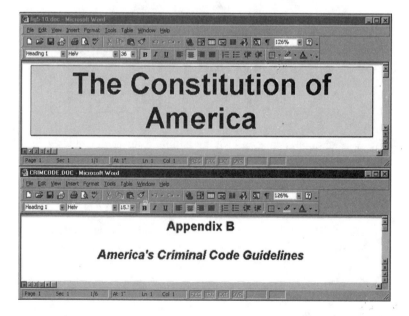

If you display multiple document windows, the window with the highlighted title bar and window buttons is the active window. It often helps to hide the ruler (select View, Ruler) to make more room to display your documents within multiple windows.

Word 2000 documents end with the `.doc` filename extension, as in `Proposal.doc` and `Sales Notes.doc`. (Filenames can have spaces in them.) You don't have to type the extension when opening or saving documents; Office 2000 automatically attaches the correct extension.

Correcting Mistakes

At any point you can *undo*, or reverse, your most recent edit or edits. Click the toolbar's Undo button. (This performs the same action as selecting Edit, Undo, and is easier to use in most cases.) If you delete a character or even an entire paragraph, for example, click Undo. Word 2000 puts the deleted text right back where it was originally!

NEW TERM   An *undo* is the reversal of an edit.

3

As you edit documents, Word 2000 changes its Edit | Undo menu option to reflect your last change; if you delete text, for example, the Edit menu's first option becomes Undo Clear, indicating that you can undo the clearing of text that you previously performed.

Word 2000 keeps track of multiple edits. Therefore, if you realize that the last three edits you made were wrong, click Undo three times and Word 2000 reverses those three edits no matter what the edits were. If you go too far, press the Redo toolbar button, and Word 2000 replaces the undo—in effect, undoing the undo! It gets confusing. If you click the arrows next to either the toolbar's Undo or Redo buttons, Word 2000 displays a list of up to 100 recent changes, which you can choose to undo or *redo as a group from that point forward*.

NEW TERM   The reversal of an undo is a *redo*.

Word 2000 can reverse any and all replacements you make with the Find and Replace dialog box.

In addition to undoing wrong edits, Word 2000 works in the background to keep your documents as safe as possible. Table 3.3 describes Word 2000's automatic file-saving features. (You can control these features through the Tools, Options dialog box.) Therefore, if you turn off your PC before saving your work, you still have the edits to the point of the most recently saved document.

TABLE 3.3. WORD 2000'S FILE-SAVING FEATURES.

Feature	Description
Automatic backup	When you begin editing an existing document, Word 2000 saves a copy of the original document with the original name and the `.bak` extension (for *backup*). No matter how much you change (or mess up) your document, the original version is always safely stored until your next editing session on that document.
AutoRecovery	Automatically saves enough of your document to restore the complete document at that point. Subsequently, if your power goes out or your computer system crashes before you have a chance to save your document and exit Word 2000, and provided that you have turned on the AutoRecovery option, Word 2000 recovers the document the next time you start Word 2000. Ordinarily, you would lose your last edits and possibly your entire document. As long as you have turned on the AutoRecovery option, Word 2000 recovers the document the next time you start Word 2000. The more frequently you set AutoRecover's timer, the more likely you will be able to recover your most recent edits if a power failure or system crash occurs.

Quitting Word 2000

After you are finished with Word 2000, you can quit by performing any of the following:

- Select File, Exit.
- Press Alt+F4.
- Double-click the Control menu icon.
- Close the window.

 Always quit Word 2000 and shut down Windows (by selecting Start, Shut Down, Shut Down) before turning off your computer; otherwise, you might lose your work.

Summary

This hour introduced Word 2000, Office 2000's word processing product. As you saw in this hour, Word 2000 makes entering text simple, and Word 2000 even corrects mistakes as you type.

One of Office 2000's many productivity factors is that the products in the Office 2000 suite often work in a similar manner. Therefore, many of the skills you learned in Word 2000 this hour carry over to the other products. If you have used Word in the past, you have already seen some of the improvements Microsoft made with Word 2000.

The next hour delves further into Word 2000 and shows you how to format your document's text. In addition, you see how the Word 2000 templates and wizards practically create your documents for you.

3

Q&A

Q What are the wavy lines I see beneath some of the that text I type?

A The red and green wavy lines indicate that Word 2000 found a spelling or grammatical error. Word 2000 is not perfect, just helpful, and sometimes Word 2000 incorrectly flags such errors when they are not really errors. You learn in Hour 5, "Managing Documents and Customizing Word 2000," how to handle the errors and teach Word 2000 what is correct.

Q Does it matter whether I press Tab or several spaces when I want to move text to the right?

A In some cases, pressing Tab and the Spacebar several times seem to produce the same visual results, but you should reserve Tab presses for those times when you want to indent or align several lines of text. You can more easily adjust tab spacing later if you want to change the indention.

Q I create special charts and tables with Word 2000, and I don't always want AutoCorrect to do its thing. How can I keep AutoCorrect from making certain corrections?

A Select the AutoCorrect corrections you need from the Tools, Options menu. If you want AutoCorrect to make a particular correction most but not all the time, you can always reverse a single AutoCorrect correction by pressing the toolbar's Undo button as soon as Word 2000 makes the AutoCorrect change.

HOUR 4

Formatting with Word 2000

This hour demonstrates Word 2000's formatting features, which add style and flair to your writing. Not only can Word 2000 help your writing read better, it can help your writing look better as well.

Word 2000 supports character, paragraph, and even document formatting. You can control every aspect of your document. If you don't want to take the time to format individual elements, Word 2000 can format your entire document automatically for you. When you begin learning Word 2000, type your text before formatting it so that you get your thoughts in the document while they are still fresh. After you type your document, you can format its text.

The highlights of this hour include the following:

- Which character formats Word 2000 supports
- What fonts are all about
- Why you should not get too fancy with most document formats

- How to apply paragraph formats
- When different views are helpful
- How to see a preview of your printed document

Simple Character Formatting

When you want to make a point, you can *format* your text. The three standard character formatting styles are underline, boldface, and italicized text. Figure 4.1 shows a document with boldfaced and italicized text on the top half and with underlined text on the bottom half.

Bold and Italicized

Figure 4.1.

Character formatting improves your documents.

Underlined

These special formatting styles are called *character formats* even though you can apply them to multiple characters, paragraphs, and complete documents as easily as you can apply them to single characters. The character formatting styles attach themselves to whatever text you select for the formatting.

NEW TERM A *format* is the shape, size, and position that you can apply to selected text, margins, headers, footers, page numbers, and virtually any other element of a document.

> *Express but don't impress.* You learn how to add a lot of fancy styles in this hour. Too many styles make your documents look busy and take away from your writing goals. Add only enough fanciness to add appeal to your writing.

To apply boldface, italic, or underlining, for example, select the text that you want to format and click the Bold, Italic, or Underline toolbar buttons. To apply formatting to a single word, first click within the word and then click the appropriate toolbar button.

> The shortcut keys Ctrl+B (boldface), Ctrl+I (italic), and Ctrl+U (underlining) apply character formatting, and your hands don't have to leave your keyboard to click the mouse. Press one of the shortcuts before you type the text you want to format. When you want to stop formatting, press the same shortcut key to deactivate the formatting.

4

Applying Fonts

One of the most common formatting changes you can make is to change the *font* used in your document. A font determines the way your characters look, from their size to their curliness to their elegance. Fonts have different names, such as Courier New and Times New Roman.

 NEW TERM The *font* is a collection of letters, numbers, and special characters that contain the same typeface, thickness, and size. Consider *font* to be synonymous with *character*.

Think about your daily newspaper. The banner across the top of the page probably looks like old Gothic letters; the headlines are more standard type. Either might or might not be boldfaced, underlined, or italicized (although a newspaper rarely applies underlining styles). Throughout your paper, the articles might contain the same font as the headline, but the headline font may be larger and heavier than the articles' font.

The size of a font is measured in *points*. One point is 1/72nd of an inch. As a standard rule of thumb, a 10- or 12-point size is standard and readable for most word processed writing. As you type and move your text cursor throughout a document, Word 2000 displays the current font name and size on the formatting toolbar. To change any selected text's font name or size, click the drop-down arrow to the right of the Font Name box, or use the Font Size drop-down list to select a new value.

NEW TERM   A *point* is a font character measurement that equals 1/72nd of an inch.

Instead of using the toolbar to apply font and other format changes, you can set formats in the Font dialog box. When you select Format, Font, Word 2000 displays the Font dialog box, as shown in Figure 4.2. You can also display the Font dialog box by right-clicking selected text and choosing Font from the pop-up menu.

Not only can you set multiple character formats from one location (the Font dialog box), but also Word 2000 displays a preview of the font in the dialog box's Preview area. Therefore, you can select various font names, sizes, and styles and see the results before actually closing the dialog box to apply those changes. When the previewed text looks the way you want, select OK and apply those changes to your selected text.

FIGURE 4.2.

Set many character formats in the Font dialog box.

If you select the Hidden character format in the Font dialog box, the hidden text appears on your screen but does not print. Hidden text is great for notes to yourself and explanatory information that supports the surrounding text that you want to print. If you use hidden text, be sure to check the Hidden text option in the Tools, Options View page. Otherwise, the hidden text won't show up on your screen.

You can quickly see a list of font styles and select one by displaying the font drop-down list as shown in Figure 4.3. After selecting text, or before typing new text, you can select a new font style from this drop-down list. Unlike previous versions of Word, the Word 2000 font style drop-down list actually shows an example of each font next to its name.

Current font style

FIGURE 4.3.

Examples of each font appear along with the font name.

Font style drop-down list box

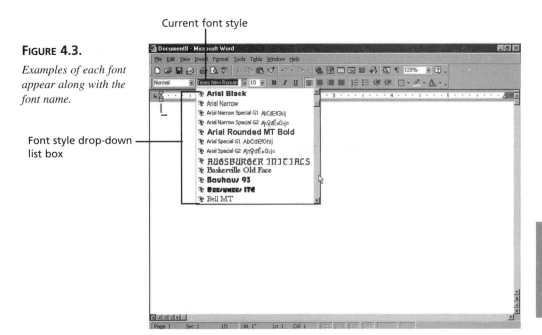

4

Applying Color

One special character format that you can apply almost as easily as the three from the preceding section is color. When you click the drop-down arrow next to the Font Color toolbar button, Word 2000 displays the small Font Color dialog box, as shown in Figure 4.4. Click a color, and Word 2000 changes your selected text to that color. In addition to text, you can apply color to the background by selecting Format, Background.

The Highlight tool on the toolbar (available when you click the same More Buttons toolbar button you click to display the Font Color button) does outline text in color, but is not a color-formatting tool. Instead, the Highlight tool works great for marking important text that you want to reference later or make stand out to the next reader. When you select text and click the Highlight tool (click the Highlight tool's drop-down arrow to change the highlighting color), Word 2000 highlights the text as though you marked your screen with a yellow highlighter pen.

The Font Color table

Click to display the
Font Color table

FIGURE 4.4.

*You can change the
color of text.*

Remember that Office 2000 now easily links with the Internet and the
Internet's fancy and colorful World Wide Web pages (see Hour 23, "Creating
Web Pages with Office 2000"). When you use Word 2000 to create a colorful
Web page, the Font Color button comes in handy.

Paragraph Formatting

Some formats work on characters; others are better suited for paragraphs. This section
describes the essentials for formatting your paragraphs so that your documents look the
way you want them to look.

As with all the formatting commands, you can apply a paragraph format
before typing to apply the formatting to all subsequent paragraphs that you
type.

Justifying Text

Perhaps the most common paragraph formats are the justification formats. When you *justify* text, you determine the text's alignment. Word 2000 supports these justification options:

- Left-justification aligns (makes even) text with the left margin.
- Center-justification centers text between the left and right margins.
- Right-justification aligns text with the right margin.
- Full-justification aligns text with both the left and right margins.

NEW TERM To *justify* means to align the text flush with the left or right margin (or both as done in a newspaper column) so that it does not show a ragged edge.

The simplest way to justify text is to click anywhere inside the paragraph that you want to justify (or select multiple paragraphs if you want to justify several) and click the toolbar's Align Left, Center, Align Right, or Justify (for full justification) buttons. As you learned in the preceding hour, the new click and type feature of Word 2000 enables you to click at the left, middle, or right of an empty line of text to justify the text that you then type there.

Although you can justify multiple paragraphs and even complete documents, a single paragraph (other than a word or sentence) is the smallest amount of text you can justify— hence, the term *paragraph format*.

Newspaper, magazine, and newsletter columns are usually fully justified. The text evenly aligns with the left and right margins.

NEW TERM *Paragraph format* refers to a format that you can apply to one or more selected paragraphs.

Setting Margins and More

The Page Setup dialog box (shown in Figure 4.5), displayed by selecting the File, Page Setup command or by double-clicking the top of the ruler, enables you to control your paragraph and page margins. Enter values for your top, bottom, left, and right margins so that your text does not print past the margin limits.

4

FIGURE 4.5.

The Page Setup dialog box enables you to set margins, page size, and page layout.

Many printers, especially laser printers, cannot print flush with the edge of the paper. Generally, one-half inch is the minimum margin size these printers allow.

The *gutter* value, if you indicate one, shifts all other measurements away from the inside margin of your page.

NEW TERM   The *gutter* is an area of a page you reserve if you plan to bind your document.

The Header and Footer values determine how far from the top and bottom of your pages the header and footer appear if you supply a header or a footer. (Hour 6, "Advanced Word 2000," describes headers and footers.)

Using Tab Settings

Click the Tabs command button in the Format, Paragraph dialog box to display the Tabs dialog box, as shown in Figure 4.6. A tab controls the vertical spacing for certain items in your text. The bottom line is that a tab keeps you from having to press your Spacebar many times when you want to insert multiple spaces in your text. In addition, a tab is more accurate when aligning text.

Table 4.1 describes each of the options in the Tabs dialog box. After you set tabs, press your Tab key as you enter paragraph text to move the cursor to the next *tab stop*.

NEW TERM   A *tab stop* is the location on a line where a Tab key press moves the cursor. You set tab stops by adding them on the ruler or from within the Tabs dialog box.

4

FIGURE 4.6.

The Tabs dialog box enables you to specify multiple tab settings.

TABLE 4.1. THE TABS DIALOG BOX OPTIONS.

Option	Description
Tab stop position	Enables you to enter individual measurement values, such as .25" to represent one-fourth of an inch. After you type a value, press Set to add that value to the list of tab settings. To clear a tab stop, select the value and click Clear. Click Clear All to clear the entire tab list.
Alignment	
Left	Left-aligns text at the tab stop (the default).
Center	Centers text at the tab stop.
Right	Right-aligns text at the tab stop.
Decimal	Aligns lists of numbers so that their decimal points align with each other.
Bar	Inserts a vertical bar at the tab stop.
Leader	
None	Removes *leader* characters. A leader is a character that provides a path for the eye to follow across the page within a tab stop. By default, Word 2000 displays nothing (blanks only) for tab areas.
....	Displays a series of periods inside the tabs (often used for connecting goods to their corresponding prices in a price list).
----	Displays a series of hyphens inside the tabs.
_____	Displays a series of underlines inside the tabs.

NEW TERM   A *leader* is a character that Word 2000 uses in a tab's blank area.

Later in this hour, the section titled "Making the Ruler Work for You" explains how to use the ruler to set and adjust tab settings.

Setting Indentation and Spacing

If you need to change *indentation* (the space between the page margin and where the text aligns) or *line spacing* (the amount of blank space between lines), select Format, Paragraph to display the Paragraph dialog box, as shown in Figure 4.7.

 Indentation is the space between the page margin and where a line, lines, or paragraph of text aligns.

 Line spacing is the blank space between lines (sometimes called the leading).

FIGURE 4.7.

The Paragraph dialog box holds indentation and spacing values.

As you change the indentation, Word 2000 updates the Preview area at the bottom of the Paragraph dialog box to show your setting results. You can type a Left or Right indentation value or click the arrows to change the current values. A Left indention value indents not only the first line of a paragraph, but the entire paragraph's left margin. A Right indention value indents from the right. You can set off a particular paragraph from surrounding paragraphs, such as a quoted paragraph, by indenting the paragraph by specifying either a Left, Right, or Full (using both) indention value.

 Do not use the Spacebar to indent text on multiple lines because the text will not align properly. Use tab stops to ensure that text aligns down the page.

The drop-down Special values—(None), First Line, and *Hanging Indent*—determine how indentation applies itself to the paragraph. If you leave (None) selected, Word 2000 indents the complete paragraph by the Left and Right indentation values that you supply. If you select First Line, Word 2000 uses the value in the By field to indent only the first line of the selected paragraph.

 NEW TERM A *hanging indent* is an indentation of all lines of a paragraph except the first line.

> If you indent the first line or apply a hanging indent, your Left and Right indentation values still apply to the entire paragraph. The first line and hanging indent values specify the *additional indenting* you want Word 2000 to perform on the first or subsequent paragraph lines.

The Spacing section enables you to specify exactly how many points you want Word 2000 to skip before or after each paragraph. You can also select multiple line spacing by selecting from the Line spacing field.

> Increase or decrease a paragraph's indentation by clicking the Decrease Indent and Increase Indent buttons on the toolbar.

Making the Ruler Work for You

As you specify indentation and tab information, the ruler updates to indicate your settings. Not only does the ruler show settings, but you can also make indentation and tab changes directly on the ruler without using dialog boxes.

Figure 4.8 shows the ruler's various tab stops and indentation handles. Click anywhere on the ruler to add a tab stop after you select the appropriate tab from the tab selection area. To remove a tab, drag the tab stop down off the ruler. By dragging an indentation handle, you can change a paragraph's indentation on-the-fly.

> Double-click the bottom of the ruler to display the Tabs dialog box, and double-click the top of the ruler to display the Page Setup dialog box.

4

FIGURE 4.8.

Use the ruler to set and change tabs and indents.

Labels pointing to figure: Hanging indent, Ruler, Center tab stop, Right tab stop, Decimal tab stop, Right Indent, First line indent, Click here to select a tab, Left indent, Left tab stop

Inserting Line and Page Breaks

Lines and pages do not always break the way you need them to. You may want to end a page early because you want to insert a chart at the top of the next page or start a new chapter, for example. Perhaps you want to put a sentence on a line by itself to make it stand out from the surrounding text. The Format, Paragraph dialog box's Line and Page Breaks tab enables you to control the way your document's lines and pages start and stop. When you click the Paragraph dialog box's Line and Page Breaks tab, Word 2000 displays Figure 4.9's settings.

A *widow* is the last line of a paragraph that prints at the top of the next page, and an *orphan* is the first line of a paragraph that prints at the bottom of a page. Usually, widowed and orphaned lines look incomplete. If you click the Widow/Orphan control option, Word 2000 adjusts page breaks, if necessary, so that two or more paragraph lines always begin a page and so that two or more paragraph lines always end a page.

Figure 4.9.

Control the way your paragraph lines break.

NEW TERM   A *widow* is the last line of a paragraph that prints at the top of a page.

NEW TERM   An *orphan* is the first line of a paragraph that prints at the bottom of a page.

The Keep Lines Together check box ensures that a page break never breaks the selected paragraph. The Keep with Next check box ensures that a page break never appears between the current paragraph and the next. The Page Break Before check box forces a page break before the selected paragraph even if a page break would not normally appear for several more lines.

By enabling the Suppress Line Numbers check box, law pleadings and other documents with line numbers will not print the lines on the selected paragraph lines. If you have set up automatic hyphenation, the Don't Hyphenate option deactivates automatic hyphenation for the selected paragraph.

Viewing Your Document's Formatting

Try this: Type and format some text. Press Shift+F1. The mouse pointer changes to a question mark. When you click over text, Word 2000 displays all the information about that selected text, including the character and paragraph formatting applied. This is neat! (Figure 4.10 shows an example.) To get rid of the formatting description, press Shift+F1 again or the Esc key.

4

FIGURE 4.10.

You can find out a lot about formats!

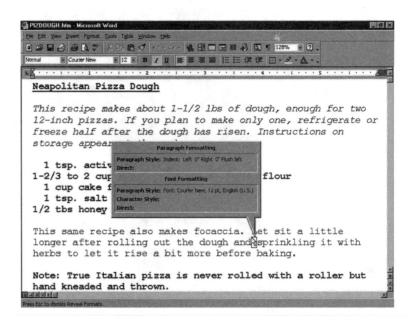

Formatting with Styles

A *style* is a collection of character and paragraph formats you can apply to your document. Each style has a name. Word 2000 comes with several styles, and you can also create your own.

 A *style* is a named collection of formatting styles applied regularly on specific kinds of text such as headings.

Click the drop-down arrow on the Style toolbar field (you may have to click the More Buttons button at the right of the toolbar to see the Style drop-down text box) to see the names of the styles. After you select a style, Word 2000 applies it to the current paragraph and subsequent paragraphs that you type. If you want to change a style's formatting or create a new style, select Format, Style to show the Style dialog box. If you want to modify the current style, click Modify; if you want to create a new style, click New.

Suppose that you routinely write résumés for other people, and you have created three separate sets of character and paragraph formats that work well, respectively, for the title of a résumé and an applicant's personal information and work history. Instead of defining each of these formats every time you create a résumé, format a paragraph with each style and store the styles under their own names (such as Résumé Title, Résumé Personal, and Résumé Work). The next time you write a résumé, you need only to click the Style toolbar button and select Résumé Title from the style list. When you then type the title, the title looks the way you want it to look without your having to designate any character or paragraph format.

Understanding Document Views

Now that you can format your document, you need to know how to display it onscreen to make the best use of the formatting during the editing process. Word 2000 supports several display views that present your document in different ways. Use the View menu to select a view, or click one of the view buttons on the horizontal scrollbar above the status bar (you must be displaying the scrollbars to see the view buttons).

The Normal View

For routine document creation and editing, the Normal view presents the cleanest screen approach and shows all character and paragraph formatting. If you choose to display special formatting characters such as italicized text, you will see those in the Normal view as well. All figures in this and the previous chapters show the Normal view.

The Web Layout View

When you want to view and edit Web pages in Word 2000, select the Web Layout view. The Web Layout view handles proper frame wrapping of text that Web pages require and display graphics in their proper orientation for a Web page. Although you can display and edit a Web page in any Word 2000 view, the Web Layout view more accurately reflects the Web page as it will appear in a browser window.

4

> **STEP-UP**
> The Web Layout view replaces the Online Layout view of previous versions of Word.

The Print Layout View

If you want to view your document exactly the way it will print, select the Print Layout view. The Print Layout view shows any details, such as headers and footers, and shows you where page breaks occur.

The Outline View

The Outline view gives you true expandable and collapsible views of your document in outline form. If you prefer to write from an outline, you can. Use the predefined heading styles to create your document's outline, and then expand on the outline when you are ready to add detail. (Figure 4.11 shows a document's Outline view.)

Surprisingly, Word 2000 offers no way to print the Outline view.

FIGURE 4.11.

If you work with outlines, the Outline view is for you.

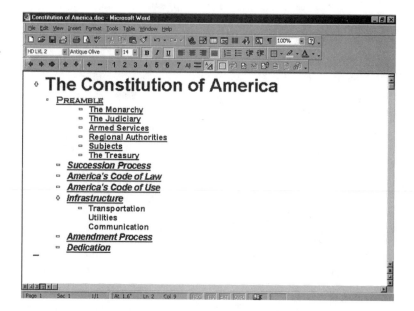

The Outline view presents the structure of the document, and shows exactly as much detail as you want to see. By clicking the heading numbers (corresponding to the styles Heading 1, Heading 2, and so on) or the plus and minus signs on the Outlining toolbar, you can see more or less detail. All the detail stays with your document, but all the detail does not appear at one time.

Full Screen View

When you need to see as much of your document as possible, select View, Full Screen. Word 2000 hides the toolbars, status bars, and menus to give more screen real estate to your document. Click the Restore window or press Esc to return to the preceding viewing state.

Print Preview

Print Preview shows how your document will look on paper. As Figure 4.12 shows, you can click Print Preview's Multiple Pages button to display several pages. You get a bird's-eye view of your printed document, which enables you to predict print format problems without wasting time or paper.

Click the Close button or press Esc to exit the preview.

FIGURE 4.12.

View how your printed document's pages will look.

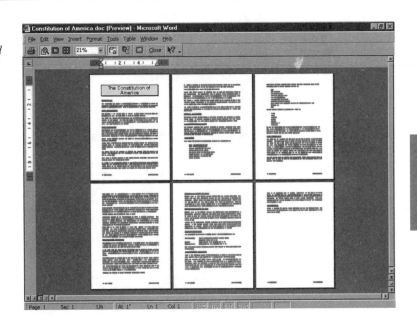

4

If you want a closer view of your Print Preview, click the magnifying glass mouse pointer anywhere on the preview to see the preview in more detail.

If you select File, Web Page Preview, Word 2000 displays the document inside your browser's window to show you how the document will look as a Web page.

Determine Your Own View

The Zoom dialog box (shown in Figure 4.13), displayed by selecting View, Zoom, enables you to adjust the display size of your characters onscreen so that you can see more text on the screen. If your margins and font size make your document's text wider than your screen size but you want to see entire lines, shrink the percentage shown in the Zoom dialog box to squeeze more text on to your screen. You can enable Word 2000 to adjust the size to fill your entire screen by selecting the Page Width option.

FIGURE 4.13.

Display as much of your text as you need to.

Inserting Numbers and Bullets

Word 2000 makes numbered and bulleted lists easy to produce. If you have set the proper AutoFormat options (see Hour 3, "Welcome to Word 2000"), follow these steps to create a properly formatted and indented numbered list:

1. Press Tab to start the first numbered item.
2. Type the number, such as 1. (follow the number with a period).
3. Press Tab.
4. Type the text that goes with the first numbered item.
5. Press Enter. The Office Assistant (if you have activated it) indicates that Word 2000 converted your previous text to a numbered list. You can change it back to regular text, deactivate the numbering, or click OK to continue the list.
6. Press Cancel if Office Assistant is present. Word 2000 automatically formats the first item and types the second number to prepare you for the next item.
7. Keep entering numbered items. When you finish, press Enter after a number, and Word 2000 converts that final numbered line to regular text.

In other words, to create a well-formatted numbered list, just start typing the list! Word 2000 formats and numbers your list after you enter the first item. If you want to convert a series of paragraphs or lines to a numbered list, select the text and click the Numbering toolbar button.

Here's another numbering trick: Before typing the numbered list, click the Numbering toolbar button. Word 2000 starts the list, types the first number for you, inserts a tab, and you only have to complete the numbered item. Word 2000 continues to add the numbers as you complete the list.

 One of the best features of Word 2000 is that you can delete and insert numbered items from and to numbered lists, and Word 2000 automatically renumbers the other items!

If you want to create a bulleted list, type the items to be bulleted, select those lines, and click the Bullets button. Again, when you add and delete items, Word 2000 automatically adds or removes the bullets and formats new items.

 Control the size of the bullets as well as the styles in your bulleted and numbered lists by selecting Format, Bullets and Numbering.

A Word About Word 2000's Wizards

This hour has discussed formatting your text and document as you type text or after you have entered the text. Word 2000's wizards, however, set up your document's format before you create your document. When you select File, New, Word 2000 displays a list of wizards and templates from which you can select.

 Templates contain formatting that you can use, as well as automated buttons that you can click to format certain text elements. Wizards are more interactive and produce more customized documents than do templates.

For example, select File, New, click the Publications tab, and double-click the Brochure Wizard icon. Word 2000 walks you through a step-by-step procedure to create a brochure.

4

Summary

This hour explained the various format options available to Word 2000 users. Keep your audience in mind; don't overdo formats or your documents will look cluttered. Keep your documents readable and remember your presentation as you format.

You can apply the character formats to individual characters as well as to selected text and the entire document. Paragraph formats control the spacing and justification of paragraphs. The views enable you to see your document from various perspectives so that you can determine whether your formats work well together. Perhaps the best indicator of style is the Print Preview, which shows how your document will look when you print it.

The next hour moves into document management and Word 2000 customization. Depending on how you use Word 2000, you might want to change the way Word 2000 behaves in certain situations.

Q&A

Q How can I type an italicized paragraph?

A Before typing any text that you want formatted in any way, set up the formatting. If you want to italicize a word, phrase, or an entire document that you are about to type, press Ctrl+I (or click the toolbar's Italic button) before you type, and Word 2000 will italicize the text. If you have already typed a paragraph that you want to italicize, select the paragraph and press Ctrl+I or click the Italic toolbar button.

Q How can I see my entire page on the screen at once?

A If you have an extremely high-resolution monitor and graphics adapter card, you can probably see an entire document page when you select the full-screen view with View, Full Screen. If you want to see the toolbars, menu, and status bar, however, you probably have to adjust the zoom factor when you select View, Zoom. After you display the Zoom dialog box, click the Page Width option to enable Word 2000 to fit the text within your screen width, or you can control the width using the Percent option. The only other way to see an entire page is to select the Print Preview mode; in Preview mode, you can make simple margin adjustments but no text changes.

Q How can I make margin adjustments in Print Preview mode?

A You should adjust the margins only when displaying a single page. Therefore, if you see multiple page previews, click the One Page button to show a single page. Then click the View Ruler bar to add a ruler to the top of the page. Use your mouse to drag and adjust the left, right, top, and bottom margins. Although such margin adjustments are not as accurate as you can set from within the Page Setup dialog box, you can visually see the results as you make margin adjustments on-the-fly.

Hour **5**

Managing Documents and Customizing Word 2000

This hour works more globally with your documents than the previous two hours. Instead of concentrating on specific editing skills, you learn how to manage your document properties. Word 2000 can keep track of several document-related items, and that tracking really comes in handy if you work in a group environment.

The proofing tools in Word 2000 are powerful and work as you type. The spell checker acts as a mentor looking over your shoulder with a dictionary, supplying you with suggested spellings for mistyped words. Additionally, Word 2000 helps with grammar, hyphenation, and synonyms.

The highlights of this hour include the following:

- What document properties are
- Where to locate and change a document's properties

- How to request the spell and grammar checker
- Why you need to proof documents manually despite the proofing tools in Word 2000
- How to customize Word 2000 to behave the way you want

Understanding Document Properties

Each Word 2000 document (as well as the other Office 2000 documents) has properties.
A *property* is information related to a particular document, such as the author's name and
creation date. If you do not specify properties, Word 2000 adds its own to your document. You see the Properties dialog box (shown in Figure 5.1) when you select File,
Properties.

NEW TERM Information related to a certain document, such as the number of paragraphs
inside the document, the document name, or the document's author, is called a
property. Other objects, such as icons, menu items, and toolbars also have properties of
their own.

FIGURE 5.1.

*Track your document's
properties.*

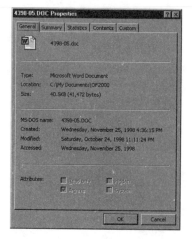

The tabs in the Properties dialog box provide the following information:

- *General*. Contains the document's file information, including the date and time you
  created, last modified, and last accessed the document.
- *Summary*. Tracks a document title, author (name to which software is registered by
  default), keywords, and comments you enter about the document.
- *Statistics*. Tracks the document's numeric statistics, such as character, word, page
  counts, and total editing time.

- *Contents*. Describes the parts of your document, such as the header, body, and footer.
- *Custom*. Keeps track of information you want in the order you specify. You can keep track of customized properties, such as the department responsible for creating or maintaining the document, a project group name that works on the document, and the person responsible for typing the document's information.

> As you add items to the Properties list box, indicate the item's data type (such as text or date) so that Word 2000 can properly format the property value that you want to track. The Custom tab is great for departments in which many people see and edit the same set of documents.

Some properties are available elsewhere in Word 2000. You can find a document's statistics, such as word and paragraph counts, for example, by selecting Tools, Word Count. Often, you can select from the menu option more quickly than displaying the document properties.

> If you create numerous documents and continually search through your disk files for particular ones, try adding search keywords to the Properties Summary page so that you can more quickly find that document using the Advanced Search option in the Open dialog box.

5

Using Word 2000's Advanced Proofreaders

Word 2000 offers these proofreading services for your writing:

- *Spell checker*. Checks your document's spelling either from beginning to end or as you enter it into the document.
- *Grammar checker*. Checks your document's grammar either from beginning to end or as you enter it into the document.
- *Thesaurus*. Provides synonyms when you need them.

NEW TERM A *thesaurus* is a list of synonyms.

- *Hyphenation*. Automatically hyphenates words at the end of lines, when appropriate, either from beginning to end or as you enter the text into the document.

STEP-UP

Previous versions of Word did not correct spelling errors as you typed your documents. You could request a manual spell check only after you typed the document. In addition, you could (and still can) right-click over a misspelled word underlined with a red wavy line and select the replacement. Only if you manually inserted an AutoCorrect entry would Word automatically correct spelling errors. Now when you type a misspelling, Word 2000 automatically substitutes the closest match in the spelling correction dictionary for the word so that you can keep typing.

Word 2000's built-in proofreading tools do not eliminate your proofing responsibilities! No matter how good Word 2000 is, Word 2000 cannot match human skills when deciphering the written language. Word 2000's spell check has no problem with this sentence, for example:

Wee road two the see too sea the waives.

The proofreading tools work only as guides to find those problems you might have missed during your own extensive proofing.

Perhaps the most important reason to learn the proofreading tools is that the other Office 2000 products use similar features. Therefore, after you learn how to use Word 2000's proofreading tools, you also know how to use the tools for an Excel 2000 worksheet or an Access 2000 database.

Using the Spell Checker

Word 2000 automatically checks your spelling and your grammar as you type your document. Any time you see red wavy underlines and green wavy underlines as you type, Word 2000 is letting you know about a possible spelling problem (the red line) or grammar problem (the green line).

Depending on the options you (or someone else) have set, your version of Word 2000 might not check both spelling and grammar as you type. Therefore, if you don't see any wavy lines, you should check your document's spelling and grammar after you have typed the document so that you don't miss anything. In addition, you may not see wavy lines if Word 2000 replaced all your misspellings with corrected entries.

To turn on and off the Check Spelling as You Type option, choose Tools, Options, and then click the Spelling & Grammar tab. On that tab, check the Check Spelling as You Type check box.

When you see a red wavy line, you can correct the problem in these ways:

- Edit the misspelling.
- Right-click the misspelling to display the pop-up menu shown in Figure 5.2. Word 2000 offers you the following options:
  - Ignore all subsequent similar misspellings (in case you want to type foreign words or formal names, but you don't want to add those words to Word 2000's spelling dictionaries).
  - Add the word to Word 2000's dictionary so that Word 2000 no longer flags the word as misspelled.
  - Select AutoCorrect and choose a correct word to add the misspelling to the AutoCorrect entries so that Word 2000 subsequently corrects the word for you on-the-fly.
  - Specify a different language dictionary to use.
  - Display Word 2000's more comprehensive Spelling dialog box, as shown in Figure 5.3.

FIGURE 5.2.

Right-click to select your spell-correction choice when Word 2000 finds a misspelling.

5

Word 2000 enables you to easily remove words that you accidentally add to your spelling dictionary. Select Tools, Options and click the Spelling & Grammar tab. Click the Dictionaries button. Select the dictionary from which you want to delete (most probably the Custom dictionary, which is the default unless you have created a new customized dictionary), and click the Edit button. Word 2000 displays the dictionary's words in a document so that you can delete the word or words you no longer want. (You can also edit any existing words or add new words.) Click the Save toolbar button. You must also turn on automatic spell checking by displaying the Spelling & Grammar page once again and checking the option labeled Check Spelling as You Type.

- Ignore the misspelling and leave the red wavy line.
- Ignore the misspelling, but check the entire document's spelling after you finish typing the document.

FIGURE 5.3.

The Spelling dialog box offers more options than the pop-up menu.

The Spelling dialog box appears when you click the pop-up menu Spelling option for a misspelled word or when you select Spelling and Grammar from the Tools menu. Table 5.1 lists the options in the Spelling dialog box.

When you check the spelling of your document from Tools, Spelling and Grammar, Word 2000 checks from the cursor's current position down to the end of your document. If you want Word 2000 to check your entire document's spelling in one step (assuming you have turned off the automatic spell checking that occurs as you type), move your cursor to the top of your document (by pressing Ctrl+Home) before requesting the spell check.

TABLE 5.1. THE SPELLING DIALOG BOX OPTIONS PROVIDE SPELLING SERVICES.

Option	Description
Ignore	Tells Word 2000 to ignore only this single occurrence of the misspelling.
Ignore All	Tells Word 2000 to ignore *all* occurrences of this misspelling in this document.
Add	Adds the word to Word 2000's spelling dictionary so that Word 2000 subsequently knows the word's spelling.
Change	Changes this single misspelling to the selected correction.
Change All	Changes all the document's misspellings of the current word to the selected correction.
AutoCorrect	Adds the misspelling and selected correction to your collection of AutoText entries.
Options	Displays the Spelling & Grammar options page (shown in Figure 5.4) on which you can modify the behavior of the spelling and grammar checker.
Undo	Undoes your most recent spell correction. The spell checker supports multiple undo levels so that you can undo more than one correction you have made.

FIGURE 5.4.

Change the Spelling & Grammar options dialog box.

5

Using the Grammar Checker

When you see a green wavy line beneath a word, Word 2000 is warning you about a possible grammar problem. Figure 5.5 shows the pop-up menu Word 2000 displays when you right-click a green wavy-lined word.

FIGURE 5.5.

Word 2000 displays a pop-up menu when you right-click a word with a green wavy underline.

Wait until you finish your document before you check the grammar. The grammar-correction process takes a few minutes to complete. In most cases, you should turn off the automatic grammar checker to speed Word 2000's response time as you type your document (to do so, select Tools, Options, select the Spelling & Grammar tab, and then uncheck the Check Grammar as You Type check box). When you finish typing the document, select Tools, Spelling and Grammar button to start the process as well.

Keep Office Assistant turned on when you check grammar. Microsoft added a lot of plain-spoken, grammar-correcting advice to the Office Assistant's repertoire of helpful topics.

As with the spelling pop-up menu, you can replace the grammar problem with the suggested word or words, ignore the suspected problem (just because Word 2000 indicates a problem does not necessarily mean that one exists), or you can start the full grammar-checking system to correct that problem as well as the rest of the document.

When you check a document's grammar from the Tools, Spelling and Grammar option (to check the entire document) or by selecting the full grammar check from the pop-up menu, Word 2000 displays the same Spelling & Grammar dialog box you see when you check for spelling only. As Figure 5.6 shows, however, the Office Assistant chimes in with its advice as well. The Office Assistant advice often provides very clear descriptions and examples of why your grammar might have a problem at the flagged location.

FIGURE 5.6.

Select your grammar-correction choice when Word 2000 finds a problem.

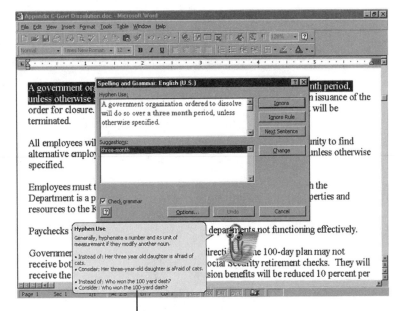

Office Assistant offers advice.

Using Automatic Hyphenation

5

Word 2000 can hyphenate your text as you type, or you can manually hyphenate your entire document. Word 2000 supports three kinds of hyphens:

- *Regular hyphens*, which Word 2000 uses to break words at the end of lines (when needed) to maintain proper document formatting. You must turn on automatic hyphenation by selecting Tools, Language, Hyphenation and checking the option labeled Automatically Hyphenate Document.

- *Optional hyphens*, which break special words (*AutoCorrect* becomes *Auto-Correct*, for example) only if those words appear at the end of lines (press Ctrl+Hyphen to indicate where you want the optional hyphen as you type the word).

NEW TERM An *optional hyphen* breaks special terms and proper names only if those words appear at the end of a line.

- *Nonbreaking hyphens*, which keep certain hyphenated words together at all times; if the hyphenated name *Brian-Kent* appears at the end of a line and you want to prevent Word 2000 from breaking apart the names at the end of a line, for example, press Ctrl+Shift+Hyphen to add that word's hyphen when you type the word.

NEW TERM   A *nonbreaking hyphen* keeps two hyphenated words together so that they never break at the end of a line.

You need to indicate optional and nonbreaking hyphens only when you type special words that Word 2000 would not typically recognize, such as company names and special terms.

You can adjust the amount of hyphenation that Word 2000 performs. Select Tools, Language, Hyphenation to display the Hyphenation dialog box, as shown in Figure 5.7. The Hyphenation zone field enables you to determine the amount of space between the end of a line's last word and the right margin. (A higher value reduces the number of hyphens that Word 2000 adds.) If you want to keep the hyphenation to a minimum, consider limiting the number of consecutive lines that Word 2000 can hyphenate at one time by specifying a Limit consecutive hyphens to field value.

FIGURE 5.7.

*Specify automatic
hyphenation.*

To hyphenate your document manually after you have created it, select Tools, Language, Hyphenation and click Manual. Word 2000 prompts for your approval at each hyphen location.

If you want to stop Word 2000 from hyphenating particular paragraphs, select those paragraphs, and then select Format, Paragraph, click the Line and Page Breaks tab, and check the Don't Hyphenate option.

If you export your document text to another program or computer system (such as a desktop publishing or typesetting system) for publication, do not have Word 2000 hyphenate your document. The target system that produces the final output should control the hyphenation, if possible. If you have Word 2000 hyphenate your document, hyphens may appear in the middle of lines if the typesetter fails to eliminate all of Word 2000's hyphens.

Using the Thesaurus

When you just can't seem to think of a particular word, you can type a *synonym* (a different word whose meaning is similar) and solicit Word 2000's thesaurus for a suggestion. To see a list of synonyms, select a word (or click anywhere in the word) and select Tools, Language, Thesaurus (or press Shift+F7). Word 2000 displays the Thesaurus dialog box, as shown in Figure 5.8.

NEW TERM   A *synonym* is a word whose meaning is similar to another.

FIGURE 5.8.

Find synonyms fast.

From the Thesaurus dialog box, you can select a replacement word (Word 2000 then automatically replaces the original word with the replacement), or use the replacement word list to look up additional synonyms. If you cannot find a good synonym for dissolve but one of the replacement words for *dissolve* is *liquefy*, for example, look up synonyms for *liquefy* by selecting the *liquefy* entry in the Thesaurus dialog box and clicking Look Up. Through this link of related words, you might find the synonym for which you are looking.

> Use the Thesaurus dialog box when you want to see antonyms (words with meanings that are opposite to the selected word). Word 2000 supplies antonyms for some of the words as well. Click the Antonyms entry to see the *antonyms*.

NEW TERM   *Antonyms* are words with opposite meanings.

Customizing Word 2000 to Work for You

If you don't like the way Word 2000 does something, you can usually customize Word 2000 to act the way you want. The Tools menu contains options that enable you to customize Word 2000:

5

- *Customize*. Enables you to change the layout of Word 2000's toolbars and menus
- *Options*. Enables you to control the behavior of most of Word 2000's automatic and manual editing features

Using the Tools, Customize Features

Figure 5.9 shows the dialog box that appears when you select Tools, Customize. (Your dialog box may show a different set of checked options from the figure's.)

FIGURE 5.9.

Customize toolbars and menus.

The Toolbars tab enables you to specify exactly which toolbars you want to see, if any, during your editing sessions. Although Word 2000 hides rarely used toolbar buttons, too many toolbars can clutter your screen and take away editing space, but different toolbars are useful at different times. Display the Tables and Borders toolbar, for example, any time you want to create or edit tables in your documents.

Most people modify the Commands tab when they want to add or remove an item from the menus in Word 2000. Select the menu from the Categories list, and Word 2000 displays that menu's items in the Commands list. You then can change a menu label or select one from the list that Word 2000 doesn't already display for that menu item. Additionally, if you start automating Word 2000 with *macros* (predefined keyboard shortcuts) or Visual Basic programs (which require some computer-programming skills), the Commands tab enables you to hook your own procedure commands to new menu items.

NEW TERM   *Macros* are predefined keyboard shortcuts.

The Options tab controls enable you to increase the size of the toolbar icons to read them more easily (at the expense of some editing area), to determine whether you want to see ToolTips, and to determine whether you want shortcut keys attached to those ToolTips.

Using the Tools, Options Features

Tools, Options is the Library of Congress of Word 2000 options. From this dialog box, you can modify the behavior of these Word 2000 features:

- *View*. Changes the way Word 2000 displays documents and windows.
- *General*. Determines colors, animation, behavior, and the measurement standard (such as inches or centimeters).
- *Edit*. Changes the way Word 2000 responds during your editing sessions.
- *Print*. Determines several printing options.
- *Save*. Specifies how you want Word 2000 to save document changes.
- *Spelling & Grammar*. Lists several spell-checking and grammar-checking settings that you can change. This is one place where you can turn these options on or off.
- *File Locations*. Enables you to set disk drive locations for common files.
- *Compatibility*. Lists a plethora of options you can change to make Word 2000 look and feel like other word processors, including previous versions of Word.
- *User Information*. Holds name, initials, and address of the registered party for use with document summaries and automatic return addresses.
- *Track Changes*. Determines the format Word 2000 uses when you make changes to documents in a group environment or when you want to track several revisions for the same document. (Word 2000 can keep track of multiple versions of a document.)

Summary

5

This hour explained how to manage your documents through the use of document properties. The document properties contain count statistics as well as other pertinent information that stays with your documents. If you work in an office environment, the properties help maintain order when many people edit the same document.

Part of managing your documents is proofing them to make them more readable and correct. The proofing tools in Word 2000 include a spell checker, grammar checker, hyphenation capabilities, and thesaurus. Although these tools don't replace human proofreading, they can help you locate problems.

You can customize almost any part of Word 2000. This hour gives you just a glimpse of the many modifications that can be made to Word 2000. Take the time to peruse the Tools, Options tabs. Even advanced Word 2000 users forget some of the options that can make their editing lives simpler. Check the options screens frequently as you learn Word 2000 and you will make Word 2000 work the way you want it to.

The next hour wraps up Word 2000 by teaching you its more advanced capabilities.

Q&A

Q Does Word 2000 update my document-property values for me?

A In some cases, Word 2000 updates your document's property values. As you type words into your document, for example, Word 2000 updates that document's word count. You must specify other user-specific properties, such as the document-search keywords and comments.

Q Why should I wait until after I create a document to proof it?

A Most Word 2000 users prefer to turn on the automatic spell checker but wait until their document is finished before hyphenating and checking the grammar. During the editing process, edits frequently change hyphenation locations; depending on your computer's speed, Word 2000 might slow down considerably to update changed hyphens when you change lines. Additionally, the grammar checker has to work constantly as you create your document, not only slowing down your edits but also indicating bad grammar in the places where you might be typing rough-draft material.

Q Should I modify Word 2000 settings if several people use the same computer?

A If you share a computer with others, you should not customize Word 2000 without telling the others what you have done. As a group, you might determine that certain Word 2000 options are better defined than others, but be sure to make customization changes only with the consent of others. Otherwise, the next person who uses Word 2000 might think Word 2000 no longer can check spelling, when in fact you have only turned off the spell checker temporarily.

HOUR 6

Advanced Word 2000

This hour wraps up our Word 2000 coverage by giving you an idea of Word 2000's uncommon features and advanced capabilities. Despite their advanced nature, Word 2000's advanced features are not difficult to use.

You will find a lot of tidbits throughout this chapter that you will use as you write. From inserting special characters to creating multiple-column newsletters, Word 2000 offers something for everybody's writing needs.

The highlights of this hour include the following:

- How to type special characters that don't appear on your keyboard
- How to insert the date, time, and page numbers in your documents
- When to add AutoText and when to add AutoCorrect entries
- How to prepare tables for your documents
- How to convert a single-column document into multiple columns
- What headers, footers, footnotes, and endnotes are all about

Using Special Characters

Symbols are special characters that don't appear on the standard keyboard. If you want to type special symbols, select Insert, Symbol to display the Symbol dialog box, shown in Figure 6.1.

 A *symbol* is a special character that doesn't appear on the standard keyboard (such as a copyright symbol).

FIGURE 6.1.

Find a symbol you want to insert.

If you don't see the symbol you want to insert, select a different font from the Font drop-down list. Many fonts, such as *WingDings*, supply special symbols from which you can choose.

> If you find yourself inserting the same symbol over and over again, consider adding that symbol to your AutoCorrect table. Click the Insert, Symbol dialog box's AutoCorrect button to see the AutoCorrect dialog box (in which Word 2000 has already inserted the symbol); type the AutoCorrect entry that you will use to produce the special symbol, press Enter, and you have created the AutoCorrect entry for that symbol.

In addition to adding a symbol-based AutoCorrect entry, you can assign a shortcut key to any symbol. Click the dialog box's Shortcut Key button, type a shortcut keystroke (such as Alt+Shift+S), and press Enter. Word 2000 then assigns that shortcut keystroke to the special symbol. Subsequently, you won't have to display the Symbol dialog box to insert special symbols, but will only have to press the appropriate keystroke.

Many special characters already have AutoCorrect and shortcut key entries. If you want to see these predefined symbols, click the Symbol dialog box's Special Characters tab to show the Special Characters page, as shown in Figure 6.2. Scroll through the list to see the predefined characters currently set.

FIGURE 6.2.

Word 2000 comes pre-defined with many shortcuts for symbols.

Inserting Dates, Page Numbers, and Comments

In addition to special characters, you can insert the date and time at the cursor's current position. Select Insert, Date and Time, and select the date and time format from Word 2000's selection list. If you click the Update Automatically option, Word 2000 constantly updates the date and time; if you leave the Update Automatically option unchecked, Word 2000 keeps the original date and time in the document.

> Press Shift+Alt+D to insert the date at the text cursor's location.

If you want Word 2000 to insert page numbers at the top or bottom of the document's printed pages, select Insert, Page Numbers. Word 2000 displays the Page Numbers dialog box. Tell Word 2000 whether you want the page numbers to appear at the top or bottom of the document pages, as well as on which portion of the page they should appear (left, center, right, inside on facing pages, or outside on facing pages).

> Word 2000 can format page numbers in several formats, such as 1, Page 1, -1-, Roman numerals, and even letters of the alphabet. Click Format to select from the various page-number format options.

6

One of the most interesting items that you can insert in a Word 2000 document is a *comment*. A comment does not print, but shows up on your screen highlighted in yellow so that you are sure to see it.

NEW TERM A *comment* is a Word 2000 document message that you can see onscreen but that does not print.

Suppose that you want to remind yourself to do something later when you edit the document, such as format the title with information you will research at another time. Just write yourself a comment! The comment acts like a yellow sticky note. The comment stays attached to your text, but you can read or remove the comment whenever you want.

To insert a comment in your text, select Insert, Comment. Word 2000 displays the comment's annotation window, as shown in Figure 6.3.

Comment is attached here

FIGURE 6.3.

Add comments to your writing.

Type comment here

Word 2000 names each of your comments using your initials (found in the document property settings). After you type your comment and click Close, Word 2000 attaches the comment to text and indicates the comment by highlighting the anchor text in bright yellow and inserting the comment name inside square brackets. Comments provide a convenient method for leaving messages for coworkers inside documents that you edit as a team.

Subsequently, when you edit your document, you see the yellow comments. If you right-click the comment, Word 2000's pop-up menu enables you to edit (or read) the comment, or delete the comment from the text.

Creating and Using AutoText Entries

Whereas AutoCorrect is great for quickly inserting formal names and common phrases, AutoText enables you to quickly insert completely formatted multilined text. AutoText is often called *boilerplate text*, which is a publishing term used for text that appears frequently.

 Boilerplate text is text that you often type, such as your company name and address.

Suppose, for example, that you often place your boldfaced, 16-point, name and address centered across the top of your personal letters. Instead of typing and formatting this text each time you need it, follow these steps to add the text as an AutoText entry:

1. Type and format the text you want to add to the AutoText entries. Make sure that it is exactly as you want it to be reproduced.

2. Select the text.

3. Select Insert, AutoText, AutoText. Word 2000 displays the AutoText page, which shows the AutoText entries currently in effect, as shown in Figure 6.4.

FIGURE 6.4.

Adding an AutoText entry makes subsequent typing easier.

6

4. Type an abbreviation for the AutoText entry in the field labeled Enter AutoText Entries Here. You can either type this text to activate the AutoText entry or you can select from the available options listed.

5. Press Enter.

When you subsequently type the AutoText entry's abbreviation and press F3, Word 2000 replaces the abbreviation with your expanded formatted AutoText entry. AutoText entries require the F3 keystroke, whereas AutoCorrect entries automatically appear when you type their abbreviations. Nevertheless, AutoText entries can be more complex and span multiple lines, whereas AutoCorrect entries are more limiting.

STEP-UP

Word 2000 contains an assortment of predefined AutoText entries. If you type Created on and press F3, for example, Word 2000 adds the current date and time to the end of the Created on text in your document. Select Tools, AutoCorrect and click the AutoText tab to see the AutoText entries defined.

If you use the predefined AutoText entries often, consider adding better shortcuts. Add a second Created on AutoText entry called cron, for example, so that you don't have to type as much to enter the AutoText in your document. To add a cron entry that mimics that of Created on, type Created on and press F3 to display the current entry. Highlight the expanded words and select Insert, AutoText, AutoText. Type the new name, cron, and click Add to add the new entry.

Adding Tables to Your Documents

Word 2000's report-creation power shines when you see how easily you can create customized tables of information inside Word 2000. *Tables* are collections of information organized in rows and columns. Tables might contain numbers, text, even graphics, or combinations of any of these. Each row and column intersection is called a *cell*. When you use both Word 2000 and Excel 2000, you might want to embed part of an Excel 2000's worksheet into a Word 2000 table. Embedded worksheets enable you to report financial data from within Word 2000. (Hour 7, "Excel 2000 Workbooks," introduces Excel 2000.)

NEW TERM   A *table* is a collection of data organized in rows and columns.

NEW TERM   A *cell* is a single table entry.

Creating a New Table

To create a new table, perform these steps:

1. Select Table, Insert, Table. Word 2000 displays the Insert Table dialog box, as shown in Figure 6.5.

FIGURE 6.5.

Use the Insert Table dialog box to prepare the new table.

2. Specify the number of columns and rows your table will need. You can change these values later if you need to. Estimate on the high end, however, because it is easier to delete additional rows and columns than to add them.

3. Enter a column width, or leave the Column Width field set to Auto if you want Word 2000 to guess the table's width. You can change a table's column width at any time (even after you enter data). You can request that Word 2000 automatically adjust each column's width to the widest data in the column by selecting the AutoFit to contents option. The Autofit to window option adjusts the column widths equally within the table's size if you resize the window that holds the table.

4. When creating your first table, press Enter. After you get used to creating tables, you can click the AutoFormat button to select from a list of predefined table formats, as shown in Figure 6.6.

FIGURE 6.6.

Word 2000 can format your table automatically.

6

5. Click OK (or press Enter) to close the dialog box. Word 2000 creates your table and outlines the table's cells in a grid format.

Word 2000 contains another tool that helps you build more customized tables. You can draw your tables by clicking the Insert Table toolbar button and dragging the resulting table of cells down and to the right until you have outlined the table size you prefer. In addition, you can draw tables freehand using the Word 2000 tools available as described in a later section titled "Drawing Tables Freehand."

Traversing the Table

One of the easiest ways to enter data in a table's cell is to click the cell (which moves the text cursor to the cell) and type. As you type past the cell's right margin, Word 2000 wraps the cell and increases the row height (if needed) to display the complete cell contents.

When you begin typing data, notice that Word 2000's automatic formatting might not match the table's data; perhaps one of the columns is too narrow or too wide. Use your mouse to adjust the size of a row or a column's width by clicking and dragging one of the table's four edges in or out. You can also expand or shrink individual columns and rows by dragging their edges.

When you move your cursor to a table's row or column edge, Word 2000 changes the mouse pointer to a table-adjuster cursor. When the mouse cursor changes, you can drag your mouse to resize the column or row.

Although you can click a cell with your mouse every time you want to enter or edit the contents of that cell, the table cursor-movement keystrokes come in handy because you can traverse the table without ever removing your hands from the keyboard. Table 6.1 describes how to traverse a table's rows and columns.

TABLE 6.1. MOVING AROUND A TABLE.

Press This...	To Move the Table's Cursor Here
Tab	The next cell
Shift+Tab	The preceding cell
Alt+PageUp	The column's top cell

Press This...	To Move the Table's Cursor Here
Alt+PageDown	The column's bottom cell
Alt+Home	The current row's first cell
Alt+End	The current row's last cell

To highlight a row, click in the margin left of the row; Word 2000 highlights the entire row. Drag your mouse down or up to select multiple rows.

Inserting New Columns and Rows

Not creating enough rows or columns for your table is one of the first table problems you will encounter. To insert or delete rows or columns, select a row or column and right-click your mouse.

Suppose that you need to insert a column. Select the column that will appear after the new column by pointing above the column until the mouse pointer changes to a down arrow. Select multiple columns by dragging your mouse to the right after you have selected one column. Right-click your mouse to display a pop-up menu. The menu will differ, depending on whether you have selected a row or column first. Select Insert Columns, and Word 2000 inserts a new column before the selected column. The right-click menu also contains a Delete Columns command.

To highlight a row, point to the margin left of the row; Word 2000 highlights the entire row. Drag your mouse down or up to select multiple rows. When you right-click your mouse, the pop-up menu contains an Insert Rows and a Delete Rows command.

After you create a simple table, click the table next to it and then select Table, Table AutoFormat to select a style, such as the shaded style in Figure 6.7. The table in Figure 6.7 is only a three-column table, but Word 2000 turned it into a professional-looking, chiseled data storehouse.

6

Drawing Tables Freehand

As you have seen, the Tables menu option gives you complete control over tables you create. Word 2000 goes one step further to help you create exactly the table you want. The toolbar's Tables and Borders tool enables you to draw tables freehand the way you might draw using a pencil and paper. The Tables and Borders tool enables you to quickly draw tables that don't necessarily have an equal number of columns for each row.

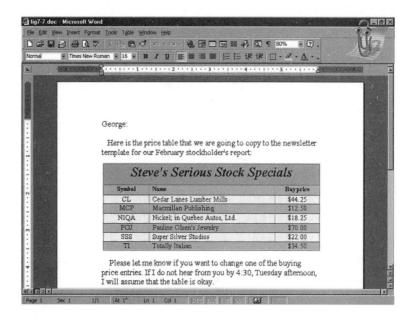

FIGURE 6.7.

Make sophisticated tables out of simple ones.

Follow these steps to use the Tables and Borders tool:

1. Click the location in your document where you want the new table.

2. Click the Tables and Borders tool. (You may have to click the More Buttons toolbar button first to locate the Tables and Borders button on your toolbar.) Your mouse cursor turns into a pencil shape, and the Tables and Borders toolbar appears.

3. Click and drag the pencil cursor diagonally down and across the page. A rectangular table outline appears. When you release the mouse, the outline becomes your table's outline.

4. Continue adding rows and columns by dragging the mouse. Notice that you can draw (by dragging) a partial row or partial column. If you draw a row or column you don't want, click the Tables and Borders Eraser tool and retrace the table lines you want to delete.

You can also change the table's line style by selecting a different style from the Tables and Borders toolbar and change the line's thickness by selecting from the Tables and Borders toolbar's Line Weight list box.

After you have drawn the table's basic outline, use the Border Color, Outside Border, and Shading Color tools to modify the table's colors. The remaining tools enable you to merge two or more cells into one, split long cells into multiple cells, change a cell's text alignment (as you might do with border columns), equally distribute columns or rows within an area, sort (alphabetically or numerically) cells within a selected row or column, and automatically sum a selected row or column.

Figure 6.8 helps to show what you can do with the freehand Tables and Borders tool. The top portion of the figure shows a table drawn freehand, and the bottom shows the results of entering the table's data and making a few simple edits using the Tables and Borders tools. Word 2000 makes tables as simple as drawing with a pencil and paper.

FIGURE 6.8.

You can format your freehand tables into professional-looking tables.

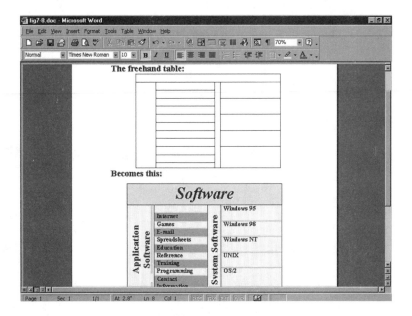

STEP-UP

Unlike previous versions of Word, Word 2000 enables you to draw multiple freehand tables next to each other as well as draw the table around existing text.

6

Creating Multiple Columns on a Page

When you want to create newspaper-style columns—such as those that appear in newsletters and brochures—configure Word 2000 to format your text with multiple columns. You can assign multiple columns to the entire document or to only a selected part of your document. Figure 6.9 shows a document with three columns and a single column at the top for the title area. Generally, you should type your document's text before breaking the document into multiple columns.

FIGURE 6.9.

You can use multiple columns for brochures and other pamphlets.

When you want to set multiple columns, follow these steps:

1. Select the text you want to convert to multiple columns. If you want to select your entire document, press Ctrl+A.

2. Select Format, Columns to display the Columns dialog box shown in Figure 6.10.

3. Click the preset column format and enter the number of columns you want to produce.

4. In the dialog box's Width and Spacing area, adjust the column width and spacing between columns if you want to adjust Word 2000's default. Generally, the default measurements work well. As you adjust the columns, Word 2000 updates the Preview area to give you an idea of the final result.

5. If you want a line between the columns, click the option labeled Line between.

6. When you click OK, Word 2000 formats your selected text into multiple columns.

To add multiple columns quickly and let Word 2000 handle the spacing (which Word 2000 generally does well), select the text that you want to format into multiple columns and then click the toolbar button's Columns button. Drag your mouse to the left to select the number of columns (from one to four). When you release the mouse, Word 2000 formats the multiple columns.

FIGURE 6.10.

Set up multiple columns with the Columns dialog box.

 If you format your document into multiple columns that are right-justified, you will probably need to hyphenate the document. Thin, justified columns often contain a lot of extra spaces that Word 2000 inserts to maintain the right-justification. You may want to select File, Print Preview to see how your overall document looks with the narrow columns.

Creating Headers and Footers

A *header* is text that appears at the top of each page (or the pages you select, such as all even pages) in your document. A *footer* appears at the bottom of your pages. You don't have to add headers and footers to each page—Word 2000 enables you to type them just once, and it automatically adds them to each page.

 A *header* contains text that appears at the top of your document pages.

 A *footer* contains text that appears at the bottom of your document pages.

To add a header or footer, follow these steps:

1. Select View, Header and Footer to display the Header and Footer toolbar, as well as outline boxes where you can type the header and footer text. Figure 6.11 shows a document that displays this toolbar, as well as the Header entry box.

6

Header entry box

FIGURE 6.11.

*Use the Header and
Footer toolbar to
adjust your docu-
ment's header and
footer.*

The First 100 Days: The Novel

Day One

"The twentieth century was not a good one for the United States," Candy judged. At 4:58 a.m., Candy
Smythe, the 28-year old ABS executive secretary, finished preparing the room for the 5:00 a.m. meeting.
"Nobody could foul up things worse than they've been over these last two years," Candy thought
solemnly. "Good grief, especially last month, nothing could beat last month," she thought. Still, here she
was, prepping ABS's executive conference room at New York City's One Rockefeller Center Plaza, for
this emergency meeting.

Header and
Footer toolbar

angry. Fred Rasner, the president of ABS News, was more than angry. He and his associates were
bewildered. Even frightened, she could see as they filed into the room quietly. They were tired too,
since most had only left a few hours ago about midnight. They all had rooms in the Waldorf Astoria
which, conveniently, was a quick three-minute walk from the office.

Page number Date Time Switch Between Header and Footer button

2. Type your header text. If you want to type footer text, click the toolbar's Switch
   Between Header and Footer button to display the footer text box and type your
   footer text. If you want to add page numbers, the date, or time to your header or
   footer text, click the appropriate toolbar buttons.

3. Click the Close button to anchor the header or footer in your document.

Word 2000 normally dims header and footer text so that you can easily distinguish
between the header, footer, and the rest of your document text when editing your document within the Page Layout view. If you want to specify that the header (or footer)
appears only on certain pages, select the File, Page Setup option and adjust the Headers
and Footers values. You must be in the Page Layout view to see headers, footers, footnotes, and endnotes in their proper places on the page.

If you want to edit a header or footer, double-click the dimmed header or
footer text while editing your document. Word 2000 opens the Header and
Footer toolbar and enables you to edit the header or footer text.

Adding Footnotes and Endnotes

A *footnote* differs from a footer in that a footnote appears only at the bottom of the page on which you include it. Word 2000 inserts a footnote reference in the text where you choose to insert the footnote; if you later add text to the page so that the footnote reference moves to the next document page, Word 2000 automatically moves the footnote as well; therefore, the footnote always appears on the same page as its reference.

NEW TERM *Footnotes* contain text that appears at the bottom of the page on which its corresponding footnote reference appears.

To insert a footnote, follow these steps:

1. Select Insert, Footnote. Word 2000 displays the Footnote and Endnote dialog box shown in Figure 6.12. *Endnotes* are footnotes that appear at the end of your document rather than at the bottom of each page. Click the option you want to add, Footnote or Endnote.

FIGURE 6.12.

Add footnotes and endnotes with this dialog box.

NEW TERM *Endnotes* are footnotes that appear at the end of your document, each with its own endnote reference number that appears in the document.

2. If you want Word 2000 to number the footnote (or endnote) sequentially starting with 1, click OK. If you want to use a different symbol for the number, click Custom mark and enter the reference you want to use.

3. Click OK. Word 2000 adds a separating line between your document and the note, adds the reference number to your document text where you inserted the footnote, and places the cursor at the bottom of the page next to the footnote reference number.

4. Type the footnote (or endnote) and click your mouse on the body of the document to resume editing.

Remember that you must display the Page Layout view to see headers, footers, footnotes, and endnotes in their proper places on the page. If you display your document in Normal view, Word 2000 displays the supplemental notes in a separate window.

6

Summary

This hour wrapped up this book's discussion of Word 2000. You learned how to add the document extras that often turn simple writing into powerful cross-referenced published works.

If you need to display tabular information, let Word 2000 create and format your tables so that your data presentation looks clean. In addition, multiple columns work well for newsletters and brochures to keep the reader's attention.

To speed up your writing, use as many AutoCorrect and AutoText entries as you can. If you repeatedly type a phrase, sentence, or block of information, that text is a good candidate for AutoCorrect or AutoText.

Hour 7 introduces you to Excel 2000. As you will see, Excel 2000 enables you to present numeric data as professionally as Word 2000 presents your documents.

Q&A

Q Should I use AutoText or AutoCorrect?

A You must decide how much formatting and effort the boilerplate text requires. If you need to type the same text often but the text consists of only a word or two and requires no special formatting, use AutoCorrect (Tools, AutoCorrect). With AutoCorrect, Word 2000 makes changes for you as you type the AutoCorrect abbreviations. (Be careful not to create AutoCorrect entries from common words, or Word 2000 might replace text that you don't always want replaced.) If the text is lengthy or requires special formatting that spans multiple lines, however, add the text as an AutoText entry. After you type the AutoText abbreviation, press the F3 key to expand the abbreviation into the formatted full text.

Q Why can't I see my headers and footers while editing my document?

A Perhaps you are displaying your document in Normal view. Select View, Page Layout to see headers and footers in their correct positions on the page.

Q What is the difference between a table and a document formatted with multiple columns?

A Both tables and multicolumn documents have multiple columns. The multicolumn document, however, is useful when you want to create a newspaper-style document with flowing columns of text and graphics. A multicolumn document might contain a table in one of its columns.

Use tables when you want side-by-side columns of related information. Use multiple columns when you want your text to snake from the bottom of one column to the top of another.

PART III

Computing with Excel 2000

Hour

HOUR 7

Excel 2000 Workbooks

This hour introduces you to Excel 2000, Microsoft's spreadsheet program. Excel 2000 is to numbers what Word 2000 is to text; Excel 2000 has been called a *word processor for numbers*. With Excel 2000, you can create numerically based proposals, business plans, business forms, accounting worksheets, and virtually any other document that contains calculated numbers.

If you are new to electronic worksheets, you will probably have to take more time to learn Excel 2000's environment than you had to learn Word 2000's. Excel 2000 starts with a grid of cells in which you place information. This hour takes things slowly to acquaint you with Excel 2000 and explains the background necessary for understanding how an Excel 2000 working area operates.

The highlights of this hour include the following:

- How to start Excel 2000
- What workbooks and worksheets are
- How to enter various kinds of Excel 2000 data
- Which keys to use to navigate through Excel 2000 data
- How to quit Excel 2000

Starting Excel 2000

You start Excel 2000 when you perform one of these actions:

- Click the New Office Document button on the Office 2000 Shortcut Bar and double-click the Blank Workbook icon to create a new Excel 2000 document. (Click the General tab, if it is not already selected, to see the Blank Workbook icon.)
- Click the New Office Document button on the Office 2000 Shortcut Bar and click one of the Excel 2000-based tabs to open an Excel 2000 template or start a wizard. (Hour 2, "Introducing Office 2000's Powerful Features," discussed templates.)
- Click the Open Office Document button on the Office 2000 Shortcut Bar and select an existing Excel 2000 workbook that you want to edit. You may have to traverse directory folders to get to the workbook that you want to open.
- Use the Windows Start menu to start Excel 2000 by clicking Microsoft Excel on the Programs menu.
- Select an Excel 2000 document from the Documents option on the Windows Start menu. Windows recognizes that Excel 2000 created the document workbook and starts Excel 2000, loading the workbook automatically. (The Documents option on the Start menu contains a list of your most recent work.)
- Click the Excel 2000 button on the Office 2000 Shortcut Bar to create a blank workbook. (Depending on your Office 2000 Shortcut Bar's setup, you might not see the Excel 2000 button.)

Figure 7.1 shows the opening Excel 2000 screen. Your screen might differ slightly depending on the options you have set.

FIGURE 7.1.

Familiarize yourself with Excel 2000's opening screen.

Labels: Menu bar, Individual cells, Formatting toolbar, Mouse pointer, Formula toolbar, Row names, Active cell, Worksheet tabs, Column names, Status bar, Office Assistant, Scrollbars

Understanding Workbooks and Worksheets

Excel 2000 enables you to create and edit *workbooks*. A workbook holds one or more *worksheets* (sometimes called *spreadsheets* or just *sheets*). A worksheet is a collection of rows and columns that holds text and numbers. Anytime you create, open, or save an Excel 2000 file, you are working with a workbook. The workbook approach keeps you from having multiple files that relate to the same project—instead, you can have all worksheets related to the same project in the same workbook (in one *.xls file). Your workbook name is the Excel 2000 name you assign when you save a file. You can save Excel 2000 worksheets and workbooks in HTML format if you want to maintain file-type consistency and if you ever want to embed your data in a Web page.

A *workbook* is a collection of worksheets stored in a single file. A workbook is useful for grouping a single project's worksheets together.

7

NEW TERM A *worksheet* is an Excel 2000 table-like document containing rows and columns that holds data and formulas.

A worksheet acts a lot like a Word 2000 table, except that Excel 2000 worksheets can do much more numeric processing than Word 2000 tables can.

> As with Word 2000 data, Excel 2000 often uses the term *document* to refer to a workbook file.

Blank Excel 2000 workbooks contain three worksheets named Sheet1, Sheet2, and Sheet3, as shown at the bottom of Figure 7.1. When you click a sheet's tab, Excel 2000 brings that sheet into view. If a workbook contains several worksheets, you might have to click one of the sheet-scrolling buttons to view additional worksheet tabs. Each column has a heading; heading names start with A, B, and so on. Each row has a heading, starting with 1, 2, and so on. The intersection of a row and column, called a *cell*, also has a name that comes from combining the row name and column number, such as C4 or A1. A1 is always the top-left cell on any worksheet. The gridlines help you to distinguish between cells, but you can turn off gridlines at any time from the Tools, Options, View page option labeled Gridlines.

NEW TERM A *cell* is the intersection of a row and column into which you enter text or numbers. A cell address is the column letter and row number location of the cell; B6 is the cell address for a cell located at column B and row 6.

> No matter how large your monitor is, you will see only a small amount of the worksheet area. Use the scrollbars to see or edit information in the off-screen cells, such as cell M17.

Every cell in your workbook contains a unique name or address to which you can refer when you are tabulating data. The cell address of the active cell (the cell that the cursor is in) appears at the left of the Formula bar. In Figure 7.1, the box reads A1 because the cursor is in cell A1.

When you move your mouse pointer across Excel 2000's screen, notice that the pointer becomes a cross when you point it to a cell area. The cross returns to its pointer shape when you point to another part of the Excel 2000 work area.

Inserting Worksheets in a Workbook

Just as Word 2000 enables you to edit multiple documents in memory at the same time, Excel 2000 enables you to edit multiple worksheets simultaneously (but those worksheets must all appear in the same workbook).

To insert a new worksheet into your workbook, right-click the worksheet tab that is to fall *after* the new worksheet. Select Insert from the pop-up menu. Excel 2000 displays the Insert dialog box, as shown in Figure 7.2, on which you can double-click the Worksheet icon and press OK. The Insert dialog box contains several kinds of items that you can add to a workbook, but worksheets are the most common items you add. The Insert, Worksheet command also inserts a new worksheet.

FIGURE 7.2.

Add a new worksheet to your workbook.

>
> If you don't like the default worksheet names (Sheet1, Sheet2, and so on), rename them by right-clicking the sheet name and selecting Rename. Type the new name. When you press Enter, the worksheet tab displays the new name.

Deleting Worksheets from a Workbook

Situations arise when you only need a single worksheet in a workbook. You might want to track your monthly household budget, for example; such a budget rarely requires multiple worksheets. For your budget, the workbook is basically the same as the worksheet, but you should pare down excess worksheets instead of wasting memory on them. Excel 2000 makes it easy to delete excess sheets. Just right-click the tab of the sheet you want to delete and select Delete from the pop-up menu.

7

You can keep multiple workbooks open at once and move between them by pressing Ctrl+F6 (the same keystroke that moves between multiple Word 2000 documents in memory). Multiple workbooks are often difficult to keep track of until you become familiar with Excel 2000 and its worksheets. Display your Window menu to see a list of open workbooks if you want to review the ones you have opened.

Working with Multiple Worksheets

To specify the maximum number of worksheets that a workbook is to hold, select Tools, Options, click the General tab, and enter a number in the Sheets in New field labeled Sheets in New Workbook. When you create a new workbook, that workbook contains the number of sheets you requested. As you can see from Figure 7.3, Excel 2000's Options dialog box resembles Word 2000's. Many of the options are identical in both products, as well as throughout the Office 2000 suite.

Enter the number of sheets here

FIGURE 7.3.

The Options dialog box enables you to specify how many worksheets to include in your workbooks.

You can refer to a specific cell located within a workbook by prefacing the cell with its workbook name, followed by an exclamation point (!), to refer to a specific worksheet's cell. For example, Sheet3!G7 refers to the seventh row of column G inside the worksheet named Sheet3. Notice that you work from right-to-left when deciphering a reference such as Sheet3!G2.

One interesting workbook feature is the capability to rearrange worksheets within a workbook, and even to move worksheets between two or more workbooks.

If you don't like the current order of the worksheets in your workbook (the worksheet tabs indicate the worksheet ordering), click and drag a worksheet's tag (the mouse cursor changes to let you know you have grabbed the worksheet) to fall before another sheet's tab. If you work with two or three particular worksheets the majority of the time, move those worksheets together so that you can move between them easily.

> Make a copy (instead of moving) of a worksheet by pressing Ctrl before you click and drag a worksheet from one location to another. Excel 2000 creates a new worksheet and uses the original worksheet for the new worksheet's data. Before you make extensive changes to a worksheet, you might want to copy it so that you can revert to the old version should anything go wrong.

Working with Multiple Workbooks

As your workbook fills up with worksheets, you need a way to manage those worksheets and move from one to another. When you then want to copy or move information from one to another worksheet, you can easily do so.

If you need to move a worksheet from one workbook to another, open both workbooks and select Window, Arrange, Tiled to display both worksheets, as shown in Figure 7.4. Drag one of the worksheet tabs to the other workbook to move the sheet. To copy instead of move, hold Ctrl while you drag the sheet name.

FIGURE 7.4.

Display both workbooks if you want to move or copy worksheets or cells between them.

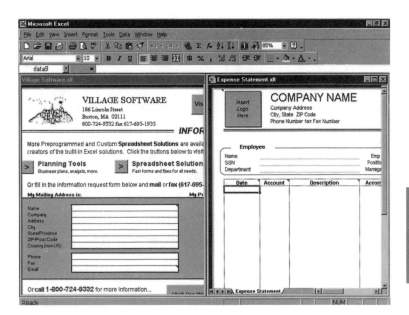

7

Entering Worksheet Data

Often, entering worksheet data requires nothing more than moving the cell pointer to the correct cell and typing the data. The various kinds of data behave differently when entered, however, so you should understand how Excel 2000 accepts assorted data.

Excel 2000 can work with the following kinds of data:

- *Labels*. Text values such as names and addresses
- *Numbers*. Numeric values such as 34, –291, 545.67874, and 0
- *Formulas*. Expressions that compute numeric results (some formulas work with text values as well)
- *Special formats*. Date and time values

As you will see in Part VII, "Combining the Office 2000 Products and the Internet," Excel 2000 works with data from other Office 2000 products. Additionally, you can *import* (transfer) data from other non-Microsoft products, such as Lotus 1-2-3.

NEW TERM   To *import* is to load data from another program into Excel 2000.

Entering Text

If you want to put text (such as a title or a name) in a cell, just place your cursor in the cell and type the text. Excel 2000 left-justifies the text in the cell. As you type, the text appears both in the cell and in the Formula bar. Remember that the Name box to the left of the Formula bar displays the name of the cell into which you are entering data. When you press Enter, Excel 2000 moves the cell pointer down one row.

> Press Tab to move the cell pointer to the right or the arrow keys to move the cell pointer in any direction after you enter data.

If you press Esc at any point during your text entry, Excel 2000 erases the text you typed in the cell and restores the original cell contents.

If your text is wider than the cell, Excel 2000 does one of two things depending on the contents of the adjacent cell to the right:

- If the adjacent cell is empty, Excel 2000 displays the entire contents of the wide cell.

- If the adjacent cell contains data, Excel 2000 truncates (cuts off) the wide cell to show only as much text as fits in the cell's width. Excel 2000 does not remove the unseen data from the cell; however, the adjacent cell, if that cell contains data, always displays instead.

Figure 7.5 shows two long *labels* (label is another name for text data) in cells C5 and C10. The same label, which is longer than standard cell width, appears in both cells. Because no data resides in D5, Excel 2000 displays all the contents of C5. The data in D10, however, overwrites the tail end of C10. C10 still contains the complete label, but only part of it is visible.

> You can increase and shrink the width and height of columns and rows by dragging the edge of the column name or row number. If you drag the right edge of column D to the right, for example, the entire column D (all rows in the column) widens.

NEW TERM   A *label* is text data inside an Excel 2000 cell.

Cell D10 contains data   No data in cell D5 to
that overwrites C10   overwrite C5

FIGURE 7.5.

Excel 2000 may or may not display all of a cell's contents.

7

Some text data, such as price codes, telephone numbers, and Zip codes, fool Excel 2000. As you see in the next section, Excel 2000 treats numeric data differently from text data when you type the data into cells. If you want Excel 2000 to treat a number (such as a Zip code) as a text entry (calculations are not performed on the cell), precede the contents with a single apostrophe ('). For example, to type the Zip code 74137, type '74137; the apostrophe lets Excel 2000 know to format the value as text.

Entering Numbers

Excel 2000 accepts numeric values of all kinds. You can type positive numbers, negative numbers, numbers with decimal points, zero-leading numbers, numbers with dollar signs, percent signs, and even *scientific notation* (a shortcut for writing extremely large and small numbers).

 Scientific notation refers to a format scientists, mathematicians, and engineers often use to write extremely large and extremely small numbers and is based on powers of 10 (such as 3.049 raised to the 1016th power).

 If you type a number but see something like 3.04959E+16 appear in the cell, Excel 2000 converted your number to scientific notation to let you know that the cell is not wide enough to display the entire number in its regular form. Excel 2000 does not extend long numbers into adjacent cells.

Excel 2000 right-justifies numbers inside cells. You can change the format for a single cell or for the entire worksheet, as you see in Hour 8, "Using Excel 2000."

Entering Dates and Times

Excel 2000 supports almost every national and international date and time format. Excel 2000 uses its AutoFormat feature to convert any date or time value that you type to a special internal number that represents the number of days since midnight, January 1, 1900. As with all Office 2000 products, Excel 2000 is Y2K-compliant meaning that Excel 2000 automatically displays all dates the user enters with four-digit year values by showing the full year. Excel 2000 should have little problem with the millennium change. Although this strange internal representation might not make sense now, you use these values a lot to compute time between two or more dates. You can easily determine how many days an account is past due, for example.

Excel 2000 uses a 24-hour clock to represent time values unless you specify a.m. or p.m. To convert p.m. times to 24-hour times, add 12 to all time values after 12:59 p.m. Thus, 7:54 p.m. is 19:54 on a 24-hour clock.

You can type any of the following date and time values to represent 6:15 p.m., July 4, 1976, or a combination of both 6:15 p.m. and July 4, 1976:

```
July 4, 1976
4-Jul-76 6:15 p.m.
6:15 p.m.
18:15
07/04/76 18:15
07-04-76 18:15
```

If you enter any of these date and time values, Excel 2000 converts them to a shortened format (such as `7/4/76 18:15`). You can enter a date, a time value, or both. As with most Office 2000 formats, you can change this default format with the Format menu. The shorter format often helps worksheet columns align better.

Navigating in Excel 2000

Your mouse and arrow keys are the primary navigation keys used to move from cell to cell. Unlike Word 2000, which uses a text cursor, Excel 2000 uses a cell pointer to show you the currently *active* cell. The active cell accepts whatever data you enter next. As you press an arrow key, Excel 2000 moves the active cell pointer in the direction of the arrow.

 The *active* cell is the current highlighted cell that accepts data you type into it.

Table 7.1 lists the most commonly used navigational keystrokes used within a worksheet. Use your mouse to scroll with the scrollbars. To scroll long distances, press Shift while you scroll with the mouse.

7

TABLE 7.1. USING THE KEYBOARD TO NAVIGATE EXCEL 2000.

This Key...	Moves to Here
Arrow keys	The direction of the arrow one cell at a time.
Ctrl+Up arrow, Ctrl+Down arrow	The topmost or bottommost row with data in the worksheet.
Ctrl+Left arrow, Ctrl+Right arrow	The leftmost or rightmost column with data in the worksheet.
PageUp, PageDown	The previous or next screen of the worksheet.
Ctrl+Home	The upper-left corner of the worksheet cell A1.
End, Arrow	The last blank cell in the arrow's direction.
Ctrl+PageUp, Ctrl+PageDown	Move to next or previous worksheet within current workbook.

Quitting Excel 2000

When you are finished with Excel 2000, quit by performing any of the following:

- Select File, Exit.
- Press Alt+F4.
- Double-click the Control icon.
- Click Excel 2000's Close button.

Always quit Excel 2000 and shut down Windows (by selecting Start, Shut Down) before turning off your computer so that you don't lose your work.

Summary

This hour introduced Excel 2000, and covered Excel 2000's screen and the concept of workbooks and worksheets. The workbook documents contain your worksheets, and your worksheets hold data, such as numbers and labels. As you see throughout this part of the book, Excel 2000 supports a tremendous number of formatting options so that you can turn your numeric data into eye-catching, appealing output.

Although Excel 2000 works best with numeric data, Excel 2000 accepts text (called labels), date, and time values as well. Excel 2000 is extremely lenient about how you type dates and times but immediately converts such values into a special internal number. This internal number enables you to calculate with dates when you need to determine the number of days between two dates or when you need to add a fixed number of days to a date to arrive at an ending date, such as a due date.

The next hour extends the concepts of this hour by showing you how to quickly add common data to an Excel 2000 worksheet. In addition, you learn how to edit the values that you type.

Q&A

Q I'm not good at math; can I use Excel 2000?

A If you were great at math, you wouldn't even need Excel 2000! Seriously, Excel 2000 does all the calculating. Your job is to place the numeric data on the worksheets so that Excel 2000 can do its thing. Many people use Excel 2000 for common household actions, such as tracking exercise routines and grocery lists. Excel 2000 is not just for accounting and mathematical applications. You learn, in Hour 9, "Editing Excel Worksheets," how to enter formulas.

Q Do I always enter the time along with the date?

A You can enter either a time value, a date value, or both when entering such information. Excel 2000 turns the information into an internal shortened format. (You can change the display format if you desire to make the data look better.) If you don't enter a date with a time value, Excel 2000 accepts the time value only and tracks just the time. If you enter a date, Excel 2000 tracks only the date.

7

HOUR **8**

Using Excel 2000

This hour teaches you how to improve the accuracy of your worksheet data. You can easily edit cell contents with the tools Excel 2000 provides.

After you master worksheet editing skills, you are then ready to see how Excel 2000's AutoCorrect feature and the spell checker work to improve worksheets. Excel 2000 can also enter values for you. When you ask Excel 2000 to fill in a series of cell values, it uses some intuitive guesswork to complete any series that you begin. If you often enter a special series of numbers or labels, you can teach Excel 2000 that series to eliminate typing when you use the series again.

The highlights of this hour include the following:

- What you do to select multiple worksheet cells
- Why the spell checker and AutoCorrect are important to numeral-based worksheets
- How Excel 2000 fills in a series of values for you
- When you must teach Excel 2000 a new series
- How to find and replace worksheet data

- Why clearing a cell does not always equate to erasing the cell's contents
- How to use comments to describe a cell

Worksheet Editing

Some of the most important Excel 2000 skills you can learn are editing skills. Entering numeric data is error-prone at its best; the faster you edit cell values accurately, the faster you complete accurate worksheets. The following sections show you the primary editing tools Excel 2000 provides.

Selecting Cells

You can select a cell, a row of cells, or a column of cells just by clicking and dragging your mouse. As you drag your mouse, Excel 2000 selects a rectangular region. You notice as you drag your mouse that Excel 2000 displays the number of rows and columns you have selected. You see the message 10R X 4C appear in the toolbar's Name box as you select 10 rows and 4 columns, for example. When you release your mouse, Excel 2000 displays the selection's upper-left corner.

Not only can you select a rectangular region of cells, you can also select disjointed regions. Select the first area, and then press Ctrl while you click another cell and drag the mouse. The selection highlight appears in both places on your screen. Remove any selection by clicking your mouse on any cell or by pressing an arrow key.

Spell Checking

No worksheet program included a spell checker before Excel. After all, worksheets are for numbers, right? Of course, the primary purpose for worksheets is formatting, arranging, and calculating numbers. Numbers without titles, however, are worthless in most instances. You have to present your numeric data in such a way that the worksheet users understand the significance of your data. Given the amount of text you enter on your worksheets, a spell checker makes sense. You can only wonder why worksheet makers did not add spell checkers long before Microsoft added one to Excel.

You can check your worksheet's spelling as follows:

- Click the Spelling toolbar button
- Select Tools, Spelling from the menu
- Press F7, the spelling shortcut key

Unlike Word 2000, Excel 2000 does not include a grammar checker or a synonym finder. Rarely do you include complete sentences on a worksheet, so the grammar checker would be wasted overhead in most cases.

8

The spell checker in Excel 2000 is the same one that Word 2000 uses (see Hour 5, "Managing Documents and Customizing Word 2000," for a quick review). The spell checker does not check every worksheet in your workbook, but only the current worksheet active on your screen. If Excel 2000 finds an error, you can choose to correct, ignore, or add the error so that the word no longer appears as an error (as might be the case for proper names).

AutoCorrect Worksheets

Use AutoCorrect as you type Excel 2000 entries just as you used AutoCorrect in Word 2000. When you type an abbreviation for an AutoCorrect entry, Excel 2000 converts that abbreviated form to the complete AutoCorrect entry for you when you press the Spacebar or leave the cell.

Word 2000, Excel 2000, and all the other core Office 2000 products share the same AutoCorrect and spelling dictionaries. Therefore, when you make changes and additions in the AutoCorrect or spelling dictionaries of Word 2000 or Excel 2000, the other products recognize those changes.

To add AutoCorrect entries, perform the same steps that you do with Word 2000:

1. Select Tools, AutoCorrect.
2. Type your abbreviated AutoCorrect entry in the Replace field.
3. Press Tab.
4. Type the replacement text in the With field.
5. Click OK to return to the worksheet editing area.

Cell Editing

Much of your Excel 2000 editing requires that you correct numeric data-entry. Of course, if you begin to type a number (or a formula, as you learn in the next hour) in a cell but realize you have made a mistake, press Backspace to erase your mistake or press the arrow keys to move the text cursor back over the entry to correct something.

If you have already moved to another cell when you recognize that you have entered an error, quickly correct the mistake like this:

1. Move the cell pointer to the cell you need to correct (click the cell to move the pointer there).

2. Press F2, which is the standard Windows editing shortcut key. (If you still have your hand on the mouse, you can double-click the cell to edit the cell's contents.) You know Excel 2000 is ready for your edit when you see the text cursor appear in the cell.

3. Move the text cursor to the mistake.

4. Press the Insert key to change from Overtype mode to Insert mode or vice versa. As with Word 2000, Overtype mode enables you to write over existing characters, whereas Insert mode shifts all existing characters to the right as you type the correction.

5. Press Enter to anchor the correction in place.

If you want to undo an edit, click the Undo button. To redo an undo, click the Redo button. As you can see, after you have mastered one Office 2000 product (as you have Word 2000), you know a lot about the other products.

Finding and Replacing

Like Word 2000, Excel 2000 contains a powerful search-and-replace operation that can search your worksheet for values and replace those values if needed.

> The find-and-replace feature in Excel 2000 works a little differently from that in Word 2000. The numeric nature of Excel 2000 requires a different type of find and replace. Therefore, read this section even if you have mastered the find-and-replace feature in Word 2000.

Figure 8.1 shows the Find dialog box in Excel 2000. You can request that Excel 2000 search by rows or columns. If your worksheet is generally longer than wide (as most are), select By Columns to speed your search. Indicate whether you want Excel 2000 to match your uppercase and lowercase search text exactly (not applicable for numeric searches), and select the proper Look In option of Formulas, Values, or Comments.

Use Formulas if you are searching for part of a formula (you learn all about formulas in the next hour), use Values if you want Excel 2000 to search only the calculated cells (not within formulas), and use Comments if you want Excel 2000 to search through cell comments. Generally, you are searching through formulas, so Excel 2000 makes Formulas the default search target.

FIGURE 8.1.

Excel 2000's Find dialog box looks for text or numbers.

The Find Entire Cells Only option indicates to Excel 2000 that a cell must contain your entire Find value and nothing else before a proper match will be made.

If you want Excel 2000 to replace the found value with another value, select the Edit, Replace command to display the Replace dialog box, as shown in Figure 8.2.

FIGURE 8.2.

Let Excel 2000 replace values for you.

Click the Replace All button if you want Excel 2000 to replace all occurrences of the found text. (Be sure you want to replace all occurrences or you'll possibly overwrite data unexpectedly.) Otherwise, click Find Next to find the next matching value and, if that is a value you want to replace, click Replace. If it is not a value you want to replace, click Find Next to locate the next occurrence.

If you want to find or replace within a limited worksheet range only, select the range before conducting the find or replace operation.

Reviewing Cut, Copy, and Paste in Excel 2000

If you have mastered the Copy, Cut, and Paste commands in Word 2000, those commands in Excel 2000 will be a breeze for you. As with Word 2000 and the other Office 2000 products, Excel 2000 uses the Windows Clipboard to hold data that you are copying, cutting, and pasting from within or between worksheets. If you open two workbooks at the same time and display both on your screen (by selecting Window, Arrange), you can easily copy, cut, and paste between the two workbooks.

To copy data from one location to another, select the cell or cells you want to copy and click the Copy toolbar button (or press Ctrl+C) to copy the worksheet contents to your Clipboard. Ctrl+A selects the entire worksheet to copy or cut. The contents stay in the original location because you elected to copy and not cut the cells. To paste the Clipboard contents to another location, select the first cell in the target location (which may reside in another workbook) and click the Paste toolbar button (or press Ctrl+V). Excel 2000 overwrites the target cells with the pasted contents, so be sure of the paste target when you paste Clipboard data.

STEP-UP

Office Assistant keeps a close eye on you at all times. If you attempt to paste data into a range that already has data, Office Assistant issues the warning shown in Figure 8.3. You can click OK to accept the overwrite or click Cancel to stop the paste.

FIGURE 8.3.

Office Assistant warns you when you are about to paste over data.

 As with all Office 2000 products, you can send up to twelve distinct items to the Clipboard and paste one or more of the copied items into your worksheet.

You can continue pasting the Clipboard to other worksheets as long as you keep selecting a target location and pressing Ctrl+V.

Excel 2000 supports drag-and-drop editing, so after you select the cells to copy, press Ctrl and drag the selection to its new location. You must drag the selection by pointing to one of the selection edges; if you attempt to drag from the center of a selected cell set, Excel 2000 changes the selection range. When you release your mouse button and the Ctrl key, Excel 2000 pastes the contents to the target location. Of course, drag-and-drop editing works only when you can see both the source and the target copy and paste locations.

To cut contents and place them elsewhere, just select the cells that you want to cut and press Ctrl+X (or click the Cut toolbar button). Excel 2000 removes the selection from its original location and places the selection on your Clipboard. You then can paste the Clipboard contents elsewhere. In effect, cutting and pasting performs a movement of the selected data. If you want to move the selection with your mouse, drag the selection without first pressing Ctrl as you did when copying the contents.

 If you want to drag and drop between two workbooks' worksheets but you only have one worksheet displayed, press the Alt key before dragging your selection. When you drag the selection over the target worksheet's name tab, Excel 2000 opens that worksheet, and you can drop the dragged contents to the open worksheet.

Clearing Data

Because of the nature of worksheets, erasing worksheet data differs from erasing word processed data. Other information on the worksheet can heavily depend on the erased data, as you see in the next hour's lesson. When you want to erase a cell's or selection's contents, first decide which of the following kinds of erasure you want to perform:

- Erase the selection and send the contents to the Clipboard (as you learned in the previous section).
- Clear only a portion of the selection, such as its formatting, comment, or data value.
- Completely erase the selection and all formatting and notes attached to the selection.
- Erase the selected cells and their position so that other cells in the row move left or cells below move up.

A worksheet's cell contains a lot more than just the numbers and text that you see on the worksheet screen. Not only can the cells contain formulas and comments, but also they often rely on other cells for information. Therefore, when you want to erase the selection, you must keep in mind how the selection affects other worksheet areas.

If you want to delete the selected cell's data, press Delete. Excel 2000 retains any formatting and comments that you had applied before you deleted the data.

If you want to more selectively erase a cell, select the Edit, Clear command and select from one of the five options listed here:

- The All option deletes the entire selection, including the contents, format, and attached comments (but not the actual cell).

- The Formats option erases only the selection's format; you can get rid of a cell's special formatting and revert to a general format without changing or erasing the contents of the cell.

- The Contents option deletes the cell contents but leaves the formatting and comments intact.

- The Comments option deletes any special comments that appear in the selected cells.

- The Hyperlinks option removes any Internet-based references within the cell.

 Reverse an accidental deletion with Undo (Ctrl+Z).

Here's a quicker way to erase the values in cells: Select the cells and drag the fill handle up and to the left. As you drag the fill handle, Excel 2000 grays the cells that are erased when you release the mouse button.

To remove the selected cells as well as their contents and close the gap left by the deleted selection, select Edit, Delete to display the Delete dialog box, as shown in Figure 8.4. Select Shift Cells Left or Shift Cells Up so that Excel 2000 knows how to close the gap that the deletion leaves.

FIGURE 8.4.

You can delete cells and move all other cells over those deleted cells.

Speed Data Entry

Excel 2000 can often predict what data you want to enter into a worksheet. By spotting trends in your data, Excel 2000 uses educated guesses to fill in cell data for you. Excel 2000 uses *data fills* to copy and extend data from one cell to several additional cells.

 NEW TERM   *Data fill* refers to the capability of Excel 2000 to spot and continue trends in data that you have started, such as a series of numbers or dates.

One of the most common data fills you perform is to use Excel 2000's capability to copy one cell's data to several other cells. You might want to create a pro forma balance sheet for the previous five-year period, for example. You can insert a two-line label across the top of each year's data. The first line would contain five occurrences of the label Year, and the second line would hold the numbers 1998 through 2002. To use the data fill feature in Excel 2000 to create the five similar labels, perform these simple steps:

1. Click the B3 cell to move the cell cursor there.

2. Type Year. Don't press Enter or any cell-moving cursor keys after you type the label.

3. Locate the cell's *fill handle*. The fill handle is the small black box located in the lower-right corner of the active cell, as shown in Figure 8.5.

Fill handle

FIGURE 8.5.

Extend a cell with the fill handle.

| NEW TERM | A *fill handle* is a cell pointer's box that you can drag to extend and copy the cell's contents. |

4. Drag the fill handle to the right across the next four columns. As you drag the fill handle, Excel 2000 displays the pop-up label Year indicating the value of the new cells.

5. Release the mouse button. Excel 2000 fills all five cells with the label.

If you drag the fill handle down, Excel 2000 copies the label down the column. Excel 2000 even fills a rectangular area if you drag the fill handle across and down the worksheet. Although the Edit, Fill command performs the same function as the fill handle, dragging the fill handle is much easier than selecting from the menu. Ctrl+D performs the same operation as Edit, Fill.

Smarter Fills with AutoFill

Even if the only fill Excel 2000 performed were the copying of data across rows and columns, the data fill would still be beneficial. Excel 2000 goes an extra step, however: It performs smart fills with a feature known as *AutoFill*. AutoFill is perhaps the single

8

reason why Excel took over the spreadsheet market a few years ago and has been the leader ever since. When you use AutoFill, Excel 2000 examines and completes data you have entered.

NEW TERM   *AutoFill* is the technique Excel 2000 uses to complete data from a cell or cell selection.

The five year pro forma period you were setting up in the preceding section included the years 1998 through 2002, for example. You can type 1998 under the first Year title and type 1999 under the second title. Select *both* cells using the same dragging technique you learned about in the Word 2000 section, and then drag the fill handle right three more cells. When you release the mouse button, you see that Excel 2000 properly fills in the remaining years, as shown in Figure 8.6.

FIGURE 8.6.

Excel 2000's AutoFill feature knows which years to fill.

If you had selected only one cell, Excel 2000 would have copied that cell's contents across the worksheet. Excel 2000 needed to see the two selected cells to notice the trend.

The years in Figure 8.6 don't exactly align under the first row, but in the next hour, "Editing Excel Worksheets," you learn how to format data to make your titles align.

Excel 2000 gets even better. If you want to use AutoFill to increment cells by a single number, as you are doing with the years, you don't really need to select two cells first. If you select any cell that contains a number, press Ctrl, and drag the fill handle, Excel 2000 adds a one to each cell to which you extend. Therefore, you could fill four years from 1999 through 2002 just by pressing Ctrl before you dragged the first year's fill handle to the right.

As you know, Excel 2000 works with text as well as with numeric values. AutoFill recognizes many common text trends, including the following:

- Days of the week names
- Days of the week abbreviations (such as Mon, Tue)
- Month names
- Month abbreviations (such as Jan, Feb)

Suppose that you want to list month names down the left of the pro forma sheet, starting in cell A5, because you need to report each month's totals for those five years. All you need to do is type January for the first month name, and drag that cell's fill handle to the twelfth cell below. Figure 8.7 shows the result.

FIGURE 8.7.

Let Excel 2000 fill in the series of month names.

Excel entered these month names

Design Your Own Fills

In addition to the month and weekday names and abbreviations, Excel 2000 can fill in any list of values. You can teach Excel 2000 a new list to use with AutoFill. After you have shown Excel 2000 the new list, anytime you type the first value and drag that cell's fill handle in any direction, Excel 2000 fills the remaining cells with your list.

To add your own AutoFill list to Excel 2000's repertoire of lists, perform these steps:

1. Select Tools, Options.
2. Click the Custom Lists tab to display the current AutoFill lists in effect.
3. Click the Add button.
4. Type your list of values for AutoFill. If you have six departments, you might enter something like Dept 1, Dept 2, Dept 3, Dept 4, Dept 5, and Dept 6. Press Enter between each value. Your screen should look like Figure 8.8.
5. Click OK to add your list to AutoFill's current list.

The next time you type the label Dept 1 in a cell and drag the fill handle to the right or down the worksheet, Excel 2000 fills in the remaining departments. If you fill only four cells, Excel 2000 uses the first four values. If you fill six or more cells, Excel 2000 fills all six departments and starts repeating the department names for any number over six.

FIGURE 8.8.

Teach Excel 2000 new AutoFill entries.

If you enter a series in a worksheet, and then decide that the series would make a great AutoFill list (in case you want to add the list to another worksheet), Excel 2000 doesn't make you re-enter the list. Just select the entire list by dragging the mouse pointer through the list. When you open the Custom Lists dialog box, click Import to add the selected range to the AutoFill entries.

AutoFill is fine for a typical range of titles and for a series of a dozen or fewer entries, but some data series consume numerous entries. When you want to enter a larger number of values in a series, perform these steps:

1. Type the first value of the series in the first cell.

2. Select the cell and all subsequent cells that will receive the rest of the series.

3. Select Edit, Fill, Series to display the Series dialog box.

4. Select Rows if you have selected cells from a row or Columns if you have selected cells from a column.

5. Select the type of series you are entering. Table 8.1 describes each of the four types from which you can choose.

6. Select the subtype. If the series is a series of months, for example, check Month.

7. Enter the Step value, which describes how each value in the series increases or decreases.

8. Enter the Stop value if necessary (you rarely need to enter one). If want to enter a series that increases every three months, for example, you check the Month option, and type 3 for the Step value, Excel 2000 will know the final month and you won't need to enter it.

   Although you won't need to indicate to Excel 2000 where to stop in most instances, a Stop value is useful if you check the Trend option in the Series dialog box. Excel 2000 starts with your initial selected value (if numeric) and estimates the values between that starting value and the Stop value that you supply.

9. Click OK to create and enter the series of values.

TABLE 8.1. TYPES OF SERIES.

Series Name	If You Type...	Excel 2000 Can Complete With
Linear	0	1, 2, 3, 4, 5
	-50, 0, 50, 100	150, 200, 250
Growth	2, 4	8, 16, 32, 64
	10, 100	1000, 10000
Date	1-Jan, 1-Apr	1-Jul, 1-Oct, 1-Jan
AutoFill	Acctg-101, Acctg-102	Acctg-103, Acctg-104
	Year '96	Year '97, Year '98

Adding Comments

As with Word 2000, you can insert *comments* in a cell. The comments act like yellow sticky notes onscreen, except that the notes in Excel 2000 aren't in the way when you don't want to see them. The comments don't appear in the cell; when you insert a comment, Excel 2000 indicates that the comment resides within the cell by flagging the cell's upper-right corner with a red triangle. When you point to the cell, Excel 2000 displays the attached comment.

NEW TERM   A *comment* is a note attached to a cell that doesn't appear as part of the cell's data.

To attach a comment to a selected cell, select Insert, Comment. Excel 2000 opens the box shown in Figure 8.9. Type your comment here. Excel 2000 automatically places your name at the beginning of the comment. The name indicates who added the comment in case you work in a multiple-user environment. (You can erase the name if you don't want to see it.) You can leave coworkers notes if you edit worksheets as a team. You can also leave yourself a note to fill in data that you might get from an outside source later.

FIGURE 8.9.

Add comments to cells.

Attached comment flags

If you select a group of cells and attach a comment, Excel 2000 attaches the comment only to the upper-left cell in the selection. Excel 2000 cannot attach a comment to an entire selection, only to individual cells.

The earlier section in this hour, "Clearing Data," tells you how to remove comments you no longer need.

Summary

Excel 2000's Copy, Cut, and Paste commands work much the same as the corresponding operations in Word 2000. This hour focused more on the differences than similarities between the products. Worksheet data differs from a word processor's, and you must handle certain kinds of Excel 2000 deletions differently from Word 2000 deletions.

This hour taught you how to speed up your data entry by using AutoFill and AutoCorrect. After you teach Excel 2000 your own special series, Excel 2000 fills in that series of values for you. Although accuracy is more important than speed, you will welcome the speedy data-entry tools Excel 2000 provides.

The next hour shows how to work with ranges, formulas, rows, and columns. Now that you have covered the groundwork, you are ready to learn about Excel 2000's powerhouse tools for worksheets.

Q&A

Q How do I know whether Excel 2000 can fill a series I have started?

A Enter the first couple of values, select the cells, and drag the selection's fill handle to the right or down, depending on your desired fill direction. As you drag the fill handle, Excel 2000 shows, in a ToolTips-like pop-up box, which values will fill in the series. If Excel 2000 does not recognize the series, the pop-up values won't be correct. You then can teach Excel 2000 the new series as explained in this hour or enter the remaining values by hand. In many instances, you will be surprised at the power of Excel 2000; if the first two values in your series are 10 and 20, for example, Excel 2000 guesses that you want to extend the series by 10s.

Q **Why does Excel 2000 sometimes select additional cells when all I want to do is extend a series?**

A You are dragging the cell's contents, *not* the fill handle. Be sure that you drag the fill handle when you want Excel 2000 to complete the series. If you drag with one of the cell's straight edges rather than its fill handle, Excel 2000 attempts to move the cell contents from their original location to your dragging target; therefore, be careful that you have grabbed the fill handle when you are ready for the fill.

Q **Why would I want to remove formatting, but not a cell's contents?**

A You learn in the next hour how to apply a lot of formats to cells. You can apply a date format to a cell, for example, so that Excel 2000 displays a date based on the value and not a number. If you format a cell for a date and later—because of editing changes, that cell no longer holds a date but a value—you will want to remove the date format. Excel 2000 uses a general numeric format for all cells to which you don't specifically apply a different format.

Hour 9

Editing Excel Worksheets

This hour teaches you additional Excel 2000 worksheet editing skills. You will be surprised how Excel 2000 helps you when you modify worksheets. Excel 2000 automatically adjusts cell range names and formulas, for example, when you rearrange your worksheet.

Understanding ranges is critical if you want to really master Excel 2000. Therefore, be sure that you master this hour. You will use range names and addresses in Excel 2000 formulas and functions.

In addition to the editing tools, you also learn how to format worksheets to make them look better. This hour teaches the formatting essentials, so you will be ready for the fancy stuff in the next hour.

The highlights of this hour include the following:

- What Excel 2000 does when you insert or delete rows and columns
- How ranges differ from selections
- Why range names are important
- What the fundamental math operators do

- How to organize formulas so that they compute in the order you want them to
- Which functions save you time and prevent errors
- How to format cells to add eye-catching appeal to your worksheet

Inserting and Deleting

As you saw in the preceding hour, the requirements for Excel 2000 are somewhat different from those for Word 2000, even though both programs perform tasks in a similar manner and with similar menu commands and dialog boxes. The nature of worksheets makes them behave differently from word processed documents. The next few sections explain how to insert and delete information from your worksheets.

Inserting Entire Cells

Inserting cells, as opposed to inserting data inside a cell, requires that the existing worksheet cells move to the right and down to make room for the new cell. When you want to insert a cell, perform these steps:

1. Select the cell that should appear *after* the inserted cell.
2. Select Insert, Cells to display the Insert dialog box.
3. Click either the Shift Cells Right option or the Shift Cells Down option to determine the direction of the shift. The shift makes room for your new cell.
4. Click OK to begin the shift.

Some people prefer to use the mouse to shift cells right or down to make room for new data. Press Shift and drag the cell's fill handle (or the selection's fill handle if you have selected a group of cells) down or to the right. Excel 2000 grays out the areas that are left blank by the shifting. You may have to experiment with inserting cells a few times by inserting and then choosing Undo (Ctrl+Z) before you get the hang of it.

Inserting Rows and Columns

To insert a row or column (and thus move the other rows down or other columns to the right), perform these steps:

1. Select the row or column that appears *after* the inserted rows or columns by clicking its header to select the entire row or column. If you want to insert more than one row or column, select that many existing rows or columns by dragging the row or column selection.
2. Select Insert, Rows or Insert, Columns. Excel 2000 shifts the existing rows or columns to make room for the new empty row or column. Instead of selecting

from the menu bar, you can point to the selected row or column and display the pop-up menu shown in Figure 9.1 by right-clicking the mouse and selecting Insert to insert the new row or column. (Excel 2000 inserts multiple rows or columns if you first selected more than one row or column.)

FIGURE 9.1.

The pop-up menu offers insert, delete, and several other options.

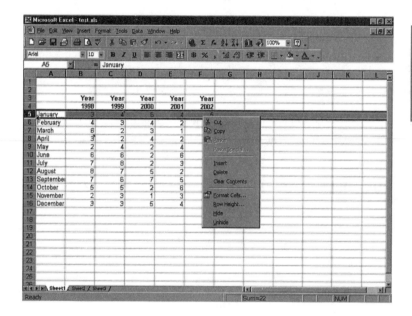

Deleting Entire Cells

When you deleted cells in the preceding hour, you learned how to remove selected cells completely from the worksheet and close the gap with the Delete dialog box. The Delete dialog box not only deletes cells, but also deletes entire rows and columns.

To delete a row or column, perform these steps:

1. Select a cell that resides in the row or column you want to delete.
2. Select Edit, Delete to display the Delete dialog box.
3. Select either the Entire Row or Entire Column option.
4. Click OK to perform the deletion. Excel 2000 shifts columns to the left or shifts rows up to fill in the missing gap.

If you want to delete multiple rows or multiple columns, select cells from each column or row you want to delete before displaying the Delete dialog box.

Deleting Rows and Columns

Perform these steps when you want to delete a row or column (as opposed to erasing the contents of a row or column):

1. Select the row or column to delete.
2. Right-click the selected row or column to display the pop-up menu.
3. Select Delete. Excel 2000 shifts the remaining part of the worksheet to close the gap.

Working with Worksheet Ranges

A *range* is a group of cells. A selected group of cells comprises a range, but ranges don't always have to be selected. A range is always rectangular. A range might be a single cell, a row, a column, or several adjacent rows and columns. The cells in ranges are always contiguous. Even though you can select noncontiguous cells, ranges always form rectangular worksheet regions. You can perform various operations on ranges, such as moving and copying.

New Term A *range* is a rectangular collection of cells.

Figure 9.2 shows three ranges on a worksheet. You can describe a range by the address of the upper-left cell of the range (the anchor point) and the address of the lower-right cell of the range. As you can see from Figure 9.2, multiple-celled ranges are designated by listing the *anchor point*, followed by a colon (:), followed by the range's lower-right cell address. Therefore, the range that begins at B3 and ends at F4 has the range of B3:F4.

New Term An *anchor point* is a range's upper-left cell address.

You will work quite a bit with ranges. One of the ways to make your worksheets more manageable is to name your ranges. You might assign the name *Titles* to your column titles, for example, *Months* to your column of month names, and so on.

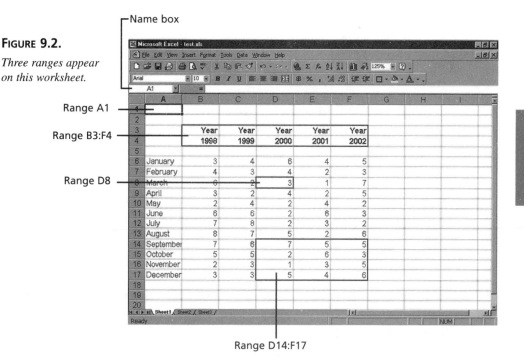

Name box

FIGURE 9.2.

Three ranges appear on this worksheet.

Range A1

Range B3:F4

Range D8

Range D14:F17

To name a range, perform these steps:

1. Select the cells that you want to include in the named range.

2. Click the Name box at the left of the Formula bar (the text box that displays cell addresses).

3. Type the range name.

4. Press Enter. When you subsequently select the range, you will see that Excel 2000 displays the *range name* rather than the range address in the Name box.

NEW TERM A *range name* is a name you assign to a range of cells. You can move a range to a new worksheet location and the range name stays the same.

Names are easier to remember than range addresses. If you create a payroll worksheet and assign the names GrossPay, NetPay, HoursWorked, TaxRate, and PayRate to the ranges that hold that data, for example, you never again have to type the range addresses. When you want to move or copy one of the ranges or use the range as a formula, just refer to the range name and let Excel 2000 figure out the correct addresses. You learn how to add ranges (including range names) to formulas in the section called "Using Formulas."

Here's an even better reason to name ranges: If you move a range, Excel 2000 moves the name with the cells! If you tracked range addresses and not names, you would constantly have to track down the latest addresses when you referred to the range. By naming ranges, you never have to worry about keeping track of addresses because the names won't change even if the addresses do.

Use meaningful names. Although AAA works as a name for a column of net sales figures, NetSales makes a lot more sense and is easier to remember. Your range names can include between 1 and 255 characters, and can contain letters, numbers, periods, and underscores. Although you cannot include spaces, you can mix uppercase and lowercase letters and include underscores to help distinguish between words in a single name.

If you create a large worksheet and you need to return to a named range to make some changes, click the Name box and type the name. Excel 2000 instantly displays that range and selects the range for you.

Fight the urge to ignore range names when you create your worksheets. The tendency is to put off naming ranges until later, and later often does not come. By naming key ranges as you create your worksheet, you more rapidly create the worksheet and the worksheet contains fewer errors.

Using Formulas

Without *formulas*, Excel 2000 would be little more than a word processor for tables of information. When you use formulas, however, Excel 2000 becomes an extremely powerful time-saving planning, budgeting, and general-purpose financial tool.

 A *formula* is a calculation that produces a result. Formulas can include math *operators*, numbers, cell addresses, and range names.

 An *operator* is a symbol that requests a mathematical calculation such as a plus sign (+).

Some people credit worksheet programs for the tremendous PC growth in the 1980s. Without formulas, worksheets would never have been able to create such a demand for personal computers.

On a calculator, you typically type a formula, and then press the equal sign to see the result. All Excel 2000 formulas *begin* with an equal sign. For example, the following is a formula:

```
=4*2-3
```

The asterisk is an operator that denotes the times sign (*multiplication*). This formula requests that Excel 2000 compute the value of 4 multiplied by 2 minus 3 to get the *result*. When you type a formula and press Enter or move to another cell, Excel 2000 displays the result, not the formula, on the worksheet.

As Figure 9.3 shows, the answer 5 appears on the worksheet, and you can see the cell's formula contents right on the Formula bar area. When entering a formula, as soon as you press the equal sign, Excel 2000 shows your formula on the Formula bar as well as in the active cell. If you click the Formula bar and then enter your formula, the formula appears in the Formula bar as well as in the active cell. By first clicking the Formula bar before entering the formula, however, you can press the left and right arrow keys to move the cursor left and right within the formula to edit it. When entering long formulas, this Formula bar's editing capability helps you correct mistakes that you might type.

FIGURE 9.3.

Excel 2000 displays a formula's result on the worksheet.

The cell's formula appears here

The formula's answer is displayed here

You can format a worksheet to show the actual formula rather than the answer, but you do something like that only when printing worksheet content listings that you want to study.

Excel's Primary Math Operators

Table 9.1 lists the primary math operators you can use in your worksheet formulas. Notice that all the example formulas begin with the equal sign.

TABLE 9.1. THE PRIMARY MATH OPERATORS SPECIFY MATH CALCULATIONS.

Operator	Example	Description
^	=7 ^ 3	Raises 7 to the power of 3 (called *exponentiation*)
/	=4 / 2	Divides 4 by 2
*	=3 * 4 * 5	Multiplies 3 by 4 by 5
+	=5 + 5	Adds 5 and 5
-	=5 - 5	Subtracts 5 from 5

NEW TERM The *exponentiation* operator raises one number to a higher power.

You can combine any and all the operators in a formula. When combining operators, Excel 2000 follows the traditional computer (and algebraic) *operator hierarchy* model. Therefore, Excel 2000 first computes exponentiation if you raise any value to another power. Excel 2000 then calculates all multiplication and division in a left-to-right order (the first one to appear computes first) before addition and subtraction (also in left-to-right order).

NEW TERM The *operator hierarchy* dictates the order that operators compute in formulas: exponentiation, multiplication and division, and then addition and subtraction.

The following formula returns a result of 14 because Excel 2000 first calculates the exponentiation of 2 raised to the third power, and then Excel 2000 divides the answer (8) by 4, and then multiplies the result (2) by 2, and finally subtracts the result (4) from 18. Even though the subtraction appears first, the operator hierarchy forces the subtraction to wait until last to compute.

```
=18 - 2 ^ 3 / 4 * 2
```

If you want to override the operator hierarchy, put parentheses around the parts you want Excel 2000 to compute first. The following formula returns a different result from the previous one, for example, despite the same values and operators used:

```
=(18 - 2) ^ 3 / 4 * 2
```

Instead of 14, this formula returns 2,048! The subtraction produces 16, which is then raised to the third power (producing 4,096) before dividing by 4 and multiplying the result by 2 to get 2,048.

Using Range Names in Formulas

The true power of Excel 2000 shows when you use cell addresses and range names in formulas. All the following are valid formulas. Cell addresses or range names appear throughout the formulas.

```
=(SalesTotals)/NumOfSales
=C4 * 2 - (Rate * .08)
=7 + LE51 - (Gross - Net)
```

When you enter formulas that contain range addresses, you can either type the full address or point to the cell address. If you want to include a complete named range in a formula (formulas can work on complete ranges, as you see later this hour), select the entire range and Excel 2000 inserts the range name in your formula. Often, finding and pointing to a value is easier than locating the address and entering the exact address.

If, for example, you are entering a formula for cells that are close to the formula's cell, when you get to the place in the formula that requires a close cell, don't type the cell address; instead, point to the cell. If you have entered a formula such as =7 + , instead of typing a cell address of LE51, you can point to that cell and Excel 2000 enters the cell's address for you. Immediately after typing the cell address for you, Excel 2000 returns your cursor to the formula (or to the Formula bar if you are entering the formula there) so that you can complete it.

After you assign a name to a cell, you don't have to remember that cell's address when you use that cell in formulas. Suppose that you are creating a large worksheet that spans many screens. If you assign names to cells when you create them, cells that you know you will refer to later during the worksheet's development, entering formulas that use that name is made easier. Instead of locating that cell to find its address, you need only to type the name when entering a formula that uses that cell.

To assign a range name to a cell or to a range of cells, select the cell or range and click the Name box at the left of the Formula bar. Type the name and press Enter. Excel 2000 assigns the name to that cell or range.

Relative Versus Absolute Cell Addressing

When you copy formulas that contain cell addresses, Excel 2000 updates the cell addresses so that they reference *relative addresses*. For example, suppose that you enter this formula in cell A1:

```
=A2 + A3
```

NEW TERM A *relative address* is an address that references cells based on the current cell's location.

This formula contains two addresses. The addresses are relative because the addresses A2 and A3 change if you copy the formula elsewhere. If you copy the formula to cell B5, for example, B5 holds this:

```
=B6 + B7
```

The original relative addresses update to reflect the formula's copied location. Of course, A1 still holds its original contents, but the copied cell at B5 holds the same formula referencing B5 rather than A1.

An absolute address is an address that does not change if you copy the formula. A dollar sign ($) always precedes an absolute address. The address B5 is an absolute address. If you wanted to sum two columns of data (A1 with B1, A2 with B2, and so on) and then multiply each sum by some constant number, for example, the constant number could be a cell referred to as an absolute address. That formula might look like this:

```
=(A1 + B1) * $J$1
```

J1 is an *absolute address*, but A1 and B1 are relative. If you copied the formula down one row, the formula would change to this:

```
=(A2 + B2) * $J$1
```

NEW TERM An *absolute address* is an address that references cells using their specific addresses and does not change when you copy the cell holding the formula.

Notice that the first two cells changed because, when you originally entered them, they were relative cell addresses. You told Excel 2000, by placing dollar signs in front of the absolute cell address's row and column references, not to change that reference when you copy the formula elsewhere.

$B5 is a partial absolute address. If you copy a formula with $B5 inside the computation, the $B keeps the B column intact, but the fifth row updates to the row location of the target cell. If you type the following formula in cell A1:

```
=2 * $B5
```

and then copy the formula to cell F6, cell F6 holds this formula:

```
=2 * $B10
```

9

You copied the formula to a cell five rows and five columns over in the worksheet. Excel 2000 did not update the column name, B, because you told Excel 2000 to keep that column name absolute (it is always B no matter where you copy the formula). Excel 2000 added 5 to the row number, however, because the row number was relative and open to change whenever you copied the formula.

The dollar sign keeps the row B absolute no matter where you copy the formula, but the relative row number can change as you copy the formula.

The bottom line is this: Most of the time, you use relative addressing. If you insert or delete rows, columns, or cells, your formulas remain accurate because the cells that they reference change as your worksheet changes.

Copying Formulas

Excel 2000 offers several shortcut tools that make copying cells from one location to another simple. Consider the worksheet in Figure 9.4. The bottom row needs to hold formulas that total each of the projected year's 12-month values.

How would you enter the total row? You could type the following formula in cell B19:

```
=B6+B7+B8+B9+B10+B11+B12+B13+B14+B15+B16+B17
```

After you have typed the formula in B19, you then *could* type the following formula in cell C19:

```
=C6+C7+C8+C9+C10+C11+C12+C13+C14+C15+C16+C17
```

You then could type the values in the remaining total cells. Instead of doing all that typing, however, copy cell B19 to cell C19. Hold Ctrl while you drag the cell edge of B19 to C19. When you release the mouse, cell C19 properly totals column C! Press Ctrl and copy C19 to D19 through F19 to place the totals in all the total cells. The totals are accurate, as Figure 9.5 shows.

If cell B19 contained absolute addresses, cells C19 through F19 would all total column B!

FIGURE 9.4.

A total row is needed for the project's yearly values.

This row needs a total

FIGURE 9.5.

Relative references make totaling these columns simple.

These were copied from B19

Recalculating Worksheets

After you set up formulas, your job is done; Excel 2000's job has just begun, however. If you change any value in the worksheet, Excel 2000 recalculates all formulas automatically! Therefore, Excel 2000 keeps your worksheet fresh and accurate as you modify values. You can use the same worksheet each month and change only the monthly data. If you leave the formulas intact, Excel 2000 computes and displays the correct answers.

You can turn off the automatic recalculation and manually recalculate when ready if you use a slow computer and want to save time when editing a large worksheet. Select Tools, Options and click the Calculation tab. Click the Manual option to force manual recalculation. If you now change the data, Excel 2000 does not recalculate your worksheet until you press F9 (the Calculate Now shortcut key).

9

Working with Functions

The previous sections explained how to enter a formula once, using relative addresses, and copy that formula to other cells. Although you only have to type the formula one time, this kind of totaling formula is tedious to type and introduces greater chance for error:

```
=B6+B7+B8+B9+B10+B11+B12+B13+B14+B15+B16+B17
```

Fortunately, Microsoft includes several built-in *functions* that perform many common mathematical calculations. Instead of writing a formula to sum a row or column of values, for example, use the Sum() function.

NEW TERM   *Functions* are built-in calculations and data manipulations that perform the work of formulas to return values.

Function names always end with parentheses, such as Average(). A function accepts zero or more *arguments*. The arguments, if any, go inside the parentheses. Always separate function arguments with commas. If a function contains only a single argument, you do not use a comma inside the parentheses. Functions generally manipulate data (numbers or text), and the argument list inside the parentheses supplies the data to the function. The Average() function, for example, computes an average of whatever list of values you pass in the argument list in Average(). Therefore, all the following compute an average from the argument list:

```
=Average(18, 65, 299, $R$5, 10, -2, 102)
=Average(SalesTotals)
=Average(D4:D14)
```

NEW TERM   An *argument* is a value on which a function operates (most often indicated by cell addresses). Arguments appear inside the parentheses of a function.

As with many functions, Average() accepts as many arguments as needed to do its job. The first Average() function computes the average of seven values, one of which is an absolute cell address. The second Average() function computes the average of a range named SalesTotals. No matter how many cells comprise the range SalesTotals, Average() computes the average. The last Average() function computes the average of the values in the range D4 through D14 (a columnar list).

The Sum() function is perhaps the most common function because you so often total table columns and rows. In the preceding section, you entered a long formula to add the values in a column. Instead of adding each cell to total the range B6:B17, you could more easily enter the following function:

=Sum(B6:B17)

If you copy this Sum() function to the other cells at the bottom of the yearly projections, you achieve the same results as the added values, but the worksheet is easier to maintain if you need to make modifications later.

Suppose that you want to track 24 biweekly totals rather than 12 monthly ones. Insert 12 additional blank rows, change the row titles (to something like JanWk12, JanWk34, FebWk12, and so on), and enter the biweekly values. You won't have to change the total calculations! When you insert rows within the Sum() range, Excel 2000 updates the range inside the Sum() function to contain the 12 new values.

Use AutoSum for Speed

Before looking at a table of common functions, Excel 2000 helps you with summing functions by analyzing your selected range and automatically inserting a Sum() function if needed. Here's how to do that:

1. Select the range that you want to sum. If you want to sum the months over the projected years for this hour's sample worksheets, for example, select the row with the January label, as shown in Figure 9.6.

2. Click the AutoSum toolbar button. Excel 2000 guesses that you want to sum the selected row and inserts the Sum() function in the cell to the right of the row.

3. Make any edits to the summed value if Excel 2000 included too many or not enough cells. You can click the cell and press F2 to edit the sum. Usually, no edits are required.

AutoSum button

FIGURE 9.6.

*Getting ready to
request a sum.*

Excel 2000 places the
Sum( ) function here

After Excel 2000 generates the Sum( ) function, you can copy the cell down the rest of
the column to add the monthly totals. However, can you see another way to perform the
same monthly totals with one selection? Select the *entire set* of monthly values with one
extra blank column at the right (the range B6:G17). Excel 2000 sees the blank column
and fills it in with each row's sum when you click AutoSum. You now can select the new
column of totals and let AutoSum compute them. Figure 9.7 shows the result of the new
sums after you add underlines and a title.

Common Functions

Functions improve your accuracy. If you want to average three cell values, for example,
you might type something like this:

```
=C2 + C4 + C6 / 3
```

This formula does not compute an average! Remember that the operator hierarchy forces
the division calculation first. If you use the Average( ) function, as shown next, you don't
have to worry as much about the calculation's hierarchy.

```
=Average(C2, C4, C6)
```

Figure 9.7.

AutoSum in action.

	A	B	C	D	E	F	G	H	I	
		Year	Year	Year	Year	Year				
		1998	1999	2000	2001	2002				
January		3	4	6	4	5	22			
February		4	3	4	2	3	16			
March		6	2	3	1	7	19			
April		3	2	4	2	5	16			
May		2	4	2	4	2	14			
June		6	6	2	6	3	23			
July		7	8	2	3	2	22			
August		8	7	5	2	6	28			
September		7	6	7	5	5	30			
October		5	5	2	6	3	21			
November		2	3	1	3	5	14			
December		3	3	5	4	6	21			
Total:		56	53	43	42	52	246			

G19   = =SUM(B19:F19)

AutoSum summed
the entire column

> Another advantage of using functions is that you can modify them more
> easily than you can long calculations. If you want to throw another cell
> value into the previous average, for example, you only need to add the
> extra cell to Average(); if you use a formula, you must remember to
> change the 3 to 4.

Table 9.2 describes common Excel 2000 built-in functions that you find a lot of uses for
as you create worksheets. Remember to start every formula with an equal sign and to
add your cell addresses to the parentheses, and you are set!

Table 9.2. Common Excel 2000 functions.

Function Name	Description
Abs()	Computes the absolute value of its cell argument. (Good for distance- and age-difference calculations.)
Average()	Computes the average of its arguments.
Count()	Returns the number of numerical arguments in the argument list. (Useful if you use a range name for the argument list.)

Function Name	Description
Counta()	Returns the number of all arguments in the argument list. (Useful if you use a range name for the argument list.)
CountBlank()	Returns the number of blank cells, if any exist, in the argument range. (Useful if you use a range name for the argument list.)
Max()	Returns the highest (maximum) value in the argument list. (Useful if you use a range name for the argument list and you need to pick out the highest value.)
Min()	Returns the lowest (minimum) value in the argument list. (Useful if you use a range name for the argument list and you need to pick out the lowest value.)
Pi()	Computes the value of mathematical pi (requires no arguments) for use in math calculations.
Product()	Computes the product (multiplicative result) of the argument range.
Roman()	Converts its cell value to a Roman numeral.
Sqrt()	Computes the square root of the cell argument.
Stddev()	Computes the argument list's standard deviation.
Sum()	Computes the sum of its arguments.
Today()	Returns today's date (requires no arguments).
Var()	Computes a list's sample variance.

Excel 2000 supports many more functions than Table 9.2 lists. Excel 2000 even supports complex mathematical, date, time, financial, and engineering functions. As you learn more about Excel 2000 and create more complex worksheets, you will run across these functions as you read through the online help.

Advanced Functions

Some of the functions require more arguments than a simple cell or range. Excel 2000 contains many financial functions, for example, that compute loan values and investment rates of return. If you want to use one of the more advanced functions, click on an empty cell and then click the Paste Function toolbar button to display the Paste Function dialog box, as shown in Figure 9.8.

FIGURE 9.8.

Let Excel 2000's Paste Function dialog box type complex functions for you.

When you select the category in the left column, the Paste Function dialog box displays a list of functions within that category. When you click one of the functions, the Paste Function dialog box gives you a helpful mini description. When you find the function you need, double-click it; Excel 2000 displays an additional dialog box that requests each of the function arguments, such as the one shown in Figure 9.9. As you continue with the Paste Function dialog box, Excel 2000 builds the function in the cell for you. As you get more proficient, you no longer need the help of the Paste Function dialog box.

FIGURE 9.9.

The Paste Function produces this dialog box that walks you through each function argument.

The Office Assistant offers more help with defining the function that you create from the Paste Function dialog box.

Introduction to Worksheet Formatting

Until now, you have seen no fancy worksheets. I kept the fancy stuff out of the way so that you could concentrate on the work at hand. It is now time to show you how to pretty things up. This hour is about to come to a close, but you still have time to learn some cell-formatting basics and you can continue with Excel 2000's more advanced formatting features in the next hour's session.

Justification

Excel 2000 right-justifies numbers (and formulas that result in numbers) and left-justifies text labels. You don't have to accept Excel 2000's default justification, however. To left-, center-, or right-justify the contents of any cell (or range), select the cell (or range) and click the Align Left, Center, or Align Right toolbar buttons. Center titles above columns and adjust your numbers to look just right.

Excel 2000 offers a trick that even some Excel 2000 gurus forget: if you want to center a title above several columns of data, type the title in a cell above the data. If you cannot center the title over the values by clicking the Center toolbar button, select all the cells around the title so that you have selected as many columns as there is data. Click the Merge and Center toolbar button. Excel 2000 centers the title, even though the title resides in a single cell, across the entire column selection.

Row and Column Height and Width

As you learn more formatting tricks, you will need to adjust certain row and column widths and heights to hold the newly formatted values. To adjust a row's height, point to the line that separates the row number from previous or subsequent rows. When the mouse pointer changes to a double-pointing arrow, drag the row's top or bottom edge up or down. Excel 2000 adjusts the entire row height as you drag your mouse. Sometimes large titles need the larger row heights. When you release the mouse, Excel 2000 anchors the new row height where you left it.

In the same manner, to change the width of a column, point to the column name's left or right edge and drag your mouse left or right. Excel 2000 adjusts the column width to follow your mouse movement. When you release the mouse, Excel 2000 anchors the new column width where you left it.

If you shrink a column width so that the column can no longer display all the data, Excel 2000 displays pound signs (#####) to warn you that you need to widen the column. Your data is still stored in the cell—it just cannot be displayed.

9

To adjust the column width so that the column (or range of columns) is exactly large enough to hold the largest data value in the column, select the column (or columns) and double-click the right edge of the column name. Excel 2000 adjusts the column to hold the widest data value in the column.

Font Changes

Feel free to change the worksheet's font to add appeal. Simple font changes, such as boldfacing, italicizing, and underlining, greatly improve the look of titles. The Bold, Italic, and Underline toolbar buttons add the proper formatting to your selected cell or range. If you select Format, Cells and click the Font tab, Excel 2000 displays the Font dialog box (virtually identical to that of Word 2000), in which you can select a new font name and size. As Figure 9.10 shows, simple font changes can make a big improvement on otherwise dull worksheets.

FIGURE 9.10.

Already this worksheet looks better.

	Year 1998	Year 1999	Year 2000	Year 2001	Year 2002	Grand Totals
Sales Factor Projections						
January	3	4	6	4	5	22
February	4	3	4	2	3	16
March	6	2	3	1	7	19
April	3	2	4	2	5	16
May	2	4	2	4	2	14
June	6	6	2	6	3	23
July	7	8	2	3	2	22
August	8	7	5	2	6	28
September	7	6	7	5	5	30
October	5	5	2	6	3	21
November	2	3	1	3	5	14
December	3	3	5	4	6	21
Total:	56	53	43	42	52	246

If you format a row with a font that's larger than the current row size, Excel 2000 adjusts the row height to make room for the new font.

Of course, you can use the Font and Font Size toolbar buttons to change a font name or size without displaying the Font dialog box.

Making Format Changes

Now that you have mastered Excel 2000 basics, it is time to learn the general format categories Excel 2000 uses for worksheet data. Table 9.3 describes each of the format categories. Unless you change the default, Excel 2000 uses the General format for data of all kinds.

TABLE 9.3. EXCEL 2000'S FUNDAMENTAL FORMATS.

Format Name	Description
General	The numeric data has no special formatting and generally appears exactly the way you enter the data.
Number	You can set the number of decimal places Excel 2000 displays for all numeric values.
Currency	Displays a dollar sign and two decimal places for dollar amounts.
Accounting	Aligns currency and decimal points in a column.
Date	Displays date and time values as values whose formats you can change.
Time	Displays only the time portion of a date and time value.
Percentage	Displays a percent sign. If you type **50** into the cell, Excel 2000 changes your value to **50%**.
Fraction	Displays numbers as fractions (great for stock quotes).
Scientific	Uses scientific notation for all numeric values.
Text	Formats *all* data as text. Great for Zip codes that are all numbers but that you never use for calculations.
Special	Formats Zip codes, phone numbers, and Social Security numbers.
Custom	Lets you define your own cell format. You can decide whether you want to see the plus or minus sign, and you can control the number of decimal places.

Format a selection by selecting Format, Cells and clicking the Number tab to display a scrolling list of formats, as shown in Table 9.3. If you select the Time format from that list, you must select one of the Time format display variations so that Excel 2000 knows how you want the time displayed.

You can also right-click the selection and select the Format Cells command from the pop-up menu. When you do, you see a dialog box that enables you to assign the formats directly to your data.

You can also use Excel's autoformatting capabilities to easily add style to your worksheet. (The next hour covers AutoFormats.)

Several formatting toolbar buttons exist that enable quick formatting of cells using the most common format styles. If you select a cell or a range of cells, you can change the selection's format more quickly with a toolbar button than with the Format, Cells dialog box. Not all Excel's formats are available through the toolbar, but these are: Currency Style, Percent Style, Comma Style, Increase Decimal (to increase the number of decimal places), and Decrease Decimal (to decrease the number of decimal places).

Summary

This hour extended your worksheet knowledge by giving you more editing tools with which to insert and delete columns, rows, and cells. After you name important worksheet ranges, you won't have to track specific addresses in your worksheet; the name is easier to remember, and Excel 2000 changes the range if you insert data in or delete it from the range.

One of the most powerful aspects of worksheets is their recalculation capability. If you change data or a formula, Excel 2000 recalculates the entire worksheet as soon as you make the change. You are always looking at the computed worksheet with up-to-date formulas, no matter what kind of data changes you make. When you add formulas to cell calculations, you not only improve your worksheet accuracy, but you finish your worksheets faster.

The next hour picks up where this one leaves off, going into formatting in more detail. Additionally, you see that graphics spruce up your worksheet and are easy to produce.

Q&A

Q What is the difference between a selection and a range?

A Selections cannot be named, and can be comprised of several disjointed areas of your worksheet. A range, on the other hand, can be named, and can be any contiguous rectangular collection of cells, including a single cell or your entire worksheet data area. Often, you select an entire range, but all selections are not ranges.

Q Why would I ever use absolute addressing?

A Relative addressing seems to make the most sense for most worksheets. If you have to rearrange your worksheet, all your relative addresses update as well. Absolute addresses are great when a formula references a single cell, such as an age or pay value, that rarely changes. You could use dollar signs to anchor the single cell in the formula that uses that cell, but keep the other addresses relative in case you need to copy the formula around the worksheet.

Q What's the difference between the formatting you get by clicking the Center toolbar button and the formatting you get by clicking the Merge and Center button?

A If you need to center the contents of one cell, both centering formats perform the same task. If want to center data (such as a title) above a range of cell columns, however, select the range the centered cell is to go over and click Merge and Center; Excel 2000 completes the centering across the multiple columns.

9

HOUR 10

Formatting Worksheets to Look Great

This hour concludes your Excel 2000 tutorial by explaining how to format your worksheet with professional styles. The AutoFormat feature in Excel 2000 quickly formats your worksheet within the boundaries you select. If you want to format your worksheet by hand, the formatting commands you learn in this hour enable you to pinpoint important data and highlight that data so that others who look at and use your worksheets find your highlighted information.

After you create and format your worksheets, use the Chart Wizard in Excel 2000 to produce colorful graphs. Often, a worksheet's trends and comparisons get lost in the numeric details. The graphs that the Chart Wizard generates look great, and Excel 2000 does all the drawing work for you.

The highlights of this hour include the following:

- What AutoFormat can do with your worksheets
- How to apply custom formats to selected cells

- When special orientation and wrapped text improve your worksheet appearance
- How to use the Chart Wizard to produce graphs that show data trends and comparisons
- How to modify your charts so that they look the way you want them to

AutoFormatting Worksheets

Before diving into additional formatting commands, you should know that the AutoFormat feature in Excel 2000 converts an otherwise dull worksheet into a nice-looking professional one. A worksheet's presentation is almost as important as the data within the worksheet. If your worksheet needs sprucing up, try AutoFormat after you have formatted individual cells because AutoFormat gives a good-looking, consistent dimension to your entire worksheet. After AutoFormat finishes, you can add finishing touches to the worksheet by adding more specific formats to highlight important cell information, such as special totals that you want to make stand out.

To use AutoFormat, press Ctrl+A to select the entire worksheet. Select Format, AutoFormat to display the AutoFormat dialog box, as shown in Figure 10.1.

FIGURE 10.1.

Let AutoFormat improve your worksheet.

Scroll through the AutoFormat samples and choose any format. When you click OK, Excel 2000 applies the format to your selected worksheet cells. Figure 10.2 shows that AutoFormat knows to highlight totals and also knows to separate headings from the data detail.

To omit certain AutoFormat format styles, click the Options button in AutoFormat to check or uncheck styles. You can keep AutoFormat from changing your worksheet's font, for example, by unchecking the Font option that appears.

FIGURE 10.2.

AutoFormat improved the appearance of this worksheet.

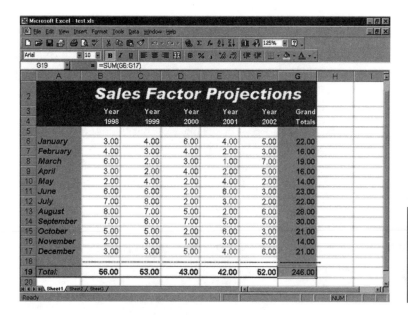

Making Your Own Default Format

Suppose that you often print worksheets to fax to others, and your fax requires boldfaced worksheets so that the recipients can read the numbers. Instead of changing your worksheet text to boldface before faxing the worksheet, you can make boldface the default font style. Excel 2000 enables you to change several of the font defaults, so if you find yourself applying the same font style over and over, consider making that style part of Excel 2000's default style.

To modify the default style, follow these steps:

1. Select Format, Style to display the Style dialog box, as shown in Figure 10.3.

FIGURE 10.3.

You can change any named style.

2. Select the default style, Normal, from the Style Name drop-down list box. (The *Normal style* is probably already the style you see when you open the dialog box.) Like Word 2000, Excel 2000 enables you to modify styles and even create customized styles of your own. When you apply the style changes you added by selecting Format, Style, Excel 2000 applies the style set by the Style dialog box to the selected cells.

NEW TERM *Normal style* is the default style Excel 2000 normally uses for all your worksheet cells.

3. To change the Normal style, click the Modify button. Excel 2000 displays the Format Cells dialog box, as shown in Figure 10.4, from which you can modify the named style.

FIGURE 10.4.

The Format Cells dialog box modifies any format currently set.

4. Click OK to close the Format Cells dialog box.

5. Click OK to close the Style dialog box. Excel 2000 applies your style to the selected cells. If you made changes to the Normal style, Excel 2000 automatically uses that format on future worksheets unless you modify the format or style.

If you plan to create additional worksheets that are similar to the one you just created, consider saving the worksheet as a template with File, Save As and then selecting the template type. When you are ready to create the next similar worksheet, load the template; your formats will already be in place.

Additional Formatting Options

Many of Excel 2000's formatting features are identical to Word 2000's, such as boldface, italics, underline, font color, and fill color (the cell's background color). In addition, you now know how to change a selection's alignment. Excel 2000 supports several special formats that go further to improve the look of your worksheets. AutoFormat uses some of these special formats, and you can create your own styles that use these formats as well.

The following sections briefly introduce you to these Excel 2000 formatting options, which provide you with additional ways to add impact to your worksheets. You can change any of these formats from the Format Cells dialog box. Open the Format Cells dialog box by selecting Format, Cells, by changing one of the stored styles as you learned in the preceding section, or by right-clicking a selection and choosing Format Cells.

10

Special Alignment

Not only can you left-justify, center-justify, and right-justify, as well as justify across selected cells, you can also orient text vertically or to whatever slant you prefer. When you click the Format, Cells Alignment tab, Excel 2000 displays the Alignment page, shown in Figure 10.5, in which you can adjust text orientation.

FIGURE 10.5.

Align text with the Format Cells dialog box Alignment page.

STEP-UP

The vertical text orientation in Excel 2000 is easier to adjust than in previous versions because Excel 2000 draws a line to show the text rotation angle as you change the angle.

When you click the Alignment dialog box's first orientation text box (the text box with the word Text dropping down the screen), Excel 2000 changes all selected cells to vertical orientation. If you want to slant text, such as titles, select a different Degree value or click the rotating text pointer to the slant you desire. When you click OK, Excel 2000 rotates the selected text to your chosen angle. Figure 10.6 shows an example of slanted titles produced by selecting a negative 45-degree angle in the Alignment dialog box. The text prints at an angle as well.

FIGURE 10.6.

You can change the vertical alignment of selected text.

Slanted text alignment ——

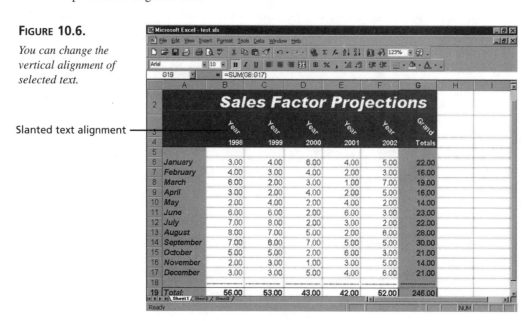

If you need to include a lot of text in one or more cells, you already know (from Hour 7, "Excel 2000 Workbooks") that Excel 2000 either truncates the cell or pours the cell's contents into the next cell to the right. Excel 2000 offers several other options, as well. When a cell requires a lot of text, select the Wrap Text option from the Alignment dialog box. Excel 2000 wraps the text within the cell's width, increasing the cell (and, therefore, row) height to display all the wrapped text. If you click the Shrink to Fit option, Excel 2000 decreases the cell's font size (as much as feasible) to display the entire cell contents within the cell's current width and height. If you click Merge Cells, Excel 2000 combines adjacent cells into a single wide cell.

Special Cell Borders

With the Format, Cells Border dialog box, shown in Figure 10.7, you can apply an outline, or *border*, around selected cells.

FIGURE 10.7.

Add borders around cells to highlight key data.

 NEW TERM A *border* is a cell outline that you can apply to enclose selected cells.

The Border page enables you to add a border to any side of the selected cells as well as diagonal lines inside the cells so that you can show a cell x'd out or otherwise cross off a cell's contents for a printed report. As you select among the Outline and Inside options, the preview area shows what the resulting border looks like.

> The Borders toolbar button is quicker to use than the Border page, but you cannot control as many border details.

Select Line Style options from the Border dialog box to change the pattern of the border that you choose. If you want to remove any selected cell's border, click None.

Special Cell Shades

The Format, Cells Patterns dialog box enables you to add color or a shading pattern to selected cells. Although the Fill Color toolbar button colors cell backgrounds more quickly than the Patterns page, the Patterns page enables you to add a shading pattern to the background.

When you click the Patterns drop-down box from the Patterns page, Excel 2000 displays pattern options, as shown in Figure 10.8.

Locked and Hidden Cells

When you create worksheets for others, you want to lock titles and formulas so that users can enter and change the data areas without harming the worksheet's format. A hidden cell is useful when you want to block a cell's value from showing temporarily.

FIGURE 10.8.

*Choose a pattern for
the selected cell.*

Available patterns

The *locked* and *hidden* cell status activates only when you activate worksheet protection by selecting Tools, Protection and selecting one of the
protection options.

NEW TERM A *locked cell* is one whose contents you cannot change if the worksheet is
protected.

NEW TERM A *hidden cell* is one whose contents you cannot see if the worksheet is protected.

The Format, Cells Protection dialog box controls the locked and hidden status of selected
cells. You can enable and disable locking as well as control the hidden status by clicking
the appropriate Protection dialog box options. Excel 2000 does not ensure that your users
won't deactivate the protection and modify the worksheet. The protection helps protect
the worksheet from accidental damage, but anyone can modify the protection status and
change locked cells.

Cell locking is great when you want to keep accidental worksheet changes from occur-
ring. If the protection needs to go further than simple safety, add a password when you
protect the selection. Only someone with the worksheet's (or workbook's) password can
unlock locked cells or show hidden cells. To add a password, select Tools, Protection.
You can add a password to the worksheet or to the entire workbook.

Creating Custom Graphs

A picture is worth a thousand words and numbers, and Excel 2000 produces
professional-looking graphs from your worksheet data. You don't need to know a lot
about graphing and charting unless you want to create extremely sophisticated Excel

2000 graphs. You can use Excel 2000's *Chart Wizard* in most cases to produce great-looking graphs quickly and easily. When you click the Chart Wizard toolbar button, Excel 2000 displays the opening screen of the Chart Wizard dialog box, as shown in Figure 10.9.

 The *Chart Wizard* is an Excel 2000 wizard that displays your worksheet data as a colorful graph.

FIGURE 10.9.

Excel 2000's Chart Wizard creates graphs for you.

10

Choosing the Chart Type

Table 10.1 describes each of the chart types that Excel 2000 creates. You can select an appropriate chart type from the Chart Wizard's opening screen. To preview your worksheet when formatted with any chart, select a chart type, and then a chart subtype, and click the button labeled Press and Hold to View Sample. Excel 2000 analyzes your worksheet data and displays a small sketch of the chart you selected.

TABLE 10.1. EXCEL 2000 CHART OPTIONS.

Chart type	Description
Column	Shows changes over time and compares values.
Bar	Compares data items.
Line	Shows trends and projections.
Pie	Illustrates the proportional size of items in the same series.
XY (scatter)	Shows relationships of several values in a series.
Area	Emphasizes the magnitude of changes over time.

continues

TABLE 10.1. CONTINUED

Chart type	Description
Doughnut	Illustrates the proportional size of items in multiple series.
Radar	Each category contains an *axis* that radiates from the center of the graph (useful for finding the data series with the most penetration, as needed in market research statistical studies).
Surface	Locates optimum combinations between two data series.
Bubble	Shows relationships between several series values, but also (with circles, or bubbles of varying sizes) shows the magnitude of data intersections.
Stock	Illustrates a stock's (or other investment's) high, low, and closing prices.
Cone, Cylinder, Pyramid	Indicates trends and comparisons with special 3D cone, cylinder, and pyramid symbols.

NEW TERM An *axis* is a graph edge that bisects the chart at right angles and indicates the data values in the chart, such as time or dollar amounts.

If you are new to graphing, you may not know which graph works best for a particular worksheet. Try one! If you see that a bar graph does not show a trend that you want to demonstrate, generate a line graph. Excel 2000 makes it easy to select from among several graphs to find the best graph for your needs.

Selecting Data for Your Graph

A *data series* is a single group of data that you might select from a column or row to graph. Unlike a range, a data series must be contiguous in the row or column with no cells in between. Often, a series is comprised of a time period, such as a week, month, or year. One person's weekly sales totals (from a group of several salespersons' weekly totals) would also form a series. Some graphs, such as pie charts, graph only a single series, whereas other graphs show comparisons between two or more data series.

NEW TERM A *data series* is a single column, row, or set of cell values that you group together, such as a given region's sales for a week, month, year, or a single sales-person.

As you look through the graph samples, if one of the series looks extremely large in comparison to the others, Excel 2000 is probably including a total column or row in the graph results. Generally, you want to graph a single series (such as monthly costs) or several series, but not the totals—the totals throw off the data comparisons. Therefore, if you see extreme ranges at the beginning or end of your graph, select only the data areas (not the total cells) from the Chart Wizard's second dialog box, shown in Figure 10.10.

You need to tell the Chart Wizard which direction the data series flows by clicking either Rows or Columns from the Chart Wizard's second dialog box.

10

FIGURE 10.10.

Be sure to select only data areas for your graph.

Click here to change selection

When you click the Next button to see the third Chart Wizard dialog box, shown in Figure 10.11, Excel 2000 enables you to enter a chart title that appears at the top of the resulting chart as well as axis titles that appear on each edge of your chart.

FIGURE 10.11.

Enter titles that you want to see on the chart.

You find other tabs in the Chart Wizard's third dialog box that enable you to control the placement of the *legend* and a *data table*.

 A *legend* describes how the chart's patterns and colors represent the information in the graph.

 A *data table* is a miniature summarized worksheet that appears beneath the graph. The table shows numerically what the graph represents graphically.

Click Next to see the final Chart Wizard dialog box, in which you determine exactly where and how to place the generated graph. Excel 2000 can create a new worksheet for the graph or embed the graph inside the current worksheet as an embedded object. You can, in turn, embed the object in other Office 2000 products, as you will learn in Part VII, "Combining the Office 2000 Products and the Internet."

Modifying the Graph

Click the Finish button to see your resulting graph. If you have chosen to embed the graph inside your current worksheet, you may have to drag the graph's *sizing handles* to expand or shrink the graph. In addition, you can drag the graph anywhere you want it to appear on your worksheet. Excel 2000 displays the floating Graph toolbar right below the graph in case you want to change it.

 Sizing handles are eight black handles that appear around certain objects, such as graphs, with which you can resize the object by dragging.

If your graph does not display data the way you prefer, you can click the Graph toolbar buttons to change the graph's properties. You can even change the graph type (from a line chart to a bar graph, for instance) from the Graph toolbar without rerunning the Chart Wizard. The Graph toolbar ensures that all data selections and titles remain in place when you change your graph. If you need to make more extensive graph changes, rerun the Chart Wizard.

In addition to using the Graph toolbar, you can often change specific parts of your graph by right-clicking the graph. If you point to your chart's title and right-click your mouse, for example, Excel 2000 displays a pop-up menu from which you can choose the title's pattern, font, and alignment.

When you single-click a graph's element, such as the legend or a charted data series, Excel 2000 displays sizing handles so that you can resize the element. If you double-click an element, Excel 2000 displays a dialog box with the element's properties, such as color and shape, so that you can modify the way the element appears on the graph.

Summary

This hour completed your Excel 2000 tutorial! You can now format your worksheets to look any way you want. If you want to let Excel 2000 give formatting a try, select your worksheet data and start Excel 2000's AutoFormat feature. Add color, patterns, shading, and borders to your worksheets.

The Excel 2000 Chart Wizard turns your data into great-looking graphical charts. By working through the Chart Wizard's dialog boxes, you give Excel 2000 all the information needed to generate custom graphs. Graphs can be used to analyze data, compare values, and often show trends faster than the worksheet's details can show.

Now that you have learned how to create great looking worksheets, you will want to show those worksheets to someone. Why not use PowerPoint 2000? The next hour introduces PowerPoint 2000, Office 2000's colorful presentation creator and editor.

10

Q&A

Q When would I want to create a style?

A If you find yourself applying the same kinds of format commands on cells quite often, consider giving that set of format commands a style name by using the Format, Style dialog box. After you create a style, you can apply that style by selecting it from the Style dialog box's list.

Q How can I change a locked cell?

A If you lock a cell, your intent is to not allow changes. Locked cells are especially useful when you create worksheets for others to use. By locking the titles and formulas, you ensure that the user can only change data areas. Nevertheless, if you need to edit a locked cell, deactivate the worksheet's protected status. After you edit the cell, activate the protection so that the worksheet is safe from inadvertent changes.

Q I get confused with all the graph terms; how do I know which chart works best for my worksheet?

A Often the best way to find the right chart type is to try a few. Excel 2000's Chart Wizard is so simple and fast that you can generate several chart types before you find just the right one. As you produce more and more charts, you begin to judge better which graphs work best for certain kinds of worksheets.

PART IV

Presenting with PowerPoint and Publisher 2000

Hour

HOUR 11

PowerPoint 2000 Presentations

This hour introduces you to PowerPoint 2000 and shows you how to get off to a good start. By using the predefined presentation tools of PowerPoint 2000, you generate good-looking presentations without needing to worry about design, format, and color specifics. After PowerPoint 2000 generates a sample presentation, you need only follow a few simple procedures to turn the sample presentation into your own.

The highlights of this hour include the following:

- How to start PowerPoint 2000
- What the AutoContent Wizard does for you
- When to use the design templates
- What a blank presentation requires
- How to exit PowerPoint 2000

Starting PowerPoint 2000

To start PowerPoint 2000, perform one of the following:

- Click the Office 2000 Shortcut Bar's New Office Document button and double-click the Blank Presentation icon to create a new PowerPoint 2000 document. (Click the General tab if it is not already selected to see the Blank Presentation icon.)

- Click the Office 2000 Shortcut Bar's Open Office Document button and from its directory select an existing PowerPoint 2000 presentation that you want to edit.

- Use the Windows Start menu to start PowerPoint 2000 by selecting Microsoft PowerPoint from the Programs menu.

- Select a PowerPoint 2000 document from the Windows Start menu's Documents option. Windows recognizes that PowerPoint 2000 created the presentation document, starts PowerPoint 2000, and loads the presentation file automatically. (The Start menu's Documents option holds a list of your most recent work.)

- Click the Office 2000 Shortcut Bar's PowerPoint 2000 button to create a blank presentation. Depending on your Office 2000 Shortcut Bar's setup, you might not see the PowerPoint 2000 button.

Unlike the other Office 2000 products, PowerPoint 2000 begins by offering a wizard-like template query that you can select for the type of presentation you want to create. Press Esc to get rid of the opening dialog box that teaches you about the PowerPoint 2000 screen.

Figure 11.1 shows the opening PowerPoint 2000 screen. Your screen might differ slightly depending on the options that you chose during installation. If your PowerPoint 2000 offers a list of options such as opening an existing presentation or creating a new one, select the option that creates a new presentation.

Toolbars Menu bar Presentation window

FIGURE 11.1.
PowerPoint 2000's opening screen.

New slide templates
Slide outline area

View buttons
Drawing toolbar

Status bar Notes page Scrollbars

11

Understanding Presentations and Slides

The primary purpose of PowerPoint 2000 is to help you design, create, and edit *presentations* and printed handouts. A presentation is a set of screens (slides) that you present to people in a group or workbook tutorial. Because PowerPoint 2000 provides a wide variety of predefined templates, you don't have to be a design specialist to create good-looking presentations.

NEW TERM A *presentation* is a set of screens that you share with a group of people as a *slide show*.

Throughout this book, the term *presentation* refers to the entire PowerPoint 2000 collection of slides; whereas, the term slide refers to an individual screen within a presentation.

NEW TERM A *slide show* is a preview of your presentation slides, one at a time, controlled manually or viewed in a timed presentation.

PowerPoint 2000 slides can contain information from the following:

- Data you type into PowerPoint 2000, including text, charts, graphs, and graphics
- Word 2000 documents
- Word 2000 document outlines
- Excel 2000 worksheets
- Excel 2000 graphs and charts
- Access 2000 databases
- Publisher 2000 publications
- Graphics programs that you use to create and edit graphics
- Other software programs whose data you import into PowerPoint 2000

Creating a New Presentation

Figure 11.1 shows the opening window that you see when you start PowerPoint 2000 and begin a new presentation. The figure shows several design templates that contain layouts you can use (templates are stored in files that contain the `.pot` extension). The design template works well for creating a PowerPoint 2000 presentation one slide at a time, but the design template might not be the best place to begin in many instances. The AutoContent Wizard, covered in the next section, is sometimes a better place to start.

Plan your presentations! Think about your target audience. Presenting identical information to two different audiences might require two completely different approaches. The same company's annual status presentation would be different for a shareholders meeting than for the board of director's meeting, for example. After you determine your target audience, think about the content of the presentation. Create an outline before you begin. In the next hour, "Editing and Arranging Your Presentation," you learn about PowerPoint 2000's outlining feature, which you can use to outline a presentation before you create the presentation slides.

AutoContent Wizard and Presentation Design

Perhaps the best place to begin creating a new presentation, particularly if you are new to PowerPoint, is the AutoContent Wizard. This wizard contains a sample presentation with sample text and a selected design. Use the wizard's dialog boxes to select a design that best suits your needs.

The AutoContent Wizard is a presentation design wizard that contains sample data from which you can select and edit to create your customized presentation.

To use AutoContent Wizard to create your presentation, follow these steps:

1. Start PowerPoint 2000.

2. Cancel the New Slide dialog box (the one you see in Figure 11.1).

3. Select File, New to display the New Presentation dialog box.

4. Click the Presentations tab to display several sample presentations.

5. Double-click the icon labeled AutoContent Wizard to start the AutoContent Wizard's question-and-answer session.

6. Answer the AutoContent Wizard's questions to design a presentation shell that best fits your application's requirements.

The AutoContent Wizard helps you to create a blank presentation in a design format that best matches the goals of your presentation. As you follow the AutoContent Wizard, you have to determine the answers to these questions: Who is your audience? What message do you want to convey? Are you selling or offering something? The best approach might be to run through the wizard once as practice to see the kinds of questions you are asked.

The AutoContent Wizard selects the best choice from among these template styles after you complete the wizard:

- Brainstorming
- Business Plan
- Certificates
- Communicating Bad News
- Company Meeting
- Corporate Financial Overview
- Corporate Home Page
- Corporate Handbook
- Employee Orientation
- Financial Plan
- Organization Management
- Marketing Plan
- Meeting Facilities Planner
- Project Status

11

- Reporting Progress
- Sales Flyers
- Team Motivation
- Technical Reporting
- Training
- Who's Who

All these AutoContent Wizard templates are available to you if you don't want to run the wizard first. PowerPoint 2000 supplies two styles for each template: one for an online intranet or Internet PowerPoint 2000 presentation, and one for a standalone PowerPoint 2000 presentation known as a standard presentation.

> You can select from a list of icons that represent these presentations from the New Presentation dialog box instead of selecting the AutoContent Wizard.

After PowerPoint 2000 creates the presentation outline, you have to fill in the details. Click any slide's icon in the left column of the presentation outline that the AutoContent Wizard produces to edit that specific slide.

Creating Presentations Using Design Templates

As you saw in Figure 11.1, PowerPoint 2000 presents you with the New Slide dialog box when you open a new presentation. If you start PowerPoint 2000 and select File, New, PowerPoint 2000 presents you with the New Slide dialog box. The New Slide dialog box contains several templates that you can use to start your presentation's first slide.

> If you click the toolbar's New button, PowerPoint 2000 does not open the New Slide dialog box but begins a new presentation with a blank slide. Therefore, despite the similar icons, the File, New command does not perform the same command as the New toolbar button.

Display the New Slide dialog box whenever you need to create a new slide for a presentation. A presentation contains one or more slides, so you need to display the New Slide dialog box every time you are ready to add the next slide to the presentation. To display the New Slide dialog box at any time, click the New Slide option in the Common Tasks menu.

Click the Common Tasks toolbar button to see the Common Tasks menu.

As you click through the templates, the New Slide dialog box displays a description in the lower-right corner, such as Chart & Text, that describes the template's most common use. Note that the AutoContent Wizard uses several of the templates for its individual slides.

When you double-click the template that best describes the slide you want to create, PowerPoint 2000 creates a new slide based on that template, as shown in Figure 11.2.

FIGURE 11.2.

A template's generated slide appears when you select a template.

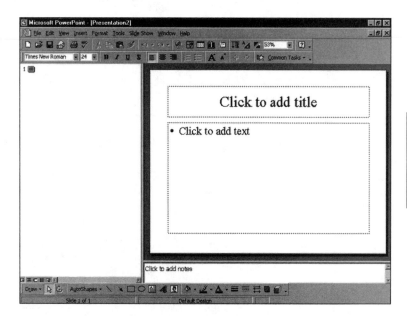

11

STEP-UP
By default, PowerPoint 2000 presents a three-pane slide view so that you can more easily manage your slides as well as edit the current slide and keep notes about the slide.

The instructions on the template's generated slide indicate what to do next. In most cases, you edit the text, possibly change colors, and perhaps add a graphics image to the slide. After you complete the slide, click the New Slide entry from the Common Tasks drop-down menu to display the New Slide dialog box and create your presentation's next slide. After you have created your final slide, you can save your presentation. You can save the presentation in PowerPoint 2000 format or in HTML for embedding into Web pages. Even if your presentation has video and other multimedia content, you can save the presentation as a Web page for viewing from a browser.

Opening a New and Blank Presentation

When you create a new presentation from scratch, you can still take advantage of the design templates. One of the design templates in the New Slide dialog box selection list is the Blank template, shown in Figure 11.3.

If you design your own slide from a blank template, you can later apply one of the template styles to the slide! Therefore, if you don't like what you generate from scratch, PowerPoint 2000 enables you to redesign the slide without requiring you to re-enter the slide's text. If you save a presentation as a template file, you can use that presentation's format for subsequent presentations.

FIGURE 11.3.

Use the Blank template to create your own slide layout.

Click here to create your own layout

Blank presentations require that you manually create every slide element, including the text, titles, and body. Most slides have a title, text, and an optional graphic image. Why not let the AutoContent Wizard or the templates start things off right? The predefined slides work for so many purposes. Resist the temptation to create your slides from scratch until you acquaint yourself with the predefined slides. In most cases, the AutoContent Wizard and templates provide exactly what your presentation needs.

After PowerPoint 2000 displays the new and empty slide, you must add text, graphics, and styles to complete the slide.

Presenting Your Work

After you create your presentation, you can present it to an audience as one or more of the following:

- Transparency overheads
- Computer screens
- Internet Web page presentations
- Audience handouts
- Workbook contents
- 35mm slides
- Color printer documents
- Reference notes for a speaker

Not only does PowerPoint enable you to create and edit presentations, but it can show your presentation as well. PowerPoint 2000 can move from screen to screen, as a slide show does, at whatever pace you request.

11

If you do not have access to a color printer, many of today's retail office product stores and retail copy centers let you take your PowerPoint 2000 presentations, on disk, to their stores where you can request color transparencies and copies of your presentations. In addition, several major photography development businesses can turn your disk-based PowerPoint 2000 presentations into 35mm slides.

Quitting PowerPoint 2000

After you have finished with PowerPoint 2000, quit by performing any of the following:

- Select File, Exit.
- Press Alt+F4.
- Double-click the Control icon.
- Click PowerPoint 2000's Close button.

Always quit PowerPoint 2000 and shut down Windows (by selecting Start I Shut Down) before turning off your computer so that you don't lose your work.

Summary

This hour introduced you to PowerPoint 2000 by showing you how to start PowerPoint 2000, how to prepare for your initial slide presentation, and how to quit. PowerPoint 2000 prepares all kinds of presentations, all of which have one or more slides (screens). Use PowerPoint 2000 to create, edit, and even present your presentations in a slide-projector format.

The AutoContent Wizard is perhaps the best way to start using PowerPoint 2000. By answering a few simple questions, AutoContent Wizard creates a presentation with sample text and formatting. To turn the generated presentation into your own, just change the text and, optionally, change the slides' design elements.

The design templates also provide help when you want to add a new slide to a presentation. When you need to create a new slide, select the closest match from the list of design templates. After the design template creates a sample slide, just edit and modify the text.

If you have a good eye for design, you can create a blank presentation from scratch. Blank presentations require the most work.

The next hour shows you how easy it is to turn the AutoContent Wizard or template-designed slides into your own.

Q&A

Q Do I begin with a PowerPoint 2000 template, the AutoContent Wizard, or a blank presentation when I want to create a presentation?

A Unlike the other Office 2000 products, you almost always create a presentation using the AutoContent Wizard or a template. A blank presentation requires you to lay out all your slide titles and text, which is too much work for most presentations. Unless your presentation requires unusual features, the AutoContent Wizard and templates produce presentations that will be close to your desired presentation.

The AutoContent Wizard is perhaps the best for PowerPoint 2000 newcomers because it presents a series of specific style choices and lays out sample text that you can easily change to fit your presentation needs.

Basically, all three presentation-generation techniques end up producing a new slide on which you must add text, modify colors, change formatting, and add optional graphics. You learn how to apply these slide edits and make improvements in the next hour.

Q I'm still confused. What is the difference between the AutoContent Wizard and the design templates?

A The AutoContent Wizard uses the design templates for its slides. The biggest difference between the two presentation-design tools is that the AutoContent Wizard creates an entire sample presentation, whereas the design templates create individual slide samples.

If you want to add a new slide to a presentation, you may want to use a design template for that individual slide. If you want PowerPoint 2000 to generate an entire set of general slides for a specific presentation, such as a corporate business meeting, you can let the AutoContent Wizard generate the entire presentation and then you can fill in the details that your presentation requires.

11

HOUR 12

Editing and Arranging Your Presentation

This hour shows you what to do after you generate a sample slide or presentation. PowerPoint 2000's AutoContent Wizard and template samples generate good-looking presentations, but it is up to you to add the specific details that you need.

First, you need to change the sample's text. In the process, you might change or add slide titles and formatting, or maybe a graphic image for more impact. This hour teaches you a few shortcuts to turn the sample presentations into the presentation you need.

The highlights of this hour include the following:

- When to use the various views that help streamline your PowerPoint 2000 work
- Why you work most often with the Normal view
- What editing tools PowerPoint 2000 supplies for your slide's text
- How the Slide Sorter view arranges your slide show
- How to select the presentation printing option you need

Getting Acquainted with PowerPoint's Views

PowerPoint 2000 requires you to change views perhaps more than any of the other Office 2000 products. Therefore, you will produce presentations more quickly if you master views now and learn the advantages and disadvantages of each view.

> **STEP-UP**
>
> When you first start PowerPoint 2000 and work on a specific presentation, PowerPoint 2000 displays a two-pane view (called the *Normal view*) with your presentation's outline in the left pane and a specific slide's content on the right. Below the right pane's slide is a special notes section on which you can type notes for the speaker (later in this section, you will read about this Notes pane).

NEW TERM The *Normal view* displays a three-pane window with your presentation's outline in the left pane, a selected slide's details in the top right pane, and a Notes pane below the slide's detail.

> The following list not only describes PowerPoint 2000's views, but also explains how to use them to convert the template and AutoContent Wizard text to a specific presentation. As you read this section, pay attention to the information that teaches how and when to edit text from the AutoContent Wizard and design templates.

PowerPoint 2000 supports the following views:

- *Normal view.* The default, two-pane view from which you can manage your presentation's slide order as well as edit specific slides.
- *Outline view.* Enables you to edit and display all your presentation text in one location rather than one slide at a time. Figure 12.1 shows the Normal view that contains a presentation's Outline view in the left pane (the Outline view comprises one-half of the Normal view) of a presentation. The large titles start new slides, and the details below the titles provide bulleted text for each slide. If you click the Outline view button, the left pane's width increases so that you can see more of the presentation's outline. While working in the Outline view, a Notes window opens under the Slide view so that you can add notes for the presentation's speaker.
- *Slide view.* Enables you to see each slide, one at a time, and edit each slide's format, color, graphics, style, or text. The Normal view displays the Slide view in its right pane. If you click the Slide view button, the right pane's width increases so that you can see more of the selected slide's details.

- *Slide Sorter view*. Displays your entire presentation so that you can add, delete, and move slides. The Slide Sorter view acts like a preview tool. You can review your presentation and use the Slide Sorter as an engine that presents your slides at a pre-set timing, using a specific transitional effect when one slide changes to another.
- *Notes Page view*. Enables you to create and edit notes for the presentation's speaker. You don't normally have to select the Notes Page view to see the Notes pane because the Notes pane always appears beneath the slide's detail in the Slide view.

Change views by clicking one of the view buttons to the left of the horizontal scrollbar or by selecting the view from the View menu. (The Notes Page view is available only from the View menu.) You work in the Outline view most often when creating and editing the text and layout order of your presentation, and you work in the Slide view most often when formatting individual slides.

NEW TERM The *Outline view* shows the table of contents and slide order of your presentation.

As Figure 12.1 shows, PowerPoint 2000 contains four buttons that you can click to change to the Normal view, the Outline view, or Slide view quickly.

FIGURE 12.1.

The Outline view shows the presentation's overall table of contents.

Slide title icons

This slide's bulleted list

View buttons

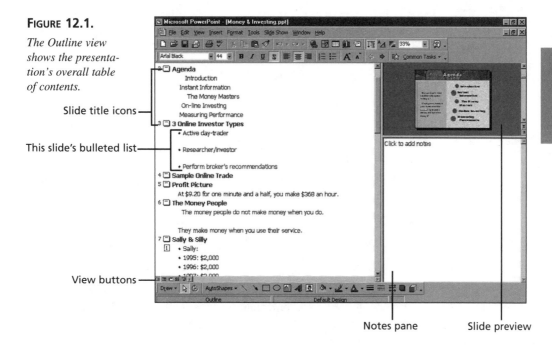

Notes pane   Slide preview

12

Using the Outline View

An outline helps you organize your presentation and sequence the slides properly. Although PowerPoint 2000 makes it easy for you to create the presentation slides themselves, the outline is easier to work with than the full slides, especially when you are still in the process of gathering your thoughts on the presentation's design and content. If you get in the habit of first creating an outline, you have less editing and slide rearranging to do later in the development of your presentation.

After you generate a sample presentation by using the AutoContent Wizard or by creating slides from the design templates, use the Outline view to work on your outline. You can reorganize your slides and edit text in this mode. Click the topic or detail you want to change and edit the text. As you enter and change Outline-view text, PowerPoint 2000 updates the Slide view in the right pane (assuming you are using the default, Normal view) so that you can get a preview of your finished slide.

All the familiar copy, cut, and paste features work in the Outline view. If you drag a title's icon or a bulleted list's item down or up the screen while in Outline view, for example, PowerPoint 2000 moves that item to its new location. When you drag a title, all the points under the title move with it. This is a good way to reorganize slides. When you drag a bulleted item, PowerPoint 2000 moves only that item.

 Unlike other Office 2000 products, PowerPoint 2000 does not copy an item if you press Ctrl before dragging the item elsewhere.

Adding and Importing New Items

To add items to the text in the Outline view, click at the end or beginning of a bulleted item to insert a new entry. If you want to insert a completely new slide, click the New Slide item in the Common Tasks dialog box, and PowerPoint 2000 displays the New Slide dialog box from which you can select a design and then enter the text. You can also click at the end of an item and press Enter to enter a blank slide.

One of PowerPoint 2000's most beneficial text features is its capability to read documents from other Office 2000 products (with the exception of FrontPage 2000). If you create a Word 2000 document that you want to include on a slide (or series of slides), select Insert, Slides from the File menu and select the Office 2000 file that you want to import to your presentation. It is best to do this in Outline view because this enables you to insert the information in the correct order and see the overall effects. The document's Heading 1 style text becomes slide titles, and the subsequent heading styles become text under the title.

> While in Word 2000, click the Present It toolbar button to turn your document into a PowerPoint 2000-ready presentation.

As with all Office 2000 products, PowerPoint 2000 recognizes HTML documents so that you can import or save Web page content.

Promoting and Demoting Elements

When you select View, Toolbars, Outlining, the Outlining toolbar appears to the left of the Outline view. The Outlining toolbar's most important feature may be its *promotion arrows*. If you type a detail item that you want to become a new slide's title, click the left arrow of the Outline toolbar (the *promote button*). To convert a title to a bulleted item, click the right arrow of the Outline toolbar (the *demote button*).

 Promotion arrows are Outlining toolbar arrow buttons that promote Outline view items to slide titles or demote slide titles to Outline view bulleted detail items.

 The *promote button* is the Outlining toolbar button that converts detail text to title text. The *demote button* is the Outlining toolbar button that converts title text to detail text.

Using the Slide View

While in Normal or *Slide view*, you can look at and edit the selected slide in the right pane's Slide view. As Figure 12.2 shows, the Slide view appears in a full-screen view when you click the Slide button. (You can adjust the far-left pane to see more of the Outline view if you wish while viewing the entire slide in the right pane.) You can make edits to your slide text and see the results of those edits as you make them.

NEW TERM The *Slide view* displays each of the presentation's slides one at a time for easier editing and formatting.

To move from slide to slide while in the Slide view, perform any of the following:

- Click the vertical scrollbar.
- Press the PageUp or PageDown keys.
- Click either the Next or Previous slide button on the vertical scrollbar.

12

Next slide's vertical scrollbar

FIGURE **12.2.**

*The Slide view shows
the layout of one of the
presentation's slides.*

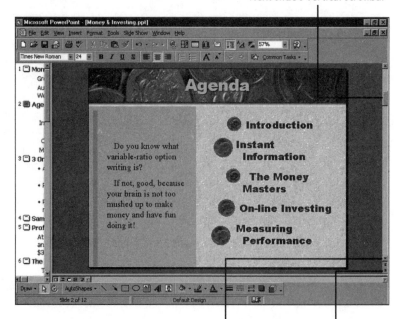

Previous slide button   Next slide button

When you want to edit a text (or graphic) object from the Slide view, click the object.
PowerPoint 2000 displays a sizing box surrounded by sizing handles. PowerPoint 2000
treats a slide's title as a single object and the slide's bulleted set of items as another
object.

To edit text, perform these steps:

1. Click the text you want to edit to display the sizing box.

2. To move the text, drag one edge of the text's resizing box in the direction you want
   to move the text.

3. To shrink or enlarge the selected text object, drag one of the sizing handles in or
   out to adjust the object's size. (PowerPoint 2000 does not shrink or enlarge text
   inside the sizing box as you resize the sizing box.)

4. After you display the sizing box, click inside the box at the point where you want
   to edit text. PowerPoint 2000 inserts the text cursor at the location of your desired
   edit. At that location, you can insert and delete text as well as change the font, color,
   and style of any text that you select using the toolbar or the Format, Font menu
   option. To increase or decrease the size of text, use the Format, Font dialog box.

Select any text, and then click the Increase Font Size toolbar button to quickly increase the font size of the selected text. The Increase Font Size button works faster than opening the Font dialog box. (A Decrease Font Size button appears as well.) You may have to click the toolbar's More Buttons button to see the Increase Font Size and Decrease Font Size buttons.

If graphics appear on the slide, double-click them to edit the images with the graphic-editing tools.

STEP-UP

If you right-click an object (such as a graphic object) while editing a slide and select the Action Settings option, PowerPoint 2000 displays the Action Settings dialog box, as shown in Figure 12.3. By assigning an Internet hyperlink address, a Windows program, or a sound wave file to a mouse click or movement, PowerPoint 2000 connects to that hyperlink location, runs the program, or plays the sound during the presentation. You can provide pushbutton access to programs and Internet Web pages while presenting your presentation!

FIGURE 12.3.

Assign events to mouse clicks and movements.

12

Using the Slide Sorter View

Use the *Slide Sorter view* to rearrange slides, not to edit text or graphics on the slides. When you display the Slide Sorter view, PowerPoint 2000 presents several of your presentation slides, as shown in Figure 12.4. The Slide Sorter view enables you to quickly and easily drag and drop slides to reorder your presentation. Although you can rearrange slides from the Outline view, the Slide Sorter view lets you see the overall visual results of your slide movements.

NEW TERM   The *Slide Sorter view* displays your slides as though they are in a projector so
            that you can easily rearrange them.

Click here to change slide transition   Slide Sorter toolbar

FIGURE 12.4.

*Rearrange slides in the
Slide Sorter view.*

Use your mouse to drag slides from one location to another in the presentation.
Remember that the Undo command (Ctrl+Z) reverses any action that you accidentally
make. You also can use the Windows Clipboard to copy, cut, and paste, although dragging
with your mouse is easier. The Clipboard holds multiple entries that you can copy, cut,
and paste as with Word and Excel. To delete a slide, click the slide once and press the
Delete key.

One of the more advanced (but useful) Slide Sorter features involves the Slide Sorter
toolbar, which appears at the top of the Slide Sorter view (refer to Figure 12.4). The toolbar's Slide Transition Effects drop-down list determines how the Slide Show feature *transitions* (dissolves) from one slide to the next when you display your presentation. The
next hour, "PowerPoint's 2000's Advanced Features," discusses PowerPoint 2000's Slide
Show in more detail. For now, click the Slide Transition Effects drop-down list to see
how PowerPoint 2000 can move from one slide to the next. The Text Preset Animation
button determines how the slide's transitional text appears during the slide show.

NEW TERM   *Transition* refers to the replacement of one slide with the next, often with a
            special effect that causes the second slide to cover the first in a unique way.

To set up slide-transition and text-animation effects, click a slide and select the desired effects from the Slide Sorter toolbar. Click the icon below each slide to see how the set transition effect will look during the slide show.

Using the Notes Pages View

When you select View, Notes Pages view, PowerPoint 2000 displays your slide, as shown in Figure 12.5, with a blank area at the bottom of the screen for speaker notes. The *Notes Pages view* contains a small version of the slide and, below it, a location for a text description of the slide. Therefore, the speaker's notes contain the slides that the audience sees as well as notes the speaker wrote to tell the audience about each slide. Your audience does not see the speaker's notes.

NEW TERM Use the *Notes Pages view* to create and keep the notes you use when presenting your slide show.

FIGURE 12.5.

Prepare speaker's notes using the Notes Pages view.

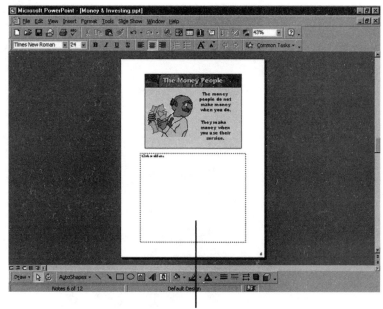

Type speaker's notes here

12

The Notes Pages are designed to be printed for the speaker. However, the speaker can also display the Notes Pages view during a presentation to eliminate paper shuffling. If the speaker's computer has two video cards and two monitors, PowerPoint 2000 can send the slides to one monitor and the speaker's slides and note pages to the other. When the speaker moves to the next slide, the speaker's notes change as well.

Use the PageUp and PageDown keys to scroll through the slides and see the speaker's notes at the bottom of each slide. If the text area is not large enough to read the notes, expand the viewing area by using the Zoom command in the Edit menu.

Saving and Printing Your Work

Be sure to save your presentation after creating and finalizing it. PowerPoint 2000 saves your presentation with the .ppt document filename extension unless you override the default file type and save your presentation in the Web-based HTML format.

Of course, you also need to print your presentation, either to paper, to a color printer, or to a printer that supports transparencies. The File, Print dialog box works differently in PowerPoint 2000 than in Word 2000 and Excel 2000. Instead of globally printing the presentation, you must indicate in PowerPoint 2000 exactly how and what you want to print.

When you display the Print dialog box, shown in Figure 12.6, open the Print What dropdown list to view the selection list.

FIGURE 12.6.

Decide exactly what you want to print.

Select your printed output

PowerPoint prints your presentation in a black-and-white format. You need to deselect the option labeled Black & White if you print to a color printer. Use the Print What dropdown list box to print your presentation in any of these styles:

- Slides only for the presentation
- Handouts (which can hold from two to six slides per page) so that you can give comprehensive notes to the audience

- Notes for the speaker
- The outline for proofreading purposes

If you want to print the entire presentation, you have to select File, Print multiple times and print a different component each time.

Summary

This hour furthered your PowerPoint 2000 knowledge by showing you how to turn a sample presentation into the presentation you want. The views are more critical in PowerPoint 2000 presentation development than in Word 2000 or Excel 2000. The views give you a completely new perspective of the presentation. In addition, you use the different views for different functions, such as editing, rearranging slides, and previewing your presentation. Whereas one view is for the audience, another view exists for the speaker.

As you might expect, you can change PowerPoint 2000 slide text easily by using the basic editing skills you have already mastered. The views enable you to view your slides, outline, and speaker's notes in their most usable form.

The next hour concludes your PowerPoint 2000 tutorial by showing how to format your slides with more detail, how to test and start the PowerPoint 2000 Slide Show, and how to spruce up your slides with graphics.

Q&A

12

Q What are the primary PowerPoint views and what does each view do?

A The two primary working views are the Outline view and the Slide view and both appear together, by default, in the Normal view. The Slide view is great for working on the color and format of each slide. Use the Outline view to keep an overall presentation goal in mind as well as to edit all your presentation's text in one location.

Q I want to use PowerPoint 2000 to present my slides, but I don't want it controlling the transition and timing of the Slide Show. Can I use PowerPoint 2000 to display my slides manually?

A You learn about the details of the PowerPoint 2000 Slide Show in the next hour, but rest assured that it supports manual slide shows in which you control the appearance of the next slide. Actually, most presenters want complete control over the timing of the slide presentations, and PowerPoint 2000 supports such manual transitions. As a matter of fact, you will probably never let it perform a completely hands-off presentation unless you use PowerPoint 2000 for a kiosk store display to promote a product as customers walk by.

Q Can I print everything (all views) with a single File, Print command?

A No, you can only print individual slide-show components, such as the speaker's notes, audience handouts, or slides from the File, Print menu. If you want to print everything and every view, select File, Print multiple times and print a different component each time.

Q I'm using a service to turn my presentation into individual color slides. Do I need the PowerPoint 2000 Slide Show?

A You learn about the Slide Show in the next hour's session. PowerPoint 2000 creates individual slides that you can print or display inside PowerPoint 2000, over a Web page, or from any other source that displays PowerPoint 2000 presentations. The Slide Show does not have anything to do with the medium on which you present your final presentation, however, so you can turn your presentation into slides without using the Slide Show.

HOUR 13

PowerPoint 2000's Advanced Features

This hour wraps up your PowerPoint 2000 tutorial by explaining how to better format your presentations. You can format your entire presentation at one time or apply styles one slide at a time.

In addition to applying global presentation and slide styles, you can edit text and other objects on specific slides. Generally, the AutoContent Wizard and the design templates create presentations that require little editing; if you want to touch up specific parts of your slides, however, PowerPoint 2000 provides the tools you need.

After you complete your presentation, use the Slide Show view to watch the presentation one screen at a time. PowerPoint 2000 follows your slide-show instructions and moves the slides forward at the pace and in the style you request.

The highlights of this hour include the following:

- How to modify your entire presentation's style
- Why you sometimes need to make minor edits to individual slides

- How to insert art and text from other programs into a slide
- When to go to the Clip Gallery for the object you need
- What PowerPoint 2000 tools you can use to work with text objects
- How to set up the Slide Show view to produce special effects
- How to prepare your slide-show presentation

Changing Your Entire Presentation's Design

PowerPoint 2000 enables you to apply a *master layout* template to your entire presentation. If you develop a presentation with the AutoContent Wizard, with individual design templates, or from scratch, you easily can change the format and look of your entire presentation.

NEW TERM *Master layout* is the term applied to a presentation's overall design.

> You might want to change your presentation's design if your target audience changes. Suppose that you give a seminar to your employees on ethics and morals in the workplace, and then learn that your local Chamber of Commerce wants to see your presentation. You should formalize the style when you present to strangers, which might require that you change your presentation's tone.

Use the following process to change the entire presentation's master layout:

1. Select Apply Design Template on the Common Tasks menu to display the Apply Design Template dialog box, shown in Figure 13.1.

2. Search through the Apply Design Template dialog box for a design you like. Double-click the design's folder to open it. PowerPoint 2000 shows a preview of that template in the Apply Design Template dialog box as you select different designs.

3. After you find and select the design template you want, click the Apply button. After PowerPoint 2000 finishes changing your presentation, page through the slides to see whether you chose a good design. You can always go back through the process to change the design again, or undo the change.

FIGURE 13.1.

Use the Apply Design Template dialog box to change the entire presentation's design.

Changing a Single Slide's Design

In the Slide or Normal view, you can change the design of an individual slide (called the slide layout) by selecting the Slide Layout option on the Common Tasks floating toolbar. PowerPoint 2000 displays the Slide Layout dialog box shown in Figure 13.2, which is the same dialog box that PowerPoint 2000 displays when you create a new slide.

NEW TERM   The term *slide layout* refers to a single slide's format and design.

> The Apply button in the Slide Layout dialog box changes to Reapply, as shown in Figure 13.2, if you click the slide's current layout.

FIGURE 13.2.

Use the Slide Layout dialog box to change a single slide's design.

13

The preceding section explained how to change the master layout of your overall presentation. If you use the Slide Layout dialog box to change an individual slide but apply a different master layout, the master layout takes precedence and changes your individual slide (if the master layout differs from the slide).

Editing Individual Slides

In most instances, the master layout and the individual slide layouts provide ample variability and style. Rarely do you have to make substantial edits to your presentation slides. Unlike most PowerPoint 2000 tutorials, this book does not go into great detail about slide editing. You don't need to edit individual slides in most cases because of the detailed layouts that PowerPoint 2000 provides.

About the only major change you must make is to add text to the slides. All the spell-checking and AutoCorrect features that were so important in Word 2000 and Excel 2000 also work for text you place in a presentation; a red wavy line beneath a word indicates that Office 2000's spell checker does not recognize the word. Correct the word, or add it to PowerPoint 2000's dictionary by right-clicking the word.

If you are importing a Word 2000 document that uses the standard styles (such as Heading 1 and Heading 2), the document automatically inserts into PowerPoint 2000 as a presentation. You can then select styles that you want to change to add flair to the presentation.

> Word 2000 documents aren't the only documents you can import into a presentation. You can import an Excel 2000 worksheet, HTML-based Web page, chart, or just about any other kind of file (including multimedia files) into a presentation, select Insert, Object, click the Create from file option, and click Browse to locate the document you want to import.

The following section describes the kinds of edits that you might want to make on individual slides when you need to hone a presentation.

Adding Text and Text Boxes

To add text to a slide, such as text that describes clip art details, add a *text box*. A text box holds text that you can format. To add a text box, follow these steps:

1. Click the Text Box button on the Drawing toolbar.
2. Drag your mouse from the text box's upper-left corner to the text box's lower-right corner. When you release the mouse, PowerPoint 2000 draws the text box, as shown in Figure 13.3.
3. Type your text.
4. Use the Formatting toolbar and the Format, Font command to modify the text style and format.

New text box

FIGURE 13.3.

You can type and format text inside a text box.

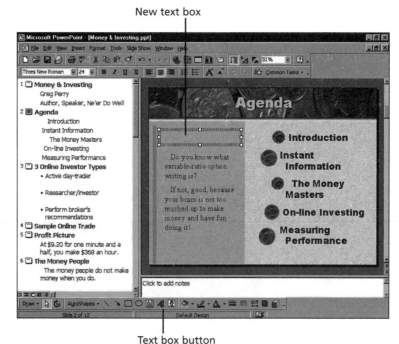

Text box button

5. Click anywhere on the slide to deselect the text box and return to the rest of your editing chores.

NEW TERM   A *text box* is a box that holds slide text.

STEP-UP

When you click the toolbar's Font drop-down list box, PowerPoint 2000 displays each font name in its own font style so that you will see how each font looks before you apply one of them.

13

Modifying, Moving and Rotating Text

You can resize the text box, change the justification and font formatting, move the text box, add a border, and change the font and background colors by right-clicking the text box or by selecting the appropriate toolbar buttons.

To change the text throughout your entire presentation, select View, Master, Slide Master to change the master layout. PowerPoint 2000 displays the Master Layout style slide, shown in Figure 13.4, which you can change to update every slide in your presentation. If you want to format a copyright message at the bottom of every slide, for example, click the slide master's footer area (to turn the footer area into a text box) and edit the text there (or delete the text to get rid of the footer throughout your presentation).

FIGURE 13.4.

Change the slide master to update every slide's text styles.

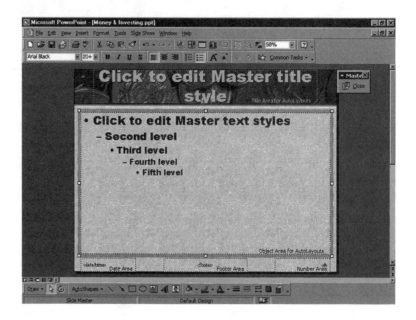

One of the neatest text-editing features is the *Free Rotate tool*. The Free Rotate tool enables you to rotate text to any angle. You might want to slant a title toward or away from text that falls below the title to add a special effect or to call out a cautionary note on a slide, for example.

NEW TERM   The *Free Rotate tool*, on the Drawing toolbar, rotates text, graphics, and any selected slide object in the degree and direction you want to rotate the object. The Free Rotate tool makes the creation of slanting titles and text as simple as dragging your mouse.

To rotate text, click the text to display the text box. Remember that a text box appears around any text, including bulleted lists and titles, when you click those objects. After you display the text box, click the toolbar's Free Rotate tool. The mouse pointer changes to a spiral-shaped pointer. Drag any of the four corners of the text box to rotate the text along an axis. (Figure 13.5 shows a rotated text box.) When you press Escape or click anywhere on the slide, the text box outline disappears and you see the rotated text.

The Free Rotate tool rotates selected bulleted lists and graphics, as well as text boxes.

FIGURE 13.5.

Use the Free Rotate tool to rotate any slide's object.

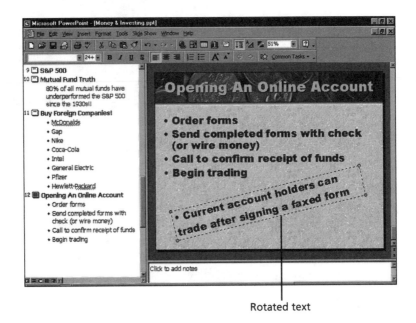

Rotated text

Adding Art

Suppose that you select a slide layout that contains a placeholder for art. Presumably, you have an art image to place on the slide or you would have chosen a different slide layout. When you select a slide layout that includes a placeholder for art, PowerPoint 2000 indicates exactly where the art is to go. Figure 13.6 shows an applied slide layout that includes a placeholder for artwork, for example. PowerPoint 2000 makes it easy to add the art. Follow the slide's instructions, and double-click the area to add the art.

13

FIGURE 13.6.

PowerPoint 2000 indicates exactly where the art is to go on the slide.

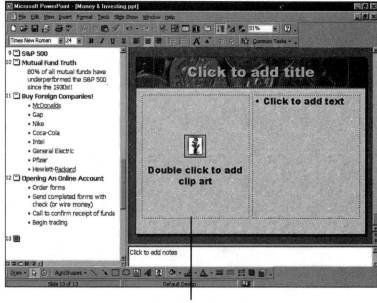

Art placeholder

When you double-click the art area, PowerPoint 2000 displays the Microsoft Clip Gallery dialog box shown in Figure 13.7. A clip (an abbreviation for clip art) is a graphic image, and the Clip Gallery is a collection of clip art images. Microsoft arranges the Clip Gallery by subject, and you can see a preview of the selected image on your screen as you look through the Clip Gallery.

 The term *clip art* refers to a stored graphic image you can place on a slide. Sometimes a clip refers to other kinds of files as well, such as a sound or video file.

 The *Clip Gallery* is a collection of clip-art images arranged by subject.

Microsoft Clip Gallery dialog box also enables you to include picture, video, and sound clip files. PowerPoint 2000 supports the insertion of these other kinds of objects; so if you want a sound to play when a slide appears, you can insert the sound file.

 If you click the button labeled Clips Online for additional clips, PowerPoint 2000 accesses the Web (logging you on if necessary) and offers thousands of additional clip files you can use in your presentation.

The Clips Online button

FIGURE 13.7.

Select art to place in your slide from Microsoft's Clip Gallery.

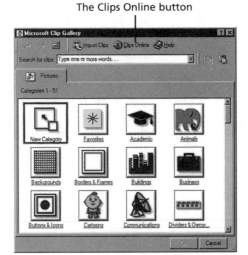

If you want to change the slide's clip art, double-click the art. PowerPoint 2000 will display the Microsoft Clip Gallery dialog box once again.

Your slide does not need to contain a placeholder for you to insert art. The placeholder enables you to more easily manage the artwork, however, and to keep the art separated from the rest of the slide's text and art. If you work with a slide layout that contains a placeholder, you can move and resize the placeholder while you add the rest of the slide's elements. When you are ready for the art, double-click the placeholder to insert the art inside the placeholder's border. Without a placeholder, your artwork overwrites existing text and graphics that already appear on the slide. You have to move and resize the inserted art manually to make it fit with the rest of the slide.

Your art does not have to reside in the Microsoft Clip Gallery for you to insert it. You can insert your own art files, such as logos and pictures, by selecting Insert, Picture, From File and then selecting your file from its directory location.

13

If you want to import a scanned or digital camera image into a slide, you don't have to leave PowerPoint 2000 to scan the image. Select Insert, Picture, From Scanner or Camera and PowerPoint 2000 starts your scanner software. Wait while you scan the image or connect your digital camera to your PC, and then insert the image into your slide.

Using PowerPoint 2000's Slide Show

One of the best ways to see the overall effect of your presentation is to run *Slide Show*. Slide Show displays your slides in sequence, moving from one slide to another, transitioning (changing) with special effects that you have set up, and moving at a preset timing that you can control.

 Slide Show is the PowerPoint 2000 slide projector that displays your presentation slides in sequence, with optional transitions between the slides.

Follow these steps to start Slide Show:

1. Finish editing your presentation and save it.
2. Select the Normal view.
3. Display the first slide in the presentation. (The Home key always takes you to the first slide, and the End key takes you to the last.)
4. Click the Slide Show view button. PowerPoint 2000 prepares the slides and displays each slide, full screen, one at a time, as you click the mouse or press PageUp and PageDown. PowerPoint 2000 halts at the last slide in the presentation.
5. Press Escape to return to the Normal view.

As you watch the slide show, pay attention to the transition and timing between slides. Remember from last hour's session, "Editing and Arranging Your Presentation," that you can control the way PowerPoint 2000 transitions between each slide from within the Slide Sorter view.

Editing Transitions

If you want more control over the transition, select the first slide (from within Slide view) whose transition you want to change and select Slide Show, Slide Transition to display the Slide Transition dialog box, shown in Figure 13.8. From the dialog box, you can control the nature of the transition (choose a transition and watch the Effect window demonstrate the transition), the timing, and the action required to change to the next slide (such as a mouse click).

FIGURE 13.8.

Select the transition effect and timing.

 To make sure the audience notices a new slide, add a sound effect to the transition. That way, when you move to the next slide, PowerPoint 2000 plays the sound you associate with the transition.

If you want to use a uniform transition for all slides, click the Apply to All button. If you want the transition to affect only the current slide, click the Apply button to close the Slide Transition dialog box.

 Run through your presentation, using all transitions, before you make your presentation to your audience. Too many transitions can be distracting and can often slow down a presentation and reduce its effectiveness.

Automating the Presentation

Of course, you want to automate your show as much as possible. If a speaker will control the presentation, he will want to use the mouse to move from slide to slide. Otherwise, you might want to run the slide show continuously as a demo or informational display, as you might do at a trade-show booth.

To automate your slide show, select Slide Show, Set Up Show to display the Set Up Show dialog box, shown in Figure 13.9.

13

Figure 13.9.

Fully automate your slide show with the Set Up Show dialog box.

Select the option that your presentation requires. If the speaker will control the show, for example, click the first option. If you want the show to run continuously, click the Browsed at a kiosk option. In addition, you can elect to show only certain slides for a particular event.

When you subsequently click the Slide Show view button, PowerPoint 2000 follows your Set Up Show dialog box instructions and displays the slides as you requested.

Using Speaker Notes

The Notes view holds your speaker notes and you can print and use those notes during your presentation. If you print handouts for your audience, PowerPoint 2000 gives you the choice of printing just the slides themselves or the slides along with your speaker notes.

Print from the Notes Pages view if you want your audience to have both the slides and the speaker notes that go along with each slide.

You can add to your speaker's notes during a presentation or take notes that you can incorporate later for the next presentation. The audience does not see the notes that you add so long as you use a separate monitor for the presentation. To take notes during a slide show presentation, right-click the current slide and select Speaker Notes. A dialog box opens to which you can add notes that PowerPoint 2000 saves as that slide's speaker notes. If you give a presentation often and think of additions during one of the presentations, you can use the Speaker Notes dialog box to remind you of additions you want to make before the next presentation.

Summary

This hour concluded the tutorial on PowerPoint 2000. You can now make presentations look professional, and you can modify individual slides when needed. In addition to mastering PowerPoint 2000's design and editing tools, you also understand how to set up and run the Slide Show viewer.

When you use PowerPoint 2000 to show your presentations, PowerPoint acts like an intelligent slide projector and displays slides at the pace you select using the transition you choose.

The next hour, "Introducing Publisher 2000," shows you how to create publications with Publisher 2000.

Q&A

Q Why would I add a text box instead of using Outline view to add the text?

A The text on the Outline view is either a title or a bulleted item. If you want to place text outside these areas, you must draw a text box. You can draw a text box anywhere on a slide, and can even overwrite parts of a clip art image with a text box. Text boxes are useful for describing figures and for placing extraneous notes on your slides.

Q What if I don't have extensive clip art to embed on my presentations?

A PowerPoint 2000 comes armed with many images, so you may not need external graphics-art packages. In addition, PowerPoint 2000 includes an Internet link, which enables you to search the Internet for clip art (as well as picture, video, and sound) files.

If you do not see the Clip Gallery when you request it, run the Office 2000 Setup program again, select the Clip Gallery, and rerun the install. (Your other files, including data and PowerPoint 2000 programs already on your disk, will not be affected.)

13

Hour **14**

Introducing Publisher 2000

This hour introduces Publisher 2000 and shows you how to turn documents that you created in other Office 2000 products into polished, professional publications. Publisher 2000 is the latest in a series of Publisher versions that Microsoft has produced over the years. In keeping with Publisher's tradition, Publisher 2000 offers new and simpler ways of producing documents that look better than ever before.

Publisher was the first product to offer wizards, the technology that all who are familiar with Microsoft products have used. You've worked with wizards already in this book (in Hour 2, "Introducing Office 2000's Powerful Features") and you know how wizards can help guide you through the document-creation process. Publisher 2000 provides wizards that help you create almost any publication you need; you'll rarely have to create a document from scratch again. Once you create a publication, you can apply wizard technology to change that publication's design.

This hour wraps up your Publisher 2000 introduction by describing many of the publications that Publisher 2000 can help you create. Once you understand the basics of how to use Publisher 2000, you can let Publisher 2000 do most of the initial design work for virtually any publication you want to create.

The highlights of this hour include the following:

- When to use Word 2000 and when to use Publisher 2000 for your publications
- How to use the Publisher 2000 wizard technology to create an initial publication design
- When to add details to the publication's design
- Why use a text frame to hold text you'll need to edit later
- How to place art in your publication
- How to use wizard technology to modify your publication after you've created it
- Where to use the many kinds of publications that Publisher 2000 helps you produce
- How to get extra wizard help when you want to design publications from scratch

Why Publisher 2000 and not Just Word 2000?

Microsoft put both Word 2000 and Publisher 2000 in Office 2000 because these products work so well together. If you want to create attention-getting publications that contain exactly the information that's important to you, *first* write your publication's text (perhaps more than one article if your publication requires multiple articles), use Word 2000's powerful word-based editing tools, and hone your words to perfection. Once you are satisfied with your writing, import that Word 2000 document into Publisher 2000. Publisher 2000 then takes over and, with Publisher 2000's help, you can turn your words into a publishable product.

Getting Acquainted with Publisher 2000

Start Publisher 2000 by selecting Microsoft Publisher from the Start, Programs option. The opening screen, shown in Figure 14.1, displays showing a catalog of wizards that create various kinds of publications for you. The catalog's left pane lists the types of publications you can create and the right pane displays samples from each type available. Scroll through the wizard samples to see all that Publisher 2000 can do for you.

FIGURE 14.1.

*From the start,
Publisher 2000 offers
wizards that help you
create eye-catching
publications.*

 If you have children, scroll down to the Airplanes amd Origami Wizards.
Publisher 2000 creates documents that include folding instructions for airplanes and other creations.

NEW TERM *Origami* is the art of folding paper into models such as birds and boats.

Creating Your First Publication

You'll use a wizard to create almost every publication in Publisher 2000. The wizards
handle most needs and, once you create a publication with a wizard, your job will be to
enter the text, import the graphics, and fine-tune the publication to meet your needs.

Get acquainted with a publication wizard by following these steps to create your first
publication:

1. If you've already started Publisher 2000 and closed the Catalog dialog box shown
   in Figure 14.1, you can start a new publication by selecting File, New and click the
   Publications by Wizard tab.

2. Select the second wizard option, Newsletters. Publisher 2000 displays a list of
   newsletter design choices in the right pane. More choices appear than will fit inside

14

the dialog box so you can scroll down the dialog box's scroll bar to see additional newsletter designs. The dialog box's preview area shows what the design will look like once you create the publication.

3. For this example, select the Floating Oval Newsletter design and click the Start Wizard button. Publisher 2000 starts the wizard, prepares your publication for the Floating Oval design, and displays the wizard's opening window with the publication's initial design as shown in Figure 14.2 after prompting you for name and address information that subsequent wizards will use.

FIGURE 14.2.

The wizard generates an initial design and helps you finish the publication.

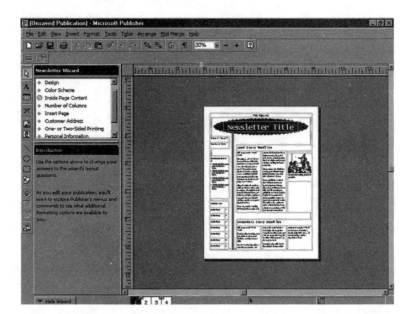

4. You can click Finish at any time before completing the wizard and finish individual wizard steps later. Click Finish now to see the wizard steps appear in the upper-left hand corner.

5. Click the Zoom control's plus sign to zoom closer into your publication and see the details better. The minus sign takes you further out so you can see the overall design once again.

6. The wizard's steps appear in the window pane labeled Newsletter Wizard. Click Color Scheme to select colors for the newsletter's elements.

7. Click different color schemes to see the effect of the color schemes applied to the sample newsletter in the right pane. For this example, select the Prairie color scheme to apply the Prairie color scheme to your publication.

8. Click the Newsletter Wizard's option labeled Number of Columns and then choose 2 columns in the pane below. The preview changes to show what the two-column newsletter will look like as Figure 14.3 shows.

FIGURE 14.3.

Publisher 2000 can convert your newsletter to multiple columns.

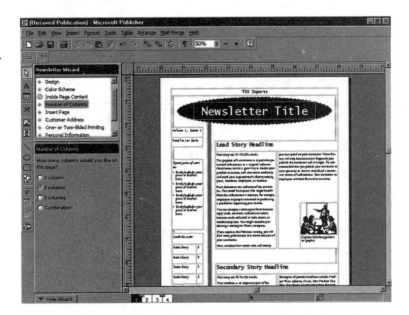

9. You can continue selecting options from the Newsletter Wizard window pane and specifying the option's details in the lower pane. The publication in the right window pane always reflects your latest selections.

If you want detailed help on a particular Publisher 2000 topic, select Help, Publisher Tutorials to display Figure 14.4's tutorial topic window. When you click on a topic, Publisher walks you through a brief, graphical tutorial of that topic.

14

FIGURE 14.4.

Publisher 2000 offers
self-guided tutorials
from the Help menu.

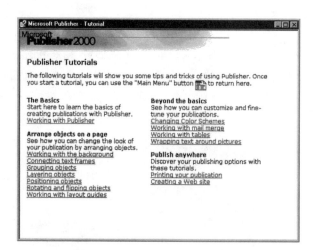

Filling in the Details

Once Publisher 2000 lays out the newsletter's design, the Newsletter wizard offers to help you more. The Newsletter wizard's steps always remain on the screen in the Newsletter Wizard pane, along with your publication, as you've seen. You can change any part of your newsletter's design, such as the color scheme, by selecting that wizard topic and changing that option.

Now that you've laid out your publication with the help of the wizard, your publication is ready for details. Those details are the pictures and text in your newsletter.

Adding Text

One of the first elements you'll add to any design is the text. The simplest text to add is the text that you type directly into your publication. Click over the newsletter's left column to highlight the column. When you begin typing, the highlighted text will automatically disappear.

Therefore, now that you've selected the first newsletter column, you can begin typing the text that you want to appear in that column. The first thing you'll notice, as soon as you begin typing, is that you cannot read what you are typing! That's okay because you can press F9 or the toolbar's + button at any time to zoom into the text that you type. Figure 14.5 shows zoomed text being entered into the first column. Use the horizontal and vertical scroll bars to bring whatever zoomed text area into view that you want to work with.

FIGURE 14.5.

Press F9 to zoom into your publication and make the text readable.

As in Word 2000, Publisher 2000 supports paragraph indention. Select Format I Indents and Lists to open a dialog box from which you can set the spacing for each paragraph's first line indention.

As you type, you'll notice that Publisher 2000 automatically hyphenates for you. You can turn off the automatic hyphenation by selecting Tools, Language, Hyphenation. In addition to turning automatic hyphenation on and off, you can control when the hyphenation occurs from the Hyphenation dialog box.

Publisher 2000 performs background spell-checking as you type the way that Excel 2000 and Word 2000 do. Also, you can select Tools, Spelling, Check Spelling (F7 is the shortcut key) to check the spelling of the entire document one final time. Publisher 2000 has no grammar checking abilities. If you create the text in Word 2000, however, you can use the Word 2000 writing tools to create accurate text and then bring the text into your publication once you've designed the publication with a Wizard. If you make a mistake while typing, Publisher 2000 supports multiple levels of undo just as Word 2000 and Excel 2000 do.

14

Continue entering text and you'll notice that Publisher 2000 supports the same AutoCorrect entries you set up in Word 2000. Use the F9 key to zoom in and then back out of your Publisher 2000. When looking at the overall publication, you can click on any column, title, or banner with text and type new text. If you click over an area where you've already entered text, Publisher 2000 lets you edit that text.

All of the character formatting options from Word 2000 and Excel 2000 are available. If you don't like Publisher 2000's default font, select Format, Font and choose a new font.

If you want to add a *drop cap* to a paragraph, select Format, Drop Cap. (The drop capital letter cannot follow a tab.) Select the type of drop cap that you want to see, click OK, and you'll see the drop cap such as the one shown in Figure 14.6.

NEW TERM A *drop cap* is a large character that begins a paragraph's first sentence.

FIGURE 14.6.

Add pizzazz to your introductory paragraphs with a fancy first letter.

Getting Text from Other Sources

You won't always want to type text directly into a publication. As a matter of fact, you'll often create the text in Word 2000 and then transfer that text to Publisher 2000. To bring text from other sources, you'll almost always do one of two things:

- Copy text from the Windows clipboard
- Import the text from its native application

Suppose you write a travel book that teaches people how to travel through Europe the fun way, as a traveler who meets the people and not as a tourist who views the sites from a bus fifty yards away. To help promote your book, you create a newsletter that acts as a sales flier for your book. You may want to copy some text from the book's manuscript into the newsletter. You certainly don't want to copy the entire book but just a paragraph or two.

Start Word 2000 (you don't have to exit Publisher 2000 to start Word 2000, of course, just click the Start button and start Word 2000 as you normally do). Load the book's document into Word 2000, select the paragraph you want to copy to the newsletter, and select Edit, Copy (Ctrl+C) to copy that paragraph to the Windows clipboard. Switch to Publisher 2000 (press Alt+Tab to switch to Publisher 2000 or click the Publisher 2000 button on your Windows taskbar), click the area that is to receive your text, and select Edit, Paste (Ctrl+V) to put the clipboard's text into your publication.

Although the clipboard is useful for copying small portions of text into your publication, you may want to import long columns of text into Publisher 2000 from a full Word 2000 document. If you work with others who write for the publications you produce, you will be able to use Wizard to lay out the publication and then import the other writers' document files directly into the newsletter columns that are to receive the writing.

To import a file from Word 2000, select Insert, Text File from the menu to display the Insert Text File dialog box. Move to the folder that contains the text document and double-click that file to import the text directly into your publication. You then can format the drop cap as well as the font and character spacing if you wish.

Text Frames

As you type, you enter text into publication elements called *text frames*. If you use the Wizard to create all your publications, you don't need to be as concerned about adding text frames as you have to be if you create a publication from scratch or if you modify a publication that a wizard designs for you. The wizard adds text frames where text is to go so that you can easily type or insert text into the frames. The frames keep the text in columns within your publication.

NEW TERM   A *text frame* holds text that you can edit.

By putting text in a text frame, and by separating the text from the other elements such as the art, Publisher 2000 lets you return to that text and edit the text using the standard insert and delete text-editing tools you are accustomed to. You can format the text, spell-check the text, and so on.

14

If Publisher 2000 did not put your text into a special text frame but simply put the text in your publication without distinguishing text from art, you would not have text-editing access to the text. Some art is textual in nature, such as fancy lettering boxed within a flowery border. You would only be able to edit such text as you might edit artwork, one *pixel* (a screen's dot from the words *picture element*) at a time.

NEW TERM   A *pixel* is a dot on your screen; many pixels work together to make up the pictures and text you see.

To add a text frame to a publication, as you would do if you were to create a publication without the help of a wizard, click the Text tool on the toolbox at the left of the Publisher 2000 screen. (The Text tool is the button with the letter *A* showing.) Once you select the Text tool, drag your mouse anywhere inside a publication to create a rectangular text frame that works just like the text frame you used to enter text in the previous section. You can add multiple columns inside a single text frame or use a different text frame for each column in your publication.

To add multiple columns to a text frame, right-click over a text frame and select Change Frame, Text Frame Properties to display the Text Frame Properties dialog box shown in Figure 14.7. Notice the options labeled Include "Continued on Page" and Include "Continued from Page" that add connecting messages to columns that continue on subsequent publication pages.

FIGURE 14.7.

Specify the number of columns you want in a text frame to make text wrap from column to column inside the frame.

If you want text to wrap across columns, continuing into subsequent columns as you type, you need to connect two text frames together. Select Tools, Text Frame Connecting to display a small Connect Frames toolbar. Click the Text Frames button (the button with two chain links) to change the mouse cursor to a pitcher shape and click on the text frame that is to connect to the original frame. (Select the frame's page number if the text is to continue into a text frame on a different page.) Once connected, Publisher 2000 ensures that overflowed text from the first text frame flows into the connected text frame, even if that text frame is on a different page.

Your Publication's Art

Working with art is actually simpler than working with text. Art resides inside art frames just as text resides inside text frames. You can change the art, resize, and move art within its frame.

When a Wizard finishes designing your publication you'll need to change the wizard's sample art to the artwork you want to use. Publisher 2000 makes replacing artwork simple. Double-click the artwork to open the Clip Gallery shown in Figure 14.8. When you select the replacement art from the Clip Gallery by double-clicking the image, Publisher 2000 places the image. You then can resize the image to fit the publication's boundaries as needed.

FIGURE 14.8.

The Clip Gallery holds art you can place in your publication.

14

If you want to use artwork from another source, such as a scanned image, you can select Insert, Picture, From File. Publisher 2000 inserts all major picture formats including GIFs, JPEGs, Kodak Photo CD, TIFF, and CorelDraw images.

Once you load the image you want to place in your publication you can move or resize that image. When you click inside an art frame, eight black *sizing handles* appear around the frame's borders. By dragging any of the resizing handles in or out you can shrink or expand the art frame and the image size changes along with the frame.

New Term *Sizing handles* are black squares that appear around an art frame that you can drag to resize an image.

If you point to the art frame's edge, without pointing to a resizing handle, the mouse cursor changes to a Move cursor. You then can drag the image (and its frame) to any location on the publication. If you move the art frame over text, Publisher 2000 formats the text around the art frame so that the art does not cover up the text as Figure 14.9 shows.

Justify both margins to get newspaper-like columns where the text aligns evenly on both sides of the column. When you move artwork into the text, as shown in Figure 14.9, the text flows more gracefully around the artwork.

Figure 14.9.

When you move an art frame into text, Publisher 2000 wraps the text around the art.

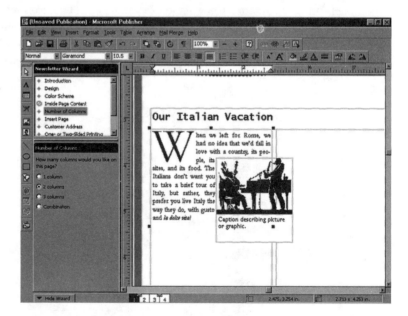

As with text, you can copy pictures from the Windows clipboard that you have copied there from another application.

Extra Shapes

The Publisher 2000 toolbox, the set of tools on the left side of your screen, includes a few drawing tools with which you can add shapes to your publication. Although these tools are not good enough to use for most original artwork, you can use the drawing tools to add lines, circles, boxes, and other simple shapes to your drawing. Many of these shapes make good borders for special text such as for emblems and callouts that you want to add to your publication.

To access the shapes, click the line, oval, or box drawing tools. A collection of special shapes appear when you click the Custom Shapes tool as shown in Figure 14.10. To draw any shape, from lines to the custom arrows, click and hold your mouse at the shape's starting point and drag the mouse to size the shape where you want it.

FIGURE 14.10.

Select a custom shape from the collection of shapes available from the toolbox.

Custom shape tools —

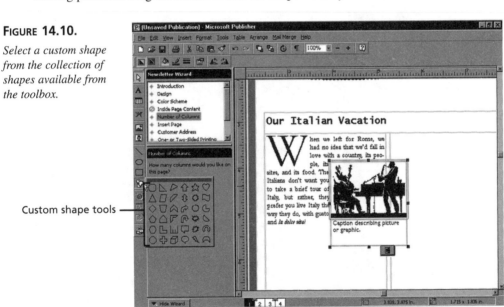

Designing with the Design Gallery

Publisher 2000 includes a design feature called the *Design Gallery*. The Design Gallery acts as a repository of pre-designed elements that you can place in your publications. For example, you may need a special banner to spruce up a newsletter's featured column. Although you can design your own eye-catching banner, why not check the Design Gallery to see if you like an example that's already there?

14

The *Design Gallery* is a collection of pre-designed objects, grouped by publication style, that gives you easy access to graphic elements such as banners, sidebars, called-out quote bubbles, and even table of contents styles.

You can explore the Design Gallery contents by following these steps:

1. Click the Design Gallery button on the toolbox. The Design Gallery button is the extra-large button at the bottom of the toolbox. The Design Gallery window opens as shown in Figure 14.11.

   Like the Clip Gallery, the Design Gallery is organized in categories listed down the left edge of the Design Gallery window. (When you add your own items to the Design Gallery, you can create new categories that will appear on the tabbed page labeled Your Objects.) Each category has its own design.

2. Click on different Design Gallery categories to see the designs available in them.

3. Once you locate the picture that represents the Design Gallery item you want to insert into your Publisher 2000, double-click the item to insert it into your publication. Publisher 2000 places the item on the Publisher 2000 editing area and closes the Design Gallery window. You can move, resize, and edit the item as if you had designed and drawn the item yourself from the shape and text tools on the toolbox.

FIGURE 14.11.

The Design Gallery contains graphic elements you can include in your publication.

Categories

Design Gallery items within each category

Scroll to see additional items

Getting Help with the Design Checker

Publisher 2000 includes a special design tool called the *Design Checker* that you use *after* you create your publication. When you select Tools, Design Checker, the Design Checker dialog box appears. To learn what kinds of design elements that Design Checker analyzes, click the Options button to display the Options dialog box shown in Figure 14.12.

 The *Design Checker* analyzes your publication and offers suggestions on how to improve your publication.

FIGURE 14.12.

The Design Checker analyzes your publication for common design problems.

As you can see, the Design Checker looks over your publication and searches for the problems listed in the Options dialog box. You can uncheck one or more of the options and click `Check selected features` if you want to limit the Design Checker just to those items you've selected. Click the option labeled `Check all problems` if you want the Design Checker to look at all elements of your publication.

The Design Checker does not leave you hanging once it finds a problem. If you click the Explain button, the help window to the right of your editing area will give instructions on how you might go about correcting the problem just found.

Even if Design Checker finds multiple problems with your publication, you don't have to wait for the Design Checker to find them all before you correct the problems. You can leave the Design Checker window on the screen but drag it out of the way while you correct the problem. Once you fix the problem, click the Design Checker's Continue button to look for additional design problems in case others appear.

14

Putting Borders Around Your Publications

You may want to place a border around your entire publication, or perhaps around a single text or art frame. A border is nice to place around smaller publications you create, such as placeholders for dinner guests. You may want to create your own business cards and place a border around your company's name.

To add a border to a publication, follow these steps:

1. Click the rectangle tool on the toolbox to activate the tool. Your mouse cursor turns into a crosshair shape.

2. Draw the box where you want the border to appear. Perhaps you are going to use the border around a headline, a photo, or even the entire publication page. If you don't draw the box the proper size, you can resize the border after you complete it.

3. Right-click over any of the box's edges to display a pop-up menu and select Change Rectangle, Line/Border Style, More Styles. The Border Style dialog box appears. Click the BorderArt tab to display the special border art shown in Figure 14.13.

FIGURE 14.13.

The Border Style dialog box determines the size, color, number of sides, and thickness of your border lines.

The BorderArt dialog box page lets you specify the size of the border and the color. In addition, you can determine if artwork that will go inside the border (if you plan to place art inside the border) is to stretch to fit the border or if the border's picture is to retain its size even if the border is much larger than the figure.

4. You can click the Create Custom button to make your own border art. Once you enter the name of a picture (from the Clip Gallery or other image), Publisher 2000 repeats that image to build a border that you can name and save in the list of borders that appear.

5. Click OK to save the border art on your editing area. You now can resize the border as you would any other box or graphic image on the publication.

Summary

This hour introduced Publisher 2000 to you and showed you how simple creating a publication can be with the wizards. The Publisher wizard lets you design the overall publication while the Design Assistant wizard guides you through the individual steps you need to finish your publication with text and art.

Enough Wizards exist to help you create just about any kind of publication you need to create. Rarely if ever will you need to create a publication from scratch. By adding text and art frames, you can customize any publication the wizards create. Publisher 2000 is more than a simple publication design tool, however. Publisher 2000 goes the next step and lets you add professional touches to your publication.

This hour also showed you how to access the design elements of Publisher 2000. In addition, you saw the many kinds of publications that Publisher 2000 can enable you to produce. Your small business will be able to use Publisher 2000 to design more than just newsletters; Publisher 2000's wizards help you produce forms, invoices, labels, and even paper-folding projects for children who may want something to do while they wait for you to finish your work at the office.

The next hour begins discussing Outlook 2000, an information manager that helps you get organized.

Q&A

Q Can I create Web pages with Publisher 2000?

A Certainly. The wizard named Web Sites gets you started. As you'll learn in Hour 24, "Introducing FrontPage 2000," FrontPage 2000 is perhaps the best tool within the Office 2000 to create and manage Web pages. You can develop the initial Web page in Publisher 2000 that you can later import into FrontPage 2000.

Q How can I place a background on my publication?

A A background image can appear on the back of your publication, acting like a watermark image that shows through. By placing the background on every page in your multi-page publication, you can add consistency to your publication's look.

The background remains blank until you add design elements, such as lines and pictures. To add work to a publication's blank background, select View, Go to Background (Ctrl+M). Publisher 2000 then temporarily hides your publication's foreground (all the elements on top of the background, including all the text and art frames). After you add whatever background images and text you want to add,

14

select View, Go to Foreground (Ctrl+M again). The publication's current page number appears at the bottom of the screen when working in the foreground.

You can hide the background on any page by selecting View, Ignore Background. The background does not go away but it does disappear from view and does not appear again until you once again select View, Ignore Background to show the background.

PART V

Organizing with Outlook 2000

Hour

Hour **15**

Outlook 2000 Basics

This hour introduces Outlook 2000, a program that could change the way you organize your life! For several years, software developers have attempted to produce an all-in-one organizing and planning program; however, these programs were separate from other programs. If you used your word processor and needed an address, you had to open a separate organization program, look up the address, and type it into the word processor. Outlook 2000 integrates with the other Office 2000 products, however, and shares a menu interface with Word and Excel.

Outlook 2000 can be addictive because it handles the details of your life so well. Not only is Outlook 2000 a truly interactive planning and scheduling program, but it is also fun to use.

The highlights of this hour include the following:

- What Outlook 2000 is all about
- How Outlook 2000 differs from Outlook Express
- What screen elements Outlook 2000 has
- How to navigate through the Calendar views

- How to schedule meetings and events
- Which tools help you manage tasks
- How to keep notes

An Outlook 2000 Overview

You can use Outlook 2000 to do the following:

- Organize your Calendar.
- Schedule meetings.
- Keep an appointment book.
- Track a prioritized to-do task list.
- Record your business and personal contacts.
- Keep a journal.
- Write notes to yourself that act like yellow sticky notes when you view them (similar to the Excel 2000 comments you learned about during Hour 8, "Using Excel 2000").
- Send and receive all your email and network documents from one location.

STEP-UP

Microsoft first introduced Outlook in Office 97. For its first version, Outlook 97 contained a rich feature set but had some problems common with many first software versions, such as its slow startup and long program-termination speed. With the improved Office 2000, you will be happy to find that the program is more efficient, contains more features, and improves the way they work.

Do not confuse Outlook 2000 with Outlook Express. Outlook Express is an add-on program that comes with Internet Explorer 4, Internet Explorer 5, and Windows 98. If you have upgraded to Internet Explorer 4 or 5 (see Hour 22, "Office 2000 and the Internet"), you also have Outlook Express. Outlook Express is a slimmed-down version of Outlook 2000. Outlook Express supports only email, a more limited contact *database* called the Windows Address Book, and a handful of other Internet-related features. Outlook Express does not replace Outlook 2000, so feel free to use Outlook 2000 rather than Outlook Express for your contact information.

NEW TERM A *database* is a collection of related information, such as the name and address information that you can store in Outlook 2000.

15

Starting Outlook 2000

Start Outlook 2000 by performing one of the following:

- Click one of several Outlook 2000-related button on the Office 2000 Shortcut Bar. The New Message button sends email, the New Appointment button creates a new appointment, the New Task button enters a new task in the scheduled task area, the New Contact button creates a new contact in your contact database, and the New Note button opens a new note to which you can add text.

- Use the Windows Start menu to start Outlook 2000 by selecting Microsoft Outlook 2000 from the Programs menu.

- Click your Windows taskbar's Outlook button. (Depending on your desktop settings, you may not see the Outlook button located in the Quick Launch toolbar.)

- Click the Office 2000 Shortcut Bar's Microsoft Outlook button to start Outlook 2000. (Depending on your Office 2000 Shortcut Bar's setup, you may not see the Outlook button.)

Figure 15.1 shows the opening Outlook 2000 screen. Your screen might differ slightly depending on the options that you chose during installation. The opening Outlook 2000 screen shows the Outlook Today view, an overview of messages, to-do tasks, and appointments for the current time period.

FIGURE 15.1.

Outlook 2000's Outlook Today opening screen summarizes your current activities and messages.

STEP-UP

Outlook 97 did not offer the Today view, the all-in-one summary screen. To locate your appointments, read email messages, and check to-do tasks, you had to navigate to different parts of the program.

Depending on your Outlook 2000 configuration, your Outlook 2000 may open to a different screen, such as the Calendar view shown in Figure 15.2. Outlook 2000's program areas appear in different window formats. The formats correspond to folders in Outlook 2000 that appear in the left-hand Shortcuts Bar. Here are the folders that you can set to appear upon startup:

- *Outlook Today*. The at-a-glance overview of your current activities, as shown in Figure 15.1.
- *Inbox*. A collection of your email messages, organized in topic folders that you set up, or contained in the default Inbox folder.
- *Calendar*. The scheduling screen where you can track appointments, as shown in Figure 15.2.
- *Contacts*. A card catalog of contact name and address information
- *Tasks*. Items you have to prioritize and complete.
- *Journal*. A log of activities you perform on the computer.
- *Notes*. Notes on any topic that you want to organize.

All of Outlook 2000's data falls within one of these folder-based formats. As you progress through the rest of this and the next hour's lesson, you will master these folders' usage and contents.

You can change the first folder that appears by selecting Tools | Options, clicking the Other tab, and then clicking the Advanced Options button. The Startup in this folder drop-down text box determines the folder that appears when you first start Outlook 2000.

Not only can you specify folders to view, but you can also specify views that are different configurations of screens with Outlook 2000 data. You can customize views so that your Outlook 2000 screens look any way you want them to look.

FIGURE 15.2.

Outlook 2000 might open in the Calendar folder, showing you the contents of your Calendar folder.

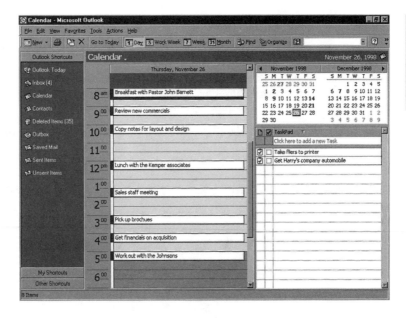

15

The Outlook 2000 screen's format differs quite a bit from that of other Office 2000 products. You won't see the typical toolbars. The following screen descriptions appear on Outlook 2000's Inbox folder view (see Figure 15.3) and elsewhere throughout Outlook 2000's screens:

- *Outlook Bar.* Contains shortcuts to some of the Outlook 2000 features. You can rearrange the Outlook Bar contents and resize its icons. The Outlook Bar enables you to access all of Outlook 2000's most frequently used areas, called *groups*. Click the group names, such as My Shortcuts, to view additional groups.

NEW TERM A *group* is an area on the Outlook Bar that separates one set of related folders from others.

- *Folder list.* Displays your Outlook 2000 data in folders, such as those described earlier in this section. Many folders exist, in addition to those described earlier, and you can create your own new folders to organize data as well. As you use Outlook 2000, you subdivide your work into the folders. Your Inbox and Outbox mail appear in folders within their respective folders in the Folder list, for example. If a number appears in parentheses after a folder name, the number represents the number of unread items in that folder. If you receive three new email messages, for example, (3) appears after the Inbox folder name.

- *Information viewer.* Displays items from the selected folder. As you work with items, both the Information viewer's format and content changes. When you look over your daily incoming mail, for example, the Information viewer displays summaries of your mail. When you want to read something specific, you can display the entire item in the Information viewer and hide the summaries. The Information viewer contains the Preview pane when you view the contents of your Inbox folder.

- *Preview pane.* Shows the selected item's contents assuming you've displayed the Preview pane from the View menu.
- *Items.* Contains the folder contents such as contacts, appointments, and email messages.

FIGURE 15.3.

The Inbox folder produces one of the most comprehensive views in Outlook 2000.

Toolbar

Items

Outlook bar

Folder List

Preview pane

If you don't see the Folder list, select View, Folder List. You can select the option once again to hide the Folder list if you decide you want more room for the items within the Information viewer window.

Using the Calendar in Outlook 2000

Outlook 2000 includes a Calendar that not only enables you to organize and track dates, but also enables you to track birthdays and anniversaries (and gives you automatic time-for-gift reminders), find open dates, keep a task list, schedule meetings. It can also remind you of appointments. The following sections show you how to use the Outlook 2000 Calendar to organize your life.

Not only does Outlook 2000 remind you of specific appointments with an audible and visible reminder, but Outlook 2000 easily sets up recurring appointments, such as weekly sales meetings or birthday reminders.

When you are ready to work with Outlook 2000's Calendar, display the Calendar by clicking the Calendar icon on the Outlook Bar at the left of the screen, selecting Calendar from the Folder list, or by selecting Go, Calendar. To display more of your Calendar, you can decrease the amount of screen space devoted to the Outlook Bar and Folder list by dragging their edges toward the left side of the screen.

You can adjust the screen columns to show more of any Outlook 2000 feature. Most Outlook 2000 users prefer to hide the Folder list, displaying it only when needed by selecting View, Folder List. Figure 15.4 shows the Outlook 2000 screen with the Calendar activated once again. Notice the Folder list is hidden to give more room to the appointments in the Calendar.

FIGURE 15.4.

Working with the Calendar.

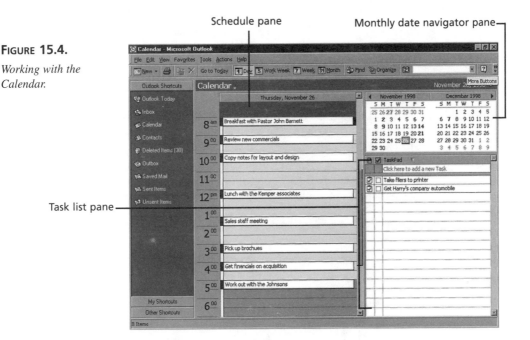

Navigating Times and Dates

Notice that the Calendar appears with these major sections:

- Monthly calendar pane (also called the Date navigator)
- Schedule pane
- Task list pane

When you first open Calendar, the monthly calendar (also called the Date navigator) always highlights the current date (getting its information from the computer's internal clock and calendar). The current date is highlighted and the current day's appointments display if you have entered any. The Calendar might show two months or just one, depending on your screen settings. You can navigate the Calendar through days and months by following these simple guidelines:

- Change days by pressing the left- or right-arrow keys or by clicking a date with your mouse.
- Change months by clicking to the left or right of the Calendar's month name or by clicking the Calendar's month name and selecting from the pop-up month list that appears.

Click through the Calendar's days and notice that the daily time planner changes days accordingly. Although you may not have any appointments set yet, you quickly see how you can look at any day's appointments by clicking that day's date. The weekend day appointment pages are darkened to remind you that you are looking at Saturday or Sunday. In addition, Outlook 2000 darkens all weekday times before 8:00 a.m. and after 5:00 p.m. The darkened areas are typical nonbusiness hours. Of course, you can enter new appointments into the darkened areas. The darkened highlight is just Outlook 2000's way of letting you know the times are not normal business hours.

> You can change the hours that Outlook 2000 designates as business hours by selecting Tools, Options and clicking the Calendar Options button. The Start time and End time list boxes hold the business hours that Outlook 2000 maintains. In addition, you can select other days to appear as workweek days in case you normally work on Saturday or Sunday. If you want Outlook 2000 to use a color that differs from the default yellow highlight, you can also select another color.

The Calendar also provides a month-at-a-glance format when you click any of the seven day abbreviations above the Calendar's day numbers. (Figure 15.5 shows the month-at-a-glance calendar that appears when you select the entire month.) When you click any of the month's weekday abbreviations in the Date navigator area, Outlook 2000 displays the schedule for the entire month. If you highlight a week in the Date navigator calendar, Outlook 2000 displays the schedule for that week.

Entire month selected

FIGURE 15.5.

The month-at-a-glance calendar provides a long-range overview of your schedule.

 If you select two or more days, Outlook 2000 displays your selection's at-a-glance planning calendar.

As you acquaint yourself with Outlook 2000's Calendar, select from the View menu to customize the screen for your particular needs. In addition, you can drag any bar separating the window panes to provide more or less room to any portion of the Outlook 2000 screen that you need.

Setting Appointments

To schedule an *appointment*, perform these steps:

1. In Day view, select the day on which you want to schedule the appointment by clicking it.

2. Select the appointment time. You might have to click the time planner's scroll bar or use your up- and down-arrow keys to see the time you want.

3. Double-click the appointment time to display the Appointment dialog box, shown in Figure 15.6.

FIGURE **15.6.**

Scheduling an appointment is easy.

4. Enter the appointment's subject and location. Outlook 2000 keeps track of your locations as you add them, so you don't have to retype them for subsequent appointments. (You need only to select them from the drop-down list.)

5. Set the start and stop times (use Tools, Options and click the Calendar options button to change the default of 30-minute appointments if you often have different appointment lengths) or click the All Day Event option if you want to schedule an all-day appointment.

6. Set your reminder time if you want a reminder. Outlook 2000 audibly and visibly reminds you of the appointment at the time you request.

7. Click the Recurrence toolbar button if the appointment occurs regularly. Outlook 2000 displays the Appointment Recurrence dialog box, shown in Figure 15.7. Set the recurrence options to enable Outlook 2000 to schedule your recurring appointment.

You could select Actions, New Recurring Appointment to go directly to the Appointment Recurrence dialog box when you set up recurring appointments.

8. Click OK to close the Appointment Recurrence dialog box.

9. Click the Save and Close button. Outlook 2000 displays your appointment in the time planner.

FIGURE 15.7.

Calendar easily accommodates appointments that occur regularly.

NEW TERM   An *appointment* is an activity for which you reserve time but which does not require other people or resources.

> If you don't run Outlook 2000 at all times in the background, it cannot remind you of pending appointments. Therefore, you should add Outlook 2000 to the Windows Startup folder so that Outlook 2000 starts automatically every time you start up your computer.

If you need to change a set appointment, double-click the appointment to display the Appointment dialog box, in which you can change the appointment details. Drag the appointment's top or bottom edges from the time planner to increase or decrease the appointment's duration. Drag the appointment's side edges to change the appointment's start time.

> Click the New Appointment button on the toolbar to schedule a new appointment without first selecting the appointment's date and time.

You can remove an appointment at any time by right-clicking over the appointment to display a pop-up menu and then selecting Delete.

Instead of using the Appointment dialog box to schedule an appointment, you can enter an appointment quickly by clicking the appointment time once to highlight it and entering the text for the appointment directly on the daily planner. When you press Enter, Outlook 2000 adds the appointment to the daily planner.

Outlook 2000 reminds you of the appointment with an audible alarm 15 minutes before the appointment. If you want to adjust the alarm lead time or make the alarm recurring, double-click the appointment entry to display the Appointment dialog box.

You may not want an audible alarm on all appointments. If you use your laptop in meetings and do not want audible alarms interrupting conversations, for example, you can remove any appointment's audible alarm by right-clicking the appointment and selecting Reminder from the pop-up menu. You can select Reminder again from that same menu to set the audible alarm once again.

Scheduling Meetings

In Outlook 2000 terminology, a *meeting* differs somewhat from an appointment. An appointment is for you; it does not involve other resources (such as people and equipment). A meeting, however, requires that you schedule more people than yourself, and perhaps requires that you reserve other resources (such as audio-visual equipment and a room in which to hold the meeting). If you work in a networked environment, Outlook 2000 can scan other people's computer schedules to help you plan meetings that others can attend.

NEW TERM A *meeting* is an appointment that involves other people and resources.

Follow these steps to schedule a meeting:

1. Create an appointment for the meeting's day and time.
2. Click the Attendee Availability tab in the Appointment dialog box. (Figure 15.8 shows the dialog box that appears.)
3. Click the Invite Others button and type (or select from the name list) the names of those attending. The list might include people or resources, such as podiums. Outlook 2000 gets the names from your Contacts folder, but you can enter new names as needed.
4. Use the scrollbars to view the free and busy times for the people you invite. You must also select the meeting time. Outlook 2000 shows you the attendees' available free time when you click AutoPick, or you can use your mouse to schedule the attendees even if their free times all conflict. (Outlook 2000 adjusts for time zones if you invite someone from another time zone.)

FIGURE 15.8.

You can schedule meetings, invite people, and reserve resources.

 Obviously, you must be organized and know the attendees quite well to have access to their schedules. Outlook 2000 will search your network for the contacts and their free times. If you are not on a network, you do not have access to the free times of the people you invite.

Click the Appointment tab to complete the dialog box. When you click Send, all recipients (if networked or available by email) get invited to your meeting by being sent the notes you entered on the Attendee Availability page.

Scheduling Events

An *event* is an activity not specifically tied to a time frame, such as a holiday or birthday. When you want to record an event, such as your boss's birthday, perform these steps:

1. Select Actions, New All Day Event. The Event dialog box appears (looking very much like the Appointment dialog box) with the tabbed Appointment page displayed.

2. Schedule the event as you do an appointment, but click the All Day Event check box to show that the event lasts the entire day (otherwise, the event automatically turns into an appointment).

3. Select the Show Time As option if you want your Calendar to show the time as Busy or Out of Office time.

4. Select an appropriate reminder time from the Reminder list, such as 2 days, to receive an audible alarm and note reminding you of the event so that you can purchase gifts or prepare for the event in some other way.

5. Click the Save and Close button to return to Calendar.

NEW TERM   An *event* is a 24-hour activity, such as a birthday or holiday.

If the event is recurring, you can select Actions, New Recurring Appointment to initiate a new recurring event. When you view the event, Outlook 2000 shows it in a *banner* (a highlighted heading) for that day in the day planner's views.

NEW TERM   A *banner* is a highlighted title that signals and describes a day's event.

Managing a Task List

A *task* is any job that you need to track, perform, and monitor to completion. Outlook 2000 tasks (like appointments and meetings) might be recurring, or they might happen only once. You can manage your Outlook 2000 task list either from the Tasks folder in the Folder list or from the Calendar folder.

NEW TERM   A *task* is any job that you need to track, perform, and monitor to completion.

> Unlike appointments, meetings, and events, tasks don't belong to any specific date or time. Tasks are jobs you need to finish but are not linked to a date or time.

To create a one-time task, perform these steps:

1. Click the New Task toolbar button or select File, New, Task. You can create a task even faster by clicking the task list's entry labeled Click Here to Add a Task.

2. Enter a task description.

3. Type the due date (the date you must complete the task, but not necessarily the day you perform the task). If you click the Due Date drop-down list, you can select from a calendar that Outlook 2000 displays. You can enter virtually any date in virtually any format, including Next Wednesday. Outlook 2000 converts your format to a supported date format.

4. Further refine your task (if you need to) by double-clicking the task to display the Task dialog box, shown in Figure 15.9. You can specify recurring tasks and assign

priority. Click the Details tab to update the status of the task as you work on it. The Details page even tracks such task-related information as mileage, time involved, and billing information.

FIGURE 15.9.

You can modify the task's specifics and status.

5. Click Save and Close to finalize the task.

After you complete a task, click the task's check box to cross the task from the list. Delete a task by selecting it and clicking the toolbar's Delete button.

If you want to remind yourself of a task's deadline, make an appointment for the deadline on the task's due date. Set the alarm for 24-hours or 2 days. When the deadline draws near, you then are reminded that the task is wrapping up fast.

Writing Yourself Notes

Outlook 2000 notes are equivalent to sticky yellow-paper notes. You can post a note inside Outlook 2000 and retrieve, edit, or delete the note later.

To see your notes, click the Notes icon on the Outlook Bar or display the Notes item from the Folder list. Double-click any note to see its contents.

To create a new note, click the New Note toolbar button to display a yellow-note window. Type your note and click the note's Close button to close the note. Resize the note by dragging its lower-right corner. Outlook 2000 tracks the note's date and time. Change the note's font by selecting a new font from the Tools, Options dialog box page and clicking the Note Options button. You can quickly select a different note color by right-clicking the note's icon when you see it in Outlook 2000.

Turn notes into appointments and tasks! Drag a note from the Notes work area to the Calendar or Tasks Outlook Bar icons. Outlook 2000 will open an appropriate dialog box with the note's contents, filling in the task or appointment's description. In the next hour, "Communicating with Outlook 2000," you learn how to work with Outlook 2000's email and journal components—you can drag notes to those Outlook 2000 programs as well.

Quitting Outlook 2000

You can quit Outlook 2000 by performing any of the following:

- Selecting File, Exit.
- Pressing Alt+F4.
- Double-clicking the Control icon.
- Clicking Outlook 2000's Close button.

Always quit Outlook 2000 and shut down Windows before turning off your computer; otherwise, you might lose your work. If an email message is in the middle of a transfer and you don't properly exit Outlook 2000, for example, you could lose some or all of that message.

Summary

This hour introduced Outlook 2000 and explained some of the ways you can use Outlook 2000 to check your Calendar; manage appointments, meetings, and events; track tasks; keep notes; and explore your computer. If you have used any other personal-information management program, you will really like the integration of Outlook 2000 into the Office 2000 and Windows environment.

The next hour shows you how to use the Contact List to find your associates quickly and easily. Additionally, the journal tracks events as they happen, including incoming mail and faxes that you receive inside the Inbox.

Q&A

Q How can I assign a task to a specific day?

A You cannot assign tasks to days. Tasks transcend days because tasks are one-time or recurring items that you must accomplish within a certain time frame, but not on a particular day. Perhaps you are only confusing Outlook 2000 terminology. If you want to assign a particular event to a time and day, assign an appointment or meeting. Tasks are items that you must accomplish and that you can track and assign to other people, but tasks are not tied to a specific time and date.

Q After I set a reminder, how does Outlook 2000 inform me of the appointment, meeting, or event?

A You must continually run Outlook 2000 during your computing sessions for Outlook 2000 to monitor and remind you of things you have to do. Outlook 2000 is one program that you probably want to add to your Windows StartUp group so that it always starts when you start Windows. Outlook 2000 cannot remind you of pending appointments if you are not running it.

Outlook 2000 tracks incoming and outgoing events. Also, as you learn in the next hour, Outlook 2000 monitors your electronic mail, faxes, and network transfers, and keeps an eye on your reminders to let you know when something is due. The only way Outlook 2000 can perform these tasks is to keep it running during your work sessions.

15

HOUR 16

Communicating with Outlook 2000

This hour concludes coverage of Outlook 2000 by showing you how to use the Journal, Contacts list, Inbox, and Outbox. The Inbox and Outbox components are central to using Outlook 2000 as a repository for your entire data throughput; these mailboxes constitute your computer's Grand Central Station. One of the most common tasks performed on the PC is the exchange of email, and Outlook 2000 makes that exchange simple.

Part of the effectiveness of Outlook 2000 hinges on how well you keep your Contacts list organized. Use Outlook 2000 to keep track of clients, friends, employees, and anyone else you contact. Outlook 2000 tracks not only routine name and address information but email addresses as well. After you set up your Contacts list, other Outlook 2000 programs (such as the Inbox) refer to the list when an address is needed. You learned in the preceding hour how to use Outlook 2000 to schedule meetings, and you can easily schedule those meetings with the contacts you record.

The highlights of this hour include the following:

- What a contact is
- How to maximize your use of the Outlook 2000 Contacts database
- When the Journal tracks items automatically
- How to enter items manually into the Journal
- How to send and receive messages
- When to use the Outlook 2000 Deleted Items folder
- How to read and reply to messages

Keeping Contacts

The Outlook 2000 *Contacts* database keeps track of your contacts so that Outlook 2000 has a central, uniform repository of information to use when you send email, hold meetings, and record calls. You can add new contacts, delete old ones you no longer need, and change information of a contact from the Contacts folder. The Contacts folder maintains name, title, address, phone, and email information on your contacts, and it offers fields that you can use for additional information such as notes, family information, and more. In addition to the recording of contact information, Outlook 2000 uses a smart name and address formatter to help ensure that your names and addresses are uniform for more accurate searching.

 A *contact* is a person or organization that you correspond with, either by mail, email, phone, or in person.

Recording Contacts

When you first use Outlook 2000, you have no contacts entered in the Contacts folder except for a sample contact that you can click to highlight and press Delete to remove. To record a new contact, perform these steps:

1. Click Contacts on the Outlook Bar, select Go, Contacts, or select Contacts from your Folder list if you have chosen to display the Folder list.

2. Click the New Contact toolbar button on the Contacts screen to open the Contact dialog box (shown in Figure 16.1).

3. Type the contact's full name. If you click the Full Name button, Outlook 2000 displays the Check Full Name dialog box, shown in Figure 16.2, to maintain separate fields for each part of the name (such as title, first name, and last name). The time you take to separate part names pays off if you use your contact information in form letters and database work.

FIGURE 16.1.

Outlook 2000 formats the entry of contact data for you.

16

Outlook 2000 automatically displays the Check Full Name dialog box if you enter a name that does not follow a typical name pattern. (Outlook 2000 displays this dialog box automatically until you uncheck the option at the bottom of the box.) If you enter only one word for a name, for example, Outlook 2000 displays the Check Full Name dialog box so you can specify whether the word is the first or last name.

FIGURE 16.2.

The Check Full Name dialog box ensures that your names are entered properly.

4. Enter the rest of the contact's information. Click the Address button to track separate parts of the contact's address using a Check Address dialog box similar to the Check Full Name dialog box. Click the drop-down Address list to record separate addresses for the same contact. You can record a business, a home, or another address, for example, by clicking the appropriate drop-down address type before entering the address. Open the phone number drop-down lists as well to store different kinds of phone numbers for your contacts.

> Notice how many phone number fields Outlook 2000 gives you to use.
> Although you see only four on the form, a phone number field for Business,
> Home, Business Fax, and Mobile, you can click the down arrow inside each
> of these fields to display a list box full of additional numbers such as
> Business 2, TTY/TDD, and Pager. Today's communication needs often require
> multiple phone numbers for the same contact, and Outlook 2000 provides
> all the number fields that you might need. Any of the list boxes on the
> Contact form drops down to provide additional choices. You can enter mul-
> tiple addresses and email accounts for each contact, for example, although
> only one physical address and one email address shows at any one time.

5. After you enter the phone numbers and email addresses, you can enter a Web page site address in case you want to record the contact's Web page or the contact's company Web page.

6. The large text box toward the bottom of the New Contact window holds any notes you want to keep for this contact.

7. Click the Details tab to record other information, such as a spouse name, with the contact. The other tabs are for advanced purposes such as keeping digitally signed security Ids, and the All Fields tab enables advanced users to rearrange the fields on a contact's form. For most Outlook 2000 users, the General and Details tabbed pages are more than adequate to hold the information a contact requires.

8. Click the Save and Close buttons to save the contact information and display a blank dialog box for your next contact.

> The contact's data page acts like an Internet Web page browser as well as a
> repository for contact data. If a contact has a Web page, enter that Web
> page's address in the Web Page field. When you return to the contact infor-
> mation and click the toolbar's Explore Web Page button, Outlook 2000
> locates and displays the contact's Web page using whatever Web browser
> (such as Internet Explorer) is installed on your system.

Be on the lookout for shortcuts as you work with Outlook 2000. Generally, you can drag and drop information instead of re-entering data when you need to transport information from one Outlook 2000 area to another. You don't even have to type in all of a client's contact information if you have that information elsewhere in Outlook 2000. Suppose, for example, that you wrote yourself a quick note with a new client's name and phone number using Outlook 2000's notes. (You learned how to take notes with Outlook 2000 in the preceding hour). You can transfer the client's information from the note to your Contacts list by dragging the note to the Contacts icon on the Outlook Bar. Outlook 2000 sets up the initial client name and number information, to which you can then add more information. Conversely, you can drag a contact to a note to place that contact information on the note.

When you close the Contact dialog box, your first contact appears in the Address Book. As you add more entries, your Contacts list grows, as shown in Figure 16.3. After you build a collection of contacts, you will click the alphabetic tabs to the right of the Address Book to locate specific contacts.

FIGURE 16.3.

Your contacts appear in Outlook 2000's Address Book.

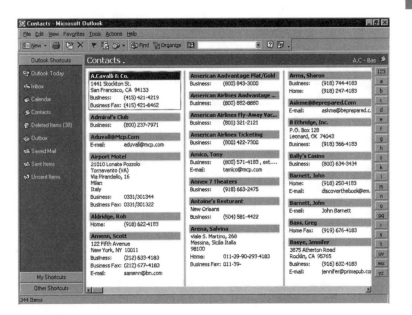

Selecting Contacts

To select a contact, display the contact name in the Address Book. After you select a contact, you can do the following things:

- Directly edit the addresses, phone numbers, and email addresses displayed on the page by clicking the appropriate fields.
- Double-click the name to open the Contact dialog box, which displays the contact information, enabling you to edit or view more detail.

- Right-click the contact name, select Call Contact, and dial the contact's phone number from the New Call dialog box (shown in Figure 16.4). If you click the Journal option, Outlook 2000 adds the call to this contact's Journal; the Journal records the call! Use the Journal to track calls such as payment requests so that you have a record of who you called and when you placed the call. The next section explains all about the Journal feature.

FIGURE 16.4.

Outlook 2000 automatically dials your selected contact.

- Right-click the contact name and click the Explore Web Page button to see the contact's Web page from within your Web browser.

- Drag the column separators right or left to see more or less of each column. If you prefer to view narrow columns in the Contact folder, you see more contacts but not the full Phone Number and Address field. If you widen the columns, you see more detail for the contacts (but fewer of them at a time).

- Right-click the contact name and select New Message to Contact to write and send an email message to the contact's first email address.

- Right-click the contact name and select the New Contact from Same Company option. Outlook 2000 creates a new contact entry and transfers all the business-related addresses and phone numbers to the new contact. You need only to fill in the new contact's name and other specifics. Likewise, Outlook 2000 enables you to create an employee Contacts list easily by transferring similar company data to each new employee you enter.

- After you double-click on a contact to open that contact's information window, you can click the toolbar's Display Map of Address button (also available from the Actions menu) to see a graphic map of the contact's general address. Outlook 2000 goes to the Web (assuming that you have Internet access) and locates the contact's address on a Microsoft Expedia Web map and shows that location such as the one shown in Figure 16.5. Not only does the map pinpoint the address, it also includes links to Web sites related to that area of the country.

FIGURE 16.5.

*View a map where
your contact resides.*

 As you get acquainted with Outlook 2000, you will learn more features that
will streamline your work. The Organize toolbar button, for example,
enables you to view your contacts in a variety of ways, even in a spread-
sheet-like format to see more contacts at one time. In Hour 21, "Office
2000's Synergy," you will learn how to write a contact a pre-addressed letter,
quickly and easily from the Contacts folder.

Keeping a Journal

The Outlook 2000 *Journal* keeps track of all your interactions with contacts, Outlook
2000 items, and activities. Although you can make manual entries, the real power of the
Journal appears when you automate Outlook 2000 to record the following types of
Journal entries:

- Track and record all items (such as email) that you send to and receive from contacts. Depending on the option you selected when you set up a contact, the Journal
  can automatically record all interactions with that contact, or you can record interactions selectively.

- Keep track of all Office 2000 documents that you create or edit. Browse the
  Journal to find a summary of the documents you created and the order in which
  you created (and edited) them.

- Track all meetings automatically.
- Track all appointments and tasks manually. (Outlook 2000 does not track appointments and tasks automatically; you must enter them yourself every time you add an appointment or task.)
- Manually record *any* activity in your Outlook 2000 Journal, including conversations around the water cooler.

NEW TERM The Outlook 2000 *Journal* keeps track of all your interactions with contacts, Outlook 2000 items, and activities.

Setting Automatic Journal Entry

Have you ever wished that you had recorded a complaint call you made when you got a bad product or service? Let Outlook 2000 track all your calls automatically! The Journal records times, dates, and people you called. As you use Outlook 2000 to make calls, record notes about the calls and track those notes in your Outlook 2000 Journal. After you open the Journal by clicking the Journal icon on the Outlook Bar or selecting Journal from the Folder list, you see a blank Journal entry such as the one shown in Figure 16.6. (Beneath the Journal's date line resides several collapsed Journal entries that you can expand to see details.)

FIGURE 16.6.

Your Journal is ready for entries.

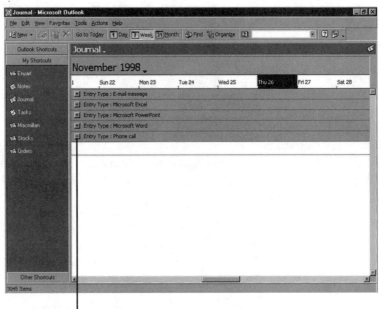

Click to expand entries

The first thing you want to do with your Journal is to designate all items that you want the Journal to track. Select Tools, Options and click the Journal Options button. Select each item from the list that you want Outlook 2000 to track. Select E-mail message, Fax, Meeting request, and Meeting response if those are the items you want the Journal to track automatically. In addition, select one or more contacts from the Contacts list, and Outlook 2000 records all activity for those specific contacts.

If you want Outlook 2000 to track document files from another program, such as Word 2000, just select that program from the list. Outlook 2000 tracks all Office 2000 document activity (if you select this option) as well as other Office 2000-aware software documents and data files. (Note that not all Windows programs are Office 2000-aware.)

16

Adding Journal Entries Manually

As mentioned earlier in this section, the Journal cannot automatically record all activity in your life; however, you can add manual entries for any activities you want recorded. If you want to record an appointment, open that appointment (from within the Calendar). If you want to record an item not related to Outlook 2000, such as a conversation, create a note for that item (see Hour 15, "Outlook 2000 Basics," for help with the note feature) and transport the information from the note to the Journal.

To record a manual Journal entry from an existing item (such as a new contact you just entered), perform these steps:

1. Double-click the item you want to record to display the Edit dialog box for the item.

2. Select the item's Actions, New Journal Entry option. The Journal now contains an icon that represents the item, such as a phone call to the contact. Double-click the Journal's icon to display the item's details.

Suppose that you wrote a letter to your phone company, for example, and you want to record the complete document in your Journal. If you have set up your Journal to track all Word 2000 documents automatically, the document appears in your Journal. If you have not set up the Journal to track Word 2000 documents automatically, however, just display the document's icon in the My Computer window on the Outlook Bar and drag the document to the Journal icon on the Outlook Bar.

You also can add a new Journal entry of any item type before you create the item. Display your Journal and select File, New. Select Journal Entry to display the Journal Entry dialog box (shown in Figure 16.7). Type a subject and select the type of Journal entry. When you click the Save and Close button, Outlook 2000 saves your entry in the Journal.

FIGURE 16.7.

Manually enter a new Journal entry.

Reviewing Journal Entries

After you set up the automatic recording, Outlook 2000 begins logging those activities. When you open the Journal for days during which some activity occurred (automatically or manually recorded), you see the Journal entry. Suppose that you want to work on files you created a few weeks ago during an end-of-month accounting close period. Open your Journal and scroll back to the date of the close. You see a list of all files that you worked on, whether those files are email messages you sent or received, notes, Word 2000 documents, or Excel 2000 worksheets.

Outlook 2000 compacts entries within the same application. Instead of seeing every Word 2000 document that you worked on this week, for example, you see a band labeled, Entry Type: Microsoft Word. Click the plus sign (+) on the band to expand the entries and see the individual Journal entries recorded for each Word 2000 file you worked on. Double-click any of the files you see to open that file. If you double-click a Word 2000 document, Word 2000 is activated and loads that document. If you double-click a contact you entered, Outlook 2000 displays that contact information.

Periodically, delete older entries from your Journal that you no longer need. The Journal entries add up quickly. When you delete a Journal entry, the files the Journal entry describes are not deleted, only their entries in the Journal are.

Mastering Outlook 2000 Mail

The Outlook Bar displays the following labeled icons:

- *Inbox*. Holds incoming email and faxes.
- *Sent Items*. Displays mail items you have sent to others.
- *Outbox*. Holds items you have queued up to send.
- *Deleted Items*. Holds items, such as email messages, that you have deleted but not removed from Outlook 2000. Select Tools, Empty Deleted Items Folder to remove the Deleted Items folder contents.

16

> When you remove an item from the Deleted Items folder, Outlook 2000 does not send the item to the Windows Recycle Bin; Outlook 2000 deletes the item completely from your system.

 The *Inbox folder* holds messages that you have received.

 The *Outbox folder* holds all your outgoing messages until you send them.

 The *Deleted Items folder* holds items you have deleted from Outlook 2000 but not completely erased from the disk. The Deleted Items folder is to Outlook 2000 what the Recycle Bin is to Windows 95.

If you want to save messages from your Inbox, move them to a different location. You can also right-click the message to move it to any folder, even one not currently listed on the Outlook bar. You can select and drag any message from the Inbox to another folder on the Outlook Bar. If you change your mind about getting rid of a message stored in your Deleted Items folder, you can move that message to a different folder. Only when you delete a message from within the Items folder is it completely deleted.

Creating and Sending Messages

One task you perform quite often is sending a message to a recipient across the Internet. To create a message, perform these steps:

1. Select File, New, Mail Message to display the Message dialog box (shown in Figure 16.8). (You can also click the New Mail Message toolbar button to open the Message dialog box more quickly than selecting from the File menu.)

2. Enter the recipient's name in the To (your primary recipient) field. If you enter a name in the Cc (carbon copy) field, Outlook Express sends a copy to that recipient and places a Cc before the name. Click these buttons if you want to select a contact in your Contacts list (highly recommended because your Contacts list holds email addresses). If you have not entered the recipient in your Contacts list, add the information now, and then close the Contacts list to return to the mail message.

   If you want to send the same message to multiple recipients, select multiple recipients from the Select Names dialog box when you click the To button to see a list of contacts. If you want to enter email addresses directly in the To field, you can separate multiple addresses with a semicolon (;).

3. Enter the message subject. Your recipient sees the subject in the list of messages that he receives.

Always enter a subject for your email messages so that your recipient knows at a glance what your message is about. This also makes it easier for you to track sent messages.

4. Type your message in the large message area at the bottom of the Message dialog box. To spell check your message, type your message, click your cursor at the beginning of the message, and then select Tools, Spelling. You can activate automatic spell checking (so that Outlook 2000 checks your spelling as you type) by selecting the appropriate option in the Tools, Options dialog box's Spelling page.

5. Click the Options tab to select certain message options (such as the message importance level and a delivery date). The recipient, like you, can order received mail by importance level when reading through the messages.

6. Click the Send button. Outlook 2000 sends the message to your folder named Outbox. If you are logged on to the Internet, Outlook 2000 sends your message immediately.

7. Select Tools, Send and Receive to send your Outbox messages. If you are logged on to the Internet when you click the Send button in step 7, Outlook 2000 finishes sending your mail and also collects any incoming messages waiting for you. If you are not logged on to the Internet, Outlook displays the Logon dialog box. Always check your Inbox for mail after sending mail from the Outbox using Tools, Send and Receive in case new mail was delivered to you.

FIGURE 16.8.

Enter the message you want to send.

16

Not all messages are text-only, and Outlook 2000 works with all file types. To attach another document file to your message, such as a Word 2000 or Excel 2000 document, click the Insert File toolbar button and select a document file from the Open dialog box that appears. The file that you attach follows any text that you typed.

Checking Mail

Regularly, you need to check your Inbox folder to see what items await you. As mentioned in step 7 of the preceding section, you must select Tools, Send and Receive to send Outbox items and receive Inbox folder items. Outlook 2000 logs you on to your Internet provider if needed. Your Inbox folder on the Outlook Bar displays a number if you have unread messages that require your attention.

If you use multiple email accounts, select the Tools, Send and Receive option and select the email account that you want to check. You might use Microsoft Network at home and a local Internet provider at work, for example. You can set up both accounts on your home and office computer and select which account's email to retrieve when you select the Tools, Send and Receive option. To add a new email account to Outlook 2000, select Tools, Accounts, Add and select the appropriate account. You may need to contact your Internet service provider to set up the appropriate properties to work with Outlook 2000 after you add an account.

If you find that Outlook 2000 logs you off your Internet provider after you retrieve your email, but you often want to remain logged on to check the Web, you can request that Outlook 2000 stay logged on. Select Tools, Account and select your Internet account. Click the Properties button and uncheck the option labeled Disconnect after Transferring Mail from Remote Mail.

When you display your Inbox folder (by clicking the Inbox icon on the Outlook Bar), you see a list of incoming message headers like the ones shown in Figure 16.9.

FIGURE 16.9.

Outlook 2000 gives you a glimpse of each message.

Outlook 2000 utilizes icons to let you know what is happening. As you read each message, the message icon changes to show that the message has been read. Revert the read message flag back to an unread state by right-clicking the message and selecting Mark as Unread from the pop-up menu. A paper clip icon appears next to each message that contains an attached file. When you open a message with an attached file, Outlook 2000 shows the attachment as an icon that you can right-click to save or open it.

To read a message, just double-click it. To reply to the sender (in effect, sending a new message to your Outbox folder), click the toolbar's Reply button and enter a reply. You can reply to the sender and all Cc recipients of the sender's message by clicking the Reply All toolbar button.

Summary

This hour explained the remaining Outlook 2000 features. You now understand contacts and the importance of entering as much information as you can about them into Outlook 2000. All Office 2000 products use the Contacts list for names and addresses. When you automate your journal, the journal contains all contacts you have elected to track.

One of the busiest Outlook 2000 areas is the messaging Inbox and Outbox folders. Outlook 2000 organizes incoming and outgoing messages and makes it easy for you to respond to messages that you receive.

The next hour, "Access 2000 Basics," begins exploring Access 2000, the Office 2000 database that is arguably the most useful and powerful PC database available today.

16

Q&A

Q What if I don't have a Web browser?

A You do have a Web browser because Office 2000 comes with one. You might not have Internet access, however. You must sign up with an Internet provider to use any Internet-based features. Hour 22, "Office 2000 and the Internet," discusses the Internet in more detail.

Q How does a message reply differ from a forwarded message?

A When you reply to a message, you create a brand new message that contains new information about the recipient's original message. If you forward a recipient's message, you send the message exactly as you first read it to another recipient (or to a list of recipients).

Q Why does Outlook 2000 not send my messages immediately after I complete them?

A Outlook 2000 does not send messages until you select Tools, Send and Receive (F5 is the shortcut key) unless you are already logged on to your Internet account. If you use the Internet in an office setting with a T1 or satellite connection, you are probably logged on to the Internet most of the time. If you use a modem to access the Internet, however, you have to initiate the logon sequence when you want to check for email.

Dialing and logging on takes time. Instead of logging on to your Internet provider every time you create an Outbox folder message, Outlook 2000 waits until you request the check for new mail to get your waiting mail and to send your outgoing mail. By waiting, Outlook 2000 only has to log on to the Internet one time to send all your messages.

PART VI

Tracking with Access 2000

Hour

HOUR 17

Access 2000 Basics

Everyone trudges through data at work and at home. A database manager, such as Access 2000, enables you to organize your data and turn raw facts and figures into meaningful information. Access 2000 processes data details, so you can spend your valuable time analyzing results. Suppose that your company keeps thousands of parts in an Access 2000 inventory database, and you need to know exactly which part sold the most in Division 7 last April. Access 2000 can find the answer for you.

This hour introduces you to the world of databases with Access 2000. The nature of databases makes Access 2000 one of the more involved programs in the Office 2000 suite of programs. Generally, people find that they can master Word 2000, Excel 2000, PowerPoint 2000, and Outlook 2000 more quickly than they can Access 2000. Access 2000 is not difficult to learn and use, but you must understand the structure of database design before you can truly understand Access 2000.

The highlights of this hour include the following:

- What a database is
- Which database-related objects Access 2000 manages

- Why databases contain tables
- What fields and records are
- How to create and modify tables

Database Basics

Whereas previous hours of this book began by showing you how to start the program, this hour begins by explaining the database concept. You need to learn a little about how a database management system organizes data before using Access 2000.

A *database* is an organized collection of data. Access 2000 is called a *database management system* because it enables you to create, organize, and manage data stored in databases.

NEW TERM   A *database* is an organized collection of related data you can easily retrieve and use.

NEW TERM   A *database management system* is a program, like Access 2000, that enables you to create, organize, and manage your data stored in databases.

> Database experts have written complete books on database theory. This hour won't give you an extremely in-depth appreciation for databases, but you learn enough to get started with Access 2000.

A database typically contains related data. In other words, you might create a home office database with your household budget, but keep another database to record your rare-book collection titles and their worth. In your household budget, you might track expenses, income, bills paid, and so forth, but that information does not overlap the book collection database. Of course, if you buy a book, both databases might show the transaction, but the two databases would not overlap.

When you design a database, define its scope before you begin. Does your home business need an inventory system? Does your home business need a sales contact? If so, an Access 2000 database works well. Only you can decide whether the inventory and the sales contacts should be part of the same system or separate, unlinked systems. The database integration of inventory with the sales contacts requires much more work to design, but your business requirements may necessitate the integration. For example, you may need to track which customers bought certain products in the past.

Not all database values directly relate to one another. Your company's loan records do not relate to your company's payroll, for example, but both probably reside in your company's accounting database. Again, you have to decide on the scope when you design your database. Fortunately, Microsoft made Access 2000 extremely flexible, so you can change any database structure when you begin using your database. The better you analyze the design up front, however, the easier your database is to create.

STEP-UP

You can read Access 97 databases from Access 2000.

17

Database Tables

If you threw your family's financial records into a filing cabinet without organizing them, you would have a mess. That is why most people organize their filing cabinets by putting related records into file folders. Your insurance papers go in one folder; your banking records go in another.

Likewise, you cannot throw your data into a database without breaking the data into separate related groups. These groups are called *tables*; a table is analogous to a folder in a filing cabinet.

NEW TERM   A *table* is a collection of data about a specific topic.

A database might contain many tables, each being a further refinement of related data. Your financial database might contain tables for accounts payable, customer records, accounts receivable, vendor records, employee records, and payroll details, such as hours worked during a given time period. The separate tables help you eliminate redundant data; when you produce a payroll report, Access 2000 retrieves some information from your employee table (such as name and pay rate) and some information from your time tables (such as hours worked).

Access 2000 is a *relational database* as opposed to a *flat file database*. That means Access 2000 uses data from multiple tables instead of requiring you to duplicate data in two or more places. Therefore, if you increase a customer's discount, you need to change the discount in only one customer table rather than in the customer table, the pricing table, and the sales table.

New Term A *relational database* relates data from multiple tables instead of requiring you to duplicate data in more than one location as opposed to a *flat file database* where the records in one file are unrelated to records in another and duplication often appears.

New Term Access 2000 stores all tables for a single database in one file that ends with the .mdb extension. By storing the complete database in one file, Access 2000 makes it easier for you to copy and back up your database. You never have to specify the .mdb extension when you create a database. As with all the Office 2000 data files, a database is referred to as a document when you want to open the database from the Office short-cut bar and menus.

> You can import data from an Access 2000 document (database table) into a Word 2000 document. This makes creating and reporting data simple.

Records and Fields

To keep track of table data, Access 2000 breaks down each table into *records* and *fields*. In a way, the table structure looks a lot like an Excel 2000 worksheet. As Figure 17.1 shows, a table's records are the rows, and a table's fields are the columns. Figure 17.1 shows an electronic checkbook register table; you usually organize your real checkbook register just like the computerized table, so you will have no problem mastering Access 2000's records and fields.

New Term A *record* is a row from a table.

New Term A *field* is a column from a table.

FIGURE 17.1.

Tables have records (rows) and fields (columns).

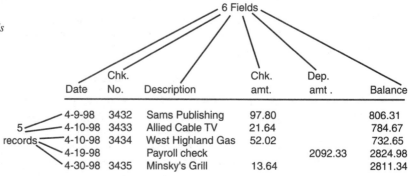

6 Fields

Date	Chk. No.	Description	Chk. amt.	Dep. amt.	Balance
4-9-98	3432	Sams Publishing	97.80		806.31
4-10-98	3433	Allied Cable TV	21.64		784.67
4-10-98	3434	West Highland Gas	52.02		732.65
4-19-98		Payroll check		2092.33	2824.98
4-30-98	3435	Minsky's Grill	13.64		2811.34

5 records

Your table fields contain different data types. As Figure 17.1 shows, one field might hold a text description, while another holds a dollar amount. Every item within the same field must be the same data type, but a table might contain several fields that differ in type. When you design your database, you are responsible for indicating to Access 2000 which data type you want for each field in your database tables.

The types of data that you can store in an Access 2000 database table are

- *Text*. Text data consists of letters, numbers, and special characters. You only report text data; you cannot calculate with it. A balance-due field would never be a text data type, but addresses, names, and Social Security numbers are examples of text fields. Generally, you store short text items (names, addresses, cities, product names, and part codes) in text fields.

- *Memo*. The memo field can hold an extremely large amount of text, including paragraphs. Memo fields consume a lot of space, and not all tables require memo fields.

- *Number*. A number field holds numbers. Use this field to calculate values.

- *Date/Time*. These fields hold date and time values (similar to the date and time format in Excel 2000). Access 2000 enables you to enter data into date and time fields using many formats. Additionally, Access 2000 respects your Windows international settings, so you are able to enter a date in your country's format.

- *Currency*. This field holds dollar amounts. Access 2000 keeps the dollar amounts rounded to the proper decimal alignment. Access 2000 recognizes your Windows international settings, and uses international money amounts when needed.

- *AutoNumber*. This field holds sequential numbers, a different number for each record in the table.

NEW TERM *AutoNumber* refers to a field data type that holds sequential numbers, one for each record in the table. Access 2000 automatically adds the AutoNumber data to tables as you add records to a table. You can use the AutoNumber field as a special record locating field because of its guaranteed unique value in the table.

- *Yes/No*. These fields hold Yes and No (or True and False) two-pronged values to indicate the existence or absence of an item or to indicate the answer to an implied question.

- *OLE object*. This is an embedded object, such as a graph you create in Excel 2000. Your Access 2000 databases can hold any kind of OLE-compatible embedded object.

17

NEW TERM *OLE*, which stands for *Object Linking and Embedding*, refers to objects from another program that you can insert into an Access 2000 table. When you change the linked object within the Access 2000 table, that change is reflected in the original file.

- *Hyperlink.* This is an Internet Web site address. Such a field can hold an Internet address for a file as well as a network or an intranet address within your system network. When the database user clicks the hyperlink, Access 2000 shows the hyperlink's Web page or network file.

> The Internet integration of Office 2000 extends to Access 2000. When you click a hyperlink Internet Web page address in a table, Access 2000 sends you to the Web page, logging you on to your Internet provider if necessary.

Using a Key Field

Every Access 2000 table requires a *primary key field*. The primary key field (often just called a key) is a field that contains no duplicate entries. Whereas a table's city field might contain multiple occurrences of the same city name, a key field must be unique for each record. You can designate a field as a key field, or you can use the AutoNumber field that Access 2000 adds to all tables as the key field.

NEW TERM A *primary key field* uniquely identifies a record.

> If you access a particular field very often, even if that field is not a key field, designate it as an *index field* in the Design view property settings. Access 2000 creates an index for every database and locates the index fields in that index. Just as an index in the back of the book speeds your searches for particular subjects, the index field speeds searches for that field.

If you were creating a table to hold employee records, a good key-field candidate would be the employee's Social Security number because every person's Social Security number is unique. If you are not sure that your data contains unique information in any field, specify the AutoNumber field that Access 2000 creates as the key.

Access 2000 uses the key field to find records quickly. When you want to locate an employee's record, for example, search by the employee's key field (the Social Security number). If you search based on the employee's name, you might not find the proper record; two or more employees might be named *John Smith*, for example.

The reason that so many companies assign you a customer number is because the customer number uniquely identifies you in their database. Although today's computerized society sometimes makes one feel like "just another number," such a customer number enables the company to keep your records more accurate and keep costs down.

Starting Access 2000

To start Access 2000, perform one of the following:

- Click the Office 2000 New Office Document button on the Shortcut Bar and double-click the Blank Database icon to create a new Access 2000 database. (If you don't see the Blank Database icon, click the General tab.)

- Click the Open Office Document button on the Shortcut Bar and select an existing Access 2000 database from its directory that you want to edit.

- Use the Windows Start menu to start Access 2000 by selecting Microsoft Access from the Programs menu.

- Select an Access 2000 database from the Documents option on the Windows Start menu. Windows recognizes that Access 2000 created the database, starts Access 2000, and loads the database automatically. (The Start menu's Documents option holds a list of your most recent work.)

- Click the Access 2000 button on the Office 2000 Shortcut Bar to create a blank database. (Depending on your Office 2000 Shortcut Bar's setup, you might not see the Access 2000 button.)

Figure 17.2 shows the opening Access 2000 screen. Your screen might differ slightly, depending on the options that you chose during installation.

The center of the opening screen contains a dialog box that guides you to your first Access 2000 operation. The dialog box enables you to do one of the following:

- Create a blank database, which requires that you manually set up the entire database structure including tables, fields, and other pertinent database-structure information.

- Start a Database Wizard that walks you through the creation of a database using predefined wizard formats.

- Open an existing database so that you can modify the database structure or work with the database information.

FIGURE 17.2.

*The opening screen
when you start
Access 2000 from the
Start menu.*

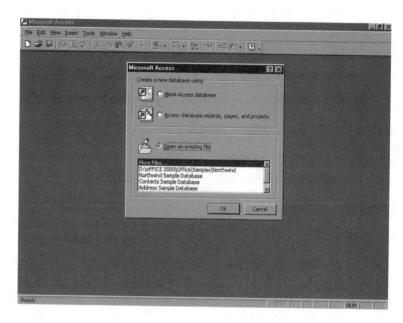

Creating an Access 2000 Database

When you start Access 2000 and see the opening dialog box, shown in Figure 17.2, select Blank Access Database and click OK to create a new database. Access 2000 prompts you for a database name and disk location using the default name db1 with the filename extension .mdb. (This same dialog box opens when you select File, New to create a new database.) You should change the db1 to something more meaningful. Enter a new name and click the Create button to display the *Database window*, shown in Figure 17.3. The Database window title bar includes the name of your database (My First in Figure 17.3) and lists the names of your database *objects*, none of which exist when you create the database. To the right of the database objects, you will find a list of three tasks Access 2000 is ready to perform. Tasks such as these appear when you select one of the database objects in the left pane. Select the first task, Create table in Design view, and Access 2000 will help you create a new table to hold data.

 The *Database window* lists your database object names and provides the central control panel for your Access 2000 work.

 Objects are tables, queries, forms, reports, pages, macros, and modules within your database.

FIGURE 17.3.

The Database window displays a list of your database objects as you create them.

A database object is a piece of an Access 2000 database. A table is an object, for example. A database report that prints database data is an object. Your data values, however, are not objects.

17

Adding Objects to Your Database

As you create your database, you add objects to the Database window's seven object categories. Any database can contain many objects from each category. The following are brief descriptions of seven kinds of Access 2000 objects:

- *Tables.* Related data within a database
- *Queries.* Stored instructions that select data from one or more tables for reporting, analysis, and data-management purposes
- *Forms.* Onscreen representations of paper forms that you and others use to enter data into tables
- *Reports.* Printed listings of database data
- *Pages. (also called Data Access Pages)* Internet-ready data table pages that you can view with Internet Explorer 5 from Web pages
- *Macros.* Stored task lists for Access 2000 commands
- *Modules.* Programs written in Visual Basic, a powerful (but advanced for nonprogrammers) programming language with which you can automate any database task

As you create your database, you create one or more instances of the database objects. You might create 25 tables and 50 reports, for example. When you want to create, edit, or work with one of the database objects, return to the Database window (the toolbar always contains a Database Window toolbar button when you are using Access 2000 but not working in the Database window) and click the tab of the object with which you need to work.

Generally, you select the object category, and then click New to create a new object in that category. Alternatively, you might select an object and click Open to work with that object.

Creating a Table

You must create tables before you can do anything with a database. The tables hold the data on which the other objects operate. As mentioned earlier in this hour, begin creating your tables from scratch until you learn more about Access 2000 and can modify tables and other database objects generated by the wizards.

To create a table, follow these steps:

1. If you have just started Access 2000 and selected the Create table in design view option, you are ready to begin creating the table. You can also click the Create table by using wizard option once you master the table-design features available. If you want to bypass the wizard, click on Tables and then click the New button from the Database window. (You can create any database object by selecting its object name from the left of the Database window and then clicking New on the Database window toolbar.) If you click New to create a table, Access 2000 will display the New Table dialog box, as shown in Figure 17.4.

FIGURE 17.4.

The New Table dialog box helps you to create tables.

2. If you display Figure 17.4's New Table dialog box, select Design View and click OK to display the *Design view* dialog box (shown in Figure 17.5). The Design view will also appear if you create the table from the option labeled Database window's Create table in Design view entry. You must now describe your table's fields in the Design view dialog box.

NEW TERM   *The Design view* displays your table's design showing the individual fields and field properties. Other Database window objects also have Design views to show their structures.

3. Type a field name, such as First Name or Quantity, for the first field in your database. The names have nothing to do with the data type that you eventually store in the table's field. The field name enables you to refer to the field as you

design your table. Only after you completely design the table do you enter data in the table. The order in which you add fields does not affect your database use. Nevertheless, try to add the fields in the general order in which you want to enter the table data.

4. Press Tab and click the drop-down list that appears in the Data Type field to select the field's data type.

5. Press Tab and type a description for the field. Some field names are optional and don't require a description, but the more you document and describe your data, the easier it is to modify your database later.

FIGURE 17.5.

Define your table's fields in the Design view dialog box.

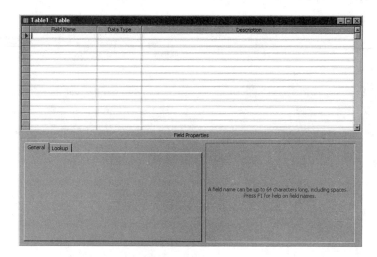

17

6. After you enter the first field's name, data type, and optional description, describe the field properties in the lower half of the Design view dialog box. Some fields do not require property settings, but most require some type of setting.

The next section describes how to set field property values.

Setting Field Properties

The lower half of the Design view contains settings for your field property values. Each field has a data type, as you already know. In addition to describing the field's data type in the Design view's upper half, you can further refine the field's description and limitations in the Field Properties section.

You can configure a different set of field property values for each data type. Text fields contain properties related to text data (such as an address or a name), for example, whereas numeric fields contain properties related to numbers (such as decimal positions).

Open the property value selection list by clicking the property values. A few common field property values that you might want to set as you create your table are as follows:

- *Field Size*. Limits the number of characters the field can hold, thereby limiting subsequent data entry of field data.
- *Format*. Displays a drop-down list with several formats that the field's data type can take.
- *Caption*. Holds a text prompt that Access 2000 displays when you enter data into this table's field. If you don't specify a caption, Access 2000 uses the field name. Access 2000 displays the caption in its status bar when you enter data into the table.
- *Default Value*. Contains the field's default value, which appears when you enter data into this table. The user can enter a value that differs from the default if desired.
- *Required*. Holds either Yes or No to determine whether Access 2000 requires a value in this field before you can save a table's data record. If you specify a field as the key field instead of letting Access 2000 add a key field, your key field must contain Yes for the Required property. If you don't want the user leaving a field blank, enter Yes for the Required property.
- *Decimal Places*. Holds the number of default decimal places shown for numbers entered into this field.

Figure 17.6 shows a completed table's Design view. The selected field's (the field with the arrow, or *field selector* in the left column) property values appear at the bottom of the dialog box. As you enter your own table fields, edit any information that you type incorrectly by clicking the field name, data type, description, or property value, and move the text cursor to the mistake to correct the problem.

Setting the Key and Saving the Table

After you complete your table's fields, you cannot close the table's Design view without designating a field as the table's primary key field. If you do not designate a key and attempt to close the table, Access 2000 warns you that no key exists. Access 2000 adds a key field using the AutoNumber format if your data does not contain a key field.

Consider adding your own key field for tables that you access often. The key field enables you to search the table more quickly. The key might be a Social Security number, a phone number, or some other code (such as a unique inventory code or customer number) that is unique for each record in the table.

FIGURE 17.6.

A more complete table definition shows you how the column names, data types, and descriptors go together.

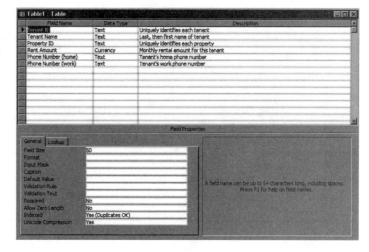

To specify a key field, select the table Design view's record by clicking to the left of the field name and then clicking the Primary Key toolbar button. Access 2000 adds a small key icon to the left of the record, indicating the table's key field.

After you add the key field, save the table by clicking the Save button on the toolbar. (If you attempt to close the table before saving it, Access 2000 prompts you for a name.) If you don't specify a new name, Access 2000 uses Table1 (and Table2, Table3, and so on as you create additional tables); however, you should use a more meaningful table name, such as Tenants, so that you can easily identify the table. When you close the table, Access 2000 returns you to the Database window where you will see the table in the right pane.

Modifying Table Structures

The beauty of Access 2000 is that, unlike other database programs, you can easily change the structure of your tables even after you have added data. Access 2000 makes it easy to add and delete fields, as well as change field properties.

Some table-structure changes affect table data. After you add data to a table, for example, you lose columns of data if you delete fields, and you lose some data through truncation if you limit a field's Size property. If you add fields to an existing table, you have to add the data for the new fields in every existing record in the table.

To modify a table, switch to the table's Design view. If you have closed the table and returned to the Database window, select the table name (which now appears in the Database window) and click Design. After you master table design changes, you are better equipped to use the Database Wizards to create initial tables that you can change to suit your specific table requirements.

Adding Fields

To add a field at the end of your table, just click the first empty Field Name box and enter the field information as you did when adding the table's initial fields.

To insert a new field between two other fields, select the field that is to appear after your new field by clicking the selection box to the left of the field name. Next, right-click the row and select Insert Rows. Access 2000 opens a new field row and enables you to enter the new field information. Figure 17.7 shows a new field being inserted into a table.

Room for new field

FIGURE 17.7.

The new field will go in the empty space.

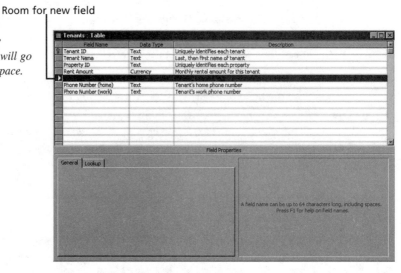

Deleting Fields

To delete a field, select the field from within the Design view and press Delete. You can delete fields from either the Datasheet view or the Design view. You can delete several fields in one operation by selecting multiple sections and dragging your mouse down several fields in the Design view.

Use Undo (Ctrl+Z) to reverse an accidental field deletion. Access 2000 supports multiple levels of Undo so that you can reverse several recent actions by issuing Undo multiple times.

Resizing and Rearranging Fields

Use your mouse to make minor adjustments to your table (such as the height of each row and the width of columns). Although the Field Size property determines the exact data storage width of each field in your table, the column widths determine how much of a field you can read while entering and editing table data and the table's structure.

At any time during your table design or data entry, you can drag a column divider left or right to increase or decrease the width of a column displayed. You can also drag a record divider up or down to increase or decrease a record height.

To rearrange the location of a field, either in Datasheet view or in the table's Design view, drag a Datasheet view field name or a Design view field selector to its new location in the table and release the mouse. Access 2000 moves the field to the location you select.

The order in which you structure a table's fields has little bearing on the table's use. You can report a table's data in any field order that you want regardless of the physical field order. Order your fields in whatever way makes the most sense to you.

Viewing Table Design and Entering Simple Data

Until now, you have worked exclusively in the Design view of the table, which describes the table's fields, properties, and key. If you open the table and click the Datasheet view toolbar button (or select from the View menu), Access 2000 changes your table's Design view to the *Datasheet view*, like the view shown in Figure 17.8. Unlike the Design view, the Datasheet view enables you to enter and edit data in the table. Unlike the Design view, however, you cannot change the table's structure from the Datasheet view apart from changing the field names. The table's Datasheet view remains empty until you type data into your table.

17

Design view tool

FIGURE **17.8.**

Use the Datasheet view to see your table's design results and enter data.

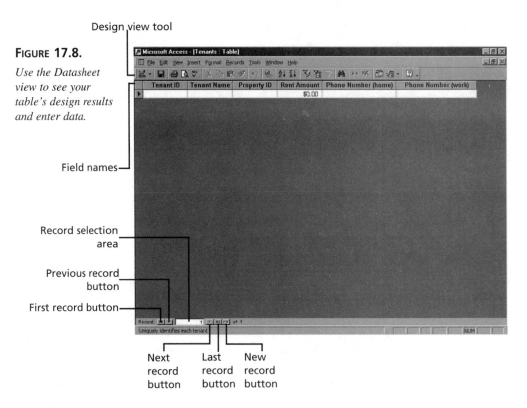

Field names

Record selection area

Previous record button

First record button

Next record button

Last record button

New record button

NEW TERM The *Datasheet view* displays your table and table data (if the table contains data) in a worksheet-like format. The Datasheet view enables you to view and edit multiple records from your table. You can enter data into your tables faster from the Datasheet view than from the other views.

The Datasheet view enables you to work with your table in row and column format, like an Excel 2000 worksheet. Until you enter data in the table, the Datasheet view shows only one empty record but as you add to the table, the Datasheet view grows to look more like an Excel worksheet with cells that represent each table's field. Although Access 2000 offers several ways to enter data into a table, the Datasheet view is the fastest and simplest if you understand records and fields. The Datasheet view is not fancy, however, and some users need more help when entering data. If you build a database application for a video store's inventory, for example, the clerk should not be adjusting the inventory table directly within the Datasheet view when a customer rents a tape. You learn in the next hour how to design forms for such data-entry that walk the user through the data-entry process for such scenarios so that the user does not inadvertently change information in the wrong record.

Although the Datasheet view is not fancy, it enables you to quickly see your table's design results and enter data. If you cannot read a full field name, drag the field separator left or right to increase or decrease the field width shown on the screen. You learned more about modifying the view in the section titled "Resizing and Rearranging Fields."

If you have not saved your table's design from within the Design view, Access 2000 prompts you for the table name before showing you the Datasheet view.

Use the toolbar or the View menu to switch back and forth between the two views. As you design a table, the two views help you pinpoint design and data problems.

17

Most Database window objects offer two views: a Design view and another view that displays the final object, such as the Datasheet view and the form's Form view.

You can even design a table from the Datasheet view, but you make more work for yourself if you do. The default Datasheet view field names are Field1, Field2, and so on until you right-click the names and change them. You cannot set specific field properties from the Datasheet view. Use the Datasheet view for simple data-entry and table-design verification unless you create only an extremely simple table.

Using Wizards to Create Databases

While you are learning Access 2000, practice designing your early databases without the help of the Access 2000 wizards. In most cases, the wizards do not create exactly the kind of database you require, and you have to change the database structure as soon as the wizard completes the database design and creation. Changing an existing database is difficult to do if you have never worked with Access 2000. The best way to gain Access 2000 mastery is to design and create your own database from scratch so that you better understand the inner workings of data.

After you master Access 2000, a wizard saves you a lot of time if you find one that creates a sample database that is close to what you need. After the wizard creates the database, you can modify the database to suit your needs.

Some of the Access 2000 Database Wizards that you can use after you master Access 2000's fundamentals are as follows:

- *Contact Management.* This wizard enables you to keep track of sales contacts.
- *Asset Tracking.* This wizard manages your company's assets.
- *Resource Scheduling.* This wizard supports the use of resources (parts, time, and people) within your organization.
- *Donations.* This wizard manages donations for nonprofit organizations.
- *Order Entry.* This wizard is a complete order-entry and transaction system.
- *Service Call Management.* This wizard enables you to track service calls that your company makes.
- *Time and Billing.* This wizard helps track expenses related to billable labor.

In addition to the wizards, Access 2000 comes with a comprehensive database called the *Northwind Traders, Inc., Database*, which you can study to learn about advanced database operations.

Quitting Access 2000

After you are finished with Access 2000, quit by performing any of the following:

- Select File, Exit.
- Press Alt+F4.
- Double-click the Control icon.
- Click Access 2000's Close button.

Always quit Access 2000 and shut down Windows before turning off your computer; otherwise, you might lose your work.

Summary

This was a theory-based hour because Access 2000 requires more preparation than the other Office 2000 products. After you learn about the elements that make up a database—tables, records, and fields—the Access 2000 mechanics are easy to understand.

To create an Access 2000 database, add tables that describe the database data. Each table contains fields and records. When you design a table, you must describe the field names and data types that the table requires.

Now that you know how to create and edit tables, you are ready to enter data and master forms in the next hour, "Entering and Displaying Access 2000 Data." By using forms for data entry and editing, you make Access 2000 tables easier to manage for you and others who use databases that you create.

Q&A

Q Would I ever want to configure a field with the AutoNumber format?

A Your data might require a unique sequential number for each record, like invoice numbers. Most often, however, Access 2000 uses the AutoNumber format for the key field that is added when you don't specify a key field.

Q Can I enter data in the Datasheet view?

A Certainly. As explained in this and the next hour, the Datasheet view is a handy view for entering simple data and for viewing multiple records of data from a table. The Datasheet view offers a worksheet-like view of your data in a row and column format. The Datasheet view gives you quick access to a table's data.

Remember that a Datasheet view shows only a single table's data at one time. It does *not* show the entire database because a database often contains multiple tables of data.

Q Can a key field contain duplicates?

A No. If you have to locate records by field and that field is not unique, you cannot make the field a key. You must decide on another key or let Access 2000 add the key field. You can speed up the access on the duplicate field by making it an Index field in the field's Design view property settings. Access 2000 sets up a special quick-find index for that field.

17

HOUR 18

Entering and Displaying Access 2000 Data

This hour explains how to use the Access 2000 tables you learned to create in the preceding hour, "Access 2000 Basics." After you master this lesson, you will be able to enter and edit database table data. After you enter the data, you need to print the data to proofread for accuracy and to keep hard copy as a backup. You don't have to master all of Access 2000's reporting tools to print good-looking reports, as you learn in this hour. When you gather a large amount of data, being able to print the data in a meaningful format is important and Access 2000 gives you the tools to do just that.

Finally, this lesson explains how to use the Form Wizard to generate forms that match your data. Forms offer a different data perspective from datasheets. The Access 2000 forms you create look like printed forms onscreen.

The highlights of this hour include the following:

- How to enter data into tables
- Which table-editing commands Access 2000 supports

- How to print tables
- When to use the Form Wizard to generate forms from tables
- How to use forms for data entry and editing
- The drawbacks of form
- How to print forms

Entering Table Data

Access 2000 gives you two primary means for adding data to tables that you create:

- Datasheet view
- Forms

The Datasheet view that you saw in the preceding hour enables you to enter, view, and edit several records at one time, and displays many records on your screen. When you use a form, on the other hand, you typically work with only one record at a time. The record takes on the format of a printed form, giving you a better focus on individual records. You learn more about forms later in this hour's section, "Using Forms to Enter and Edit Data." The next section focuses on the Datasheet view.

Using the Datasheet View

In the preceding hour, you learned how to display the Datasheet view. The Datasheet view offers one of the simplest ways to enter and edit data in an Access 2000 database. The rest of this section shows you how Access 2000 makes entering data easy.

Entering Data

To enter data in the Datasheet view after you have displayed the Datasheet view, just click the Datasheet view's first field and enter the field information. When you enter data into the first field, Access 2000 opens an additional blank record below the one you are entering. Access 2000 always leaves room for additional records. As you enter data, press Tab, Shift+Tab, or the arrow keys to move from field to field. You can also click any field into which you want to enter data. As you enter data, watch the status bar at the bottom of your screen. If you entered a description for a field, Access 2000 displays that description in the status bar when you enter data in that field.

If, while entering data, you see a number automatically appear in a field, don't panic. Access 2000 is automatically entering an AutoNumber field (such as a key field).

Figure 18.1 shows a Datasheet view that contains several records. The record pointer always moves as you enter and edit data to show the current record. The asterisk to the left of the empty record indicates a new record into which you can enter data.

FIGURE 18.1.

A Datasheet view can show several records of data.

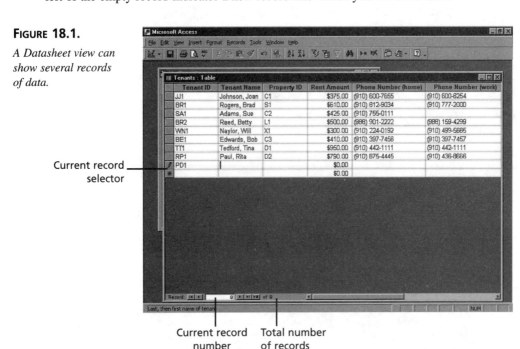

Current record selector

Current record number		Total number of records

18

 Often, multiple records contain the same data in certain fields (as is the case with city and state names in a table). Press Ctrl+' to copy the preceding record's field value into the current field's cell.

As you enter data, take advantage of Office 2000's AutoCorrect feature. When you enter AutoCorrect abbreviations and shortcuts, Access 2000 substitutes the shortcut with the AutoCorrect correction. Access 2000 does not automatically enable the Office 2000 automatic spell checker because much of your table data contains formal names that would appear to the spell checker as misspellings. You can check your table's spelling by selecting Tools, Spelling.

To change a mistake, such as a transposed number, click the mistake to insert the text cursor in the Datasheet view's field and correct the entry. You can also press the arrow keys to move to any field, and press F2 to edit the field's text.

After you finish entering or editing a table's data, save the table and click its Close button to return to the Database window. If you have not saved the table before attempting to close it, Access 2000 prompts you for a name. By default, Access 2000 uses the names Table1, Table2, and so on, but you should rename the tables to reflect the data they contain.

Formatting Your Data

Access 2000 is forgiving when you enter special data such as dates, times, monetary amounts, and memo field values. You can basically enter data in these fields in whatever way seems best to you! You can enter a date in a date field, for example, using any of the following formats:

```
05/12/1999
5/12/1999
May 12, 1999
May 12 1999
```

Access 2000 uses a predefined date format to display dates and times in the Datasheet view, so after you type a date, it can be immediately reformatted to match this view. By default, Access 2000 uses the date format mm/dd/yyyy.

STEP-UP

Unlike Access 97, Access 2000 defaults to a four-digit year value when displaying dates. The new century change requires that a four-digit date be adhered to. Although some Access 2000 date formats display using a two-digit year, Access 2000 stores the year as a four-digit year.

As with dates, you can enter time in several common ways. Add a.m. or p.m. or use 24-hour clock time. Access 2000, by default, formats your time values to the hh:mm:ss format.

Press Ctrl+; to enter the current date in a field, and press Ctrl+: to enter the current time. Access 2000 gets these values from your computer's clock and calendar setting. Ctrl+; causes the date to display using the format *dd/mm/yyyy* (unless your Windows International settings determine a different date format) although Access 2000 stores the date using the current four-digit year.

Access 2000 currency fields accept a wide variety of formats. You can type a dollar sign (or whatever currency symbol matches your Windows International Country setting), decimals, and even insert commas in currency values. After you enter a currency amount, Access 2000 displays the amount with the default format. The default currency format uses a dollar sign. If you fail to type the dollar sign, Access 2000 supplies one automatically.

Access 2000 automatically adjusts to the current Windows International settings. Your Windows Control Panel contains an icon labeled Regional Settings. The language specified in your PC's Regional Settings determines how Access 2000 displays data. Therefore, you can maintain one database for multiple users around the world. The PC running the Access 2000 database determines, therefore, how the data appears on the screen and in reports.

> If you need to format a currency amount in a different format from your Windows International Settings, you can do so by specifying the format in the Design view's property settings.

18

If you enter a format that Access 2000 does not recognize, such as placing two decimal points inside a single dollar amount, Access 2000 displays a dialog box (shown in Figure 18.2), indicating you should correct the value before entering the next field.

FIGURE 18.2.

Access 2000 lets you know if you enter a bad format.

Access 2000 does not let you leave a record that contains a bad format. Therefore, when you close your tables, you can be assured that Access 2000 saves all the data with the proper data type. Although the data values may not be correct, you will know that the data does fit within the specified formats you have declared for the table.

Editing Data

All the editing skills you mastered with the other Office 2000 products work with Access 2000. You can rearrange the order of fields and records by dragging them with your mouse. You can select more than one field or record at a time by dragging your mouse through the record selectors or field names or by holding Shift while you click record selectors or field names. Press Ctrl+A to select all records in the table.

To delete one or more records or fields, select the records or fields you want to delete and right-click them. Select Delete Column or Delete Record.

> When you right-click the selected records or fields, the pop-up menu provides quick Cut, Copy, and Paste commands as well as Insertion commands for records and fields. Use the Hide command to temporarily hide records and fields (they physically stay in the table) that you want out of the way while you work with other data, and reveal the data when you are ready to work with the entire table again. Additionally, you can *sort* records in *ascending order* or *descending order* with the right-click's pop-up menu options.

NEW TERM To *sort* is to alphabetize or numerically order table records.

NEW TERM To sort by *ascending order* is to sort from low to high order.

NEW TERM To sort by *descending order* is to sort from high to low order.

> If you often need to adjust the width or height of records and fields, consider changing your table's font size and style (by selecting Format, Font).

Navigating Large Tables

Use the record selector at the bottom of the Datasheet view to move through and jump over large blocks of records that don't interest you at the time. The record selector works somewhat like a VCR, enabling you to move forward and backward through your data.

Here are a few pointers:

- Click Next Record to move the record selector to the next record.
- Click Previous Record to move the record selector to the previous record.
- Click First Record to move to the table's first record.
- Click Last Record to move to the table's last record.
- Click the Record Number area and type a new record number to jump directly to that record.

Simple Printing

Access 2000 includes powerful reporting tools, but they take some time to master. You learn about reporting in Hour 20, "Advanced Access 2000." If you just want to print a listing of your data, however, you can do so easily from the Datasheet view. Access 2000 automatically prints the Datasheet view with field titles.

Perhaps you need to check a table listing for errors, or you want a printed listing (called a *hard copy*) so that you can proofread the data values that you entered. Before printing, display a preview (like the one shown in Figure 18.3) by selecting File, Print Preview. Move the magnifying glass mouse cursor over any portion of the preview and click to see a close-up.

Figure 18.3.

Get a preview of printed datasheet tables.

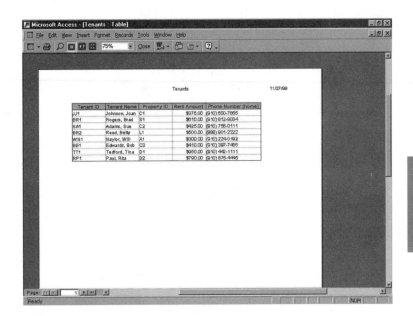

18

NEW TERM   A *hard copy* is a printed listing of your data.

To print a Datasheet view's table, select File, Print (or click the Printer button on the toolbar).

Using Forms to Enter and Edit Data

When you computerize your records, you want to make it as easy as possible for people to enter, edit, and view data in your database. Often, Access 2000 reduces paperwork. A credit agency might use Access 2000 to keep track of loan applications that borrowers fill out, for example. As borrowers bring in their completed applications, a clerk types the data from the application into an Access 2000 table. Although a Datasheet view would work fine for the data entry, a *form* works even better! The form can, onscreen, mimic the look and feel of paper forms that many people are accustomed to using. You do not have to keep files of paper forms now that you use Access 2000.

An Access 2000 *form* enables you to enter data into your tables using the familiar format of a paper form.

Using the Form Wizard to Generate Forms

You probably want to use the Form Wizard to create your first form. The Form Wizard generates simple forms that work well in most cases.

Follow these steps to start the Form Wizard:

1. Display the Database window.
2. Click the Forms tab to display the Forms page.
3. Click New to display the New Form dialog box (shown in Figure 18.4).

Creating a new form.

4. Click to highlight the Form Wizard option.
5. Select the table in the lower part of the dialog box to use as a basis for the form. If your database contains multiple tables, those tables appear in the drop-down list.
6. Click OK to display the opening Form Wizard dialog box (shown in Figure 18.5). This dialog box lists the available fields that you can include for your selected table.

FIGURE 18.5.

The opening Form Wizard dialog box shows your selected table and its available fields.

You may or may not want to include every field on every form you create. Suppose, for example, that you want to create a form for your company's personnel that contains employee names and extension numbers, but not employee pay rates. Therefore, the next step in creating your form is to indicate to Access 2000 which fields to include.

To select table fields for the form, select a field and click the button labeled >. Access 2000 adds that field to the selected field list. To include all the fields, click the button labeled >>. The Form Wizard sends all the table's fields to the selected field list.

If you send a field to the form accidentally, select that field and click the button labeled < to remove the field from the form. Clicking << removes all the fields, so you can start over if you want to rearrange the fields or copy new ones from scratch.

Click the Next button to display the Form Wizard layout dialog box (shown in Figure 18.6). Click the different options to see a preview of how that option changes the form's layout.

FIGURE 18.6.

Select a layout for your form.

> The Tabular and Datasheet form layouts are similar to the Datasheet view. The Columnar and Justified layouts look more like typical paper forms. As you click each option, Access 2000 displays that option's resulting form layout.

When you click the Next button, the Form Wizard displays a dialog box from which you can select a form style (as shown in Figure 18.7). Click through the style selections to see a preview of those available. Many styles have unique personalities that can add eye-catching appeal to an otherwise dull form.

FIGURE **18.7.**

The Form Wizard supports several form styles.

When you click the Next button, you see the Form Wizard's closing dialog box, which asks for a form title (the default title is the name of your selected table). Click Finish to generate the form.

After you learn more advanced Access 2000 commands (see Hour 20), such as how to use the form-creation and editing tools, you can open the generated form's Design view and change specific parts of the form. The Form Wizard generates your form, and you can then modify the form to look exactly the way you want it. For now, the Form Wizard's generated forms work well.

In some cases, generated forms contain problems but you can correct those problems with a little editing from the form's Design view. Figure 18.8 shows a generated form with a record's data, for example. The Form Wizard automatically uses field names for the form prompts and data descriptions. If your field names are long, the Form Wizard may not display the entire field name for the prompt. Also, some data does not align properly, such as the Rent Amount field shown in Figure 18.8. In addition, if your table does not contain many fields, the form does not take up the full screen and may look too small. You can maximize the form onscreen or resize the form to a smaller window.

Figure 18.8 shows the form in the *Form view*. The Form view displays records in the form-like format. Access 2000 also contains a form's Design view (not unlike the table's Design view), in which you can edit the form and change its appearance.

Figure 18.8.

The Form Wizard generates good forms, but they sometimes have problems.

Value appears too far to the right

Long field names do not display

New Record button

  New Term *Form view* is Access 2000's display of forms with record data appearing in the form fields.

> When using forms, you must understand how all the data types appear. If your table contains Yes/No data-type fields, those fields appear with an *x* to indicate the Yes value. If you name a rental property's tenant field Pet Deposit?, for example, and assigned the Yes/No data type to the field, those owners who pay a pet deposit have an *x* for this field value. Memo fields hold a lot of data, so if you use a memo field, keep typing when the text cursor reaches the right side of the field. Access 2000 scrolls the field to enable you to continue. Form views display memo fields with scrollbars, so you can look at all the data in the fields.

18

Navigating Forms

Forms typically show only single records. Unlike the Datasheet view, the form is a much better tool for working with single records. In the Datasheet view, you can often see many records but not all the fields in those records, because the fields rarely fit on the Datasheet view screen. The form shows only a single record, but often manages to include all fields from the records because of the form layout.

Access 2000 offers several ways to move through records in the Form view. Press up arrow, down arrow, Tab, and Shift+Tab to move from one field to another. Press PageUp and PageDown to move to the preceding and next table record, respectively. The record number appears at the bottom of the form window's record selection control. As in the Datasheet view, you can click the record selection control to move from record to record.

To jump to a record quickly, press F5, type a record number, and press Enter. F5 sends the cursor to the record selector so that you can find a different table record.

Editing Forms

As you move through the form records, feel free to change data in the record. The record selector arrow changes to an editing pencil to show that you are editing the record. If you use Tab or Shift+Tab to move from field to field, press F2 when the highlight appears over the field you want to edit. When you change data from within the Form view, Access 2000 changes the data in the underlying tables.

 To add records from the Form view, click the record selector's New Record button to display a new one that you can fill out.

Printing Forms

If you select File, Print from the Form view, Access 2000 prints the forms. Unlike the onscreen Form view, Access 2000 prints as many forms on the page as fit (select the File, Print Preview to see what will print, like the preview shown in Figure 18.9).

FIGURE 18.9.

Access 2000 prints multiple records per form.

Summary

This hour extended your Access 2000 knowledge by showing you how to use the Datasheet view to enter and print data. You also learned how to create and use forms. Access 2000 replaces the paper forms you are used to and provides a form-like approach to data entry and editing.

The Form Wizard quickly generates nice forms for you from your table data. The Form Wizard is a great place to start designing your forms because it analyzes your table and generates a form based on that analysis.

The next hour, "Retrieving Your Data," teaches you how to filter data and use queries so that you can work with subsets of table data.

Q&A

Q **When I open a table's Datasheet view, why does the data appear in a different order from the order in which I entered it?**

A Access 2000 sorts data, in an ascending order, according to the table's selected key field. Your Datasheet views always appear in the order sorted by the key field unless you change the sort order by right-clicking the field that you want to sort by. Access 2000 uses the key field to locate records quickly when you search for data.

Q **Why should I use the Form Wizard but not the Table Wizard when I begin learning Access 2000?**

A You must understand tables, records, and fields before you use the Table Wizard to generate tables because you almost always have to modify the Table Wizard's generated table to suit your exact needs. Therefore, it helps, when starting out, to create tables from scratch and learn how tables work. After you learn how to use the table's Datasheet and Design views, you are better equipped to edit tables generated with the Table Wizard.

The Form Wizard looks at tables that you generated and creates simple data-entry forms with the format and layout that you request. Forms require less editing when you generate them from the Form Wizard than tables do. You will be pleased with the Form Wizard from the moment you create your first form.

Q **Can I edit the AutoNumber field?**

A If you let Access 2000 create and enter your table's key field, you should also let Access 2000 maintain the AutoNumber that it enters for you. When you create reports, you can hide the AutoNumber field so that the field does not appear with the data that others see. The AutoNumber field is Access 2000's bookkeeping field when you fail to designate a key. Access 2000 keeps the table sorted in the key order, and you should not bother with this field. If you want, rearrange the table to move the AutoNumber field to the far-right side of the Datasheet view. Then you rarely see the field when you work with the data.

HOUR 19

Retrieving Your Data

This hour teaches you about Access 2000 filters and queries. Although your database contains a lot of data, you rarely want to see all that data simultaneously. Generally, you want to see only data subsets. Filters and queries produce those subsets for you.

When you view data subsets, you prevent unwanted data from getting in the way of the information with which you need to work. The power of queries is that you can select records and fields from multiple tables and view that selected data subset from within a single Datasheet or Form view.

The highlights of this hour include the following:

- What a filter is
- Why you sometimes use Filter by Selection and sometimes use Filter by Form
- When a filter limits you
- Why queries are more robust than filters
- How to use the query wizards
- How to use the Query Design view to create and edit queries
- Where to specify advanced selection criteria

Using Data Filters

A *filter* is a subset of data from a table. Suppose that you want to see only certain records from a table, such as all customers who are past due. Instead of hiding the records that you don't want to see, create a filter. The filter removes unwanted records from view. The records don't go away, and you don't have to unhide the records later (as you do when you actually hide records by right-clicking over a column or row in the Datasheet view and selecting Hide Columns or Hide Row). A filter works like a short-term record hider, putting certain records out of the way while you work with the filtered data.

NEW TERM   A *filter* temporarily creates a subset of records from a table by screening out unwanted data.

Access 2000 supports three filtering approaches:

- *Filter by Selection.* Filters data based on selected table data
- *Filter by Form.* Enables you to choose the data fields that you want Access 2000 to use for filtering
- *Advanced Filter/Sort.* Controls advanced filtering options from the Access 2000 menu bar

The easiest and most common filter options are Filter by Selection and Filter by Form, which the following two sections describe.

> Access 2000 includes an Advanced Filter/Sort option on the Records I Filter menu, but you will almost always prefer creating a query to using the advanced filter. In addition, Access 2000 supports a Filter Excluding Selection that filters the opposite of Filter by Selection. A query is easier to save and work with in the future than a filter.

Filter by Selection

Filter by Selection works by example. Suppose that you want to display only those table records that contain a specific field value; for example, you need to work only with customer records from Brazil. If your customer table contains a Country field with scattered Brazil entries, you can filter out all those records that do *not* contain Brazil in their Country fields.

You can practice working with filters by opening the sample Northwind Traders database that comes with Access 2000. Perform the following steps to design a filter that filters out records that don't contain Brazil:

1. Display the Datasheet view for the customer table.

2. Locate one record with Brazil in the Country field. You may have to click the horizontal scrollbar to see the Datasheet view to the left to see the Country field.

3. Double-click the single field value that contains Brazil to select that value. If you select only the first part of the field instead of selecting the entire field, such as the letter *B* only, you filter all records that do not start with *B*.

4. Click Filter by Selection on the toolbar. Access 2000 filters out all records that don't match your selected *criteria*. Figure 19.1 shows a filtered Datasheet view that displays only records containing a Brazil entry in their Country field. Before the filter, this Datasheet view held 91 records. By locating the example field and clicking once, you just changed the display to those records that only contain Brazil for the Country field value.

New Term   The term *criteria* refers to a specific request pattern that you want Access 2000 to use to find a value.

5. To return to the full Datasheet view, click the toolbar's Remove Filter button.

As you can see, a filter removes unwanted records; Access 2000 filters those unwanted records from view.

> To filter all records that contain your selected values, leaving all those that don't contain the selected value, select Records, Filter, Filter Excluding Selection. The Filter Excluding Selection option works like a reverse filter.

19

> You do not first have to locate a customer record from Brazil to create the previous list's filter. If you right-click any field value in the table and then type a value in the pop-up menu's Filter For text box, Access 2000 applies the Filter by Selection command to your entered filter value. Therefore, you can type Brazil in the Filter For text box, press Enter, and more quickly create the same filter that the previous steps created.

FIGURE 19.1.

Filter by selection filters out all unwanted records.

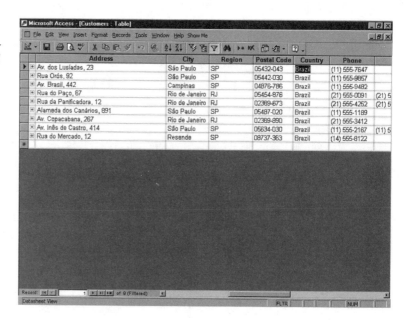

Filter by Form

Filter by Form enables you to filter by multiple values rather than by only one value. You can apply a Filter by Form from both the Datasheet and Form views.

Perform these steps to use Filter by Form:

1. Click the Filter by Form button. Access 2000 displays a single blank record. If you have recently created a filter, that previous filter's selection value appears in the single row that displays. You can erase the value and enter a different one.

2. Scroll to the field you want to filter by and select the empty field.

3. Click the field's drop-down arrow that appears. Access 2000 displays a scrolling drop-down list of every value (without duplicates) that appears in that field within the current table.

4. Select the value by which you want to filter.

5. Optionally, click another empty field value and select from that field's drop-down list of available values. You can select as many filtering field values as you need. Unlike the Filter by Selection, which enables you to filter only by one field value, Filter by Form enables you to filter by several fields.

6. Click the Apply Filter button to display the filtered records.

7. Click the Remove Filter button (this button is called the Apply Filter button before you begin filtering) when you are ready to return to the full-record view.

If you filter by a date field, Access surrounds the filtered value with pound signs (#). You often see pound signs around dates, such as #7/4/1999#; this enables Access 2000 to distinguish the date from a formula.

Access 2000 can perform an Or filter, meaning that Access 2000 filters to find all records that include one or more of your selected filter field values. If you want to find all customers who live in New York or who live in Maine, for example, select New York, click the Or tab at the bottom of the Filter by Form window, and select Maine. You can continue adding *or conditions* to select from one of several fields.

New Term An *or condition* occurs when Access 2000 performs a search or filter on one or more value matches at the same time.

Although Access 2000 uses an or condition to select from one of several field values, it uses an *and condition* to select across fields. That means that if you select Brazil for the Country field filter and Rio for the City field filter, Access 2000 filters to find all records with both Brazil as a country and Rio for the city. If a record contains the country Brazil but San Paulo for the city, such a filter would not keep that record.

New Term An *and condition* occurs when Access 2000 performs a search or filter on multiple value matches at the same time.

19

Using Queries

A *query* is really nothing more than a question you ask Access 2000 about your data. Access 2000 does not understand questions the way you generally ask them, so you must ask your question with its special query format. A query differs somewhat from a filter. A query is the request that produces a subset of data. A filter, on the other hand, just temporarily hides certain data from your Access 2000 views so that you can see only a subset of data from a table.

New Term A *query* is a stored set of database record selection commands. The query indicates to Access 2000 exactly which data you want to view or edit, based on search criteria that you specify.

A query is an object, just like tables and forms are objects. Therefore, you see the Queries object page on the Database window and you create, edit, and execute queries from this page. As with other objects, queries have names that you give them. Many queries are nothing more than named filters; however, filters go away when you are finished with them, whereas you can recall a query later by its name. If you want to reapply a filter, however, you must reproduce the filter.

Although you cannot name filters, you can turn a Filter by Form request into a named query. When you enter the Filter by Form request, click the Save as Query toolbar button. Access 2000 prompts you for a query name and stores the filter as a query. Often, creating a named query from a Filter by Form is faster than generating a new query from scratch if you only want to create a simple query that filters records.

Queries are often much more advanced than filters. A query enables you to specify selected records from a table or from another query. You can create a query that selects records and fields from multiple tables. The data subset that a query generates often becomes a table-like Datasheet view from which you can report. You can build a query that extracts certain records and fields from three tables, for example, and then generate a report from those extracted records and fields.

Not only can you create a query that extracts fields and records, but also you can specify the exact order of the resulting data subset, sort the subset, and use powerful extraction criteria to select data based on very specific requirements.

The created data subset is sometimes called a *dynaset*.

Creating a Query with the Query Wizard

Although you can build a query from scratch, the Query Wizard can do the dirty work for you in most cases.

Access 2000 includes these four query wizards:

- *Simple Query Wizard.* Extracts fields from one or more tables and from other queries.
- *Crosstab Query Wizard.* Creates a worksheet-like query that summarizes field values and cross-tabulates matching values.

- *Find Duplicates Query Wizard.* Creates a data subset from two or more tables or queries that contain matching values in one or more fields that you select.

- *Find Unmatched Query Wizard.* Creates a data subset from two or more tables or queries that contain no duplicate records.

When you create a new query, a list of these four query-based wizards appear in a list you can select from. In addition, a fifth entry appears labeled Design View. The Design View entry is misleading because this is not a wizard, but a query-building screen from which you must build the query from scratch without the help from any wizard.

You use the Simple Query Wizard often because of its general-purpose design. When you create a new query by clicking New on the Queries Database window page, Access 2000 displays the New Query dialog box (shown in Figure 19.2).

FIGURE 19.2.

Begin creating your query in the New Query dialog box.

Follow these steps to build your first query using the Simple Query Wizard:

1. After opening your database, click Queries in the Database window.

2. Click the Database window's New button to open the New Query window.

3. Select the Simple Query Wizard from the New Query dialog box and click OK. Access 2000 starts the wizard and displays the Simple Query Wizard dialog box shown in Figure 19.3.

4. Select a table or an existing query that holds the data you want the query to extract. (You can build queries from tables or from other queries.) Access 2000 displays fields from the selected table (or query) in the Available Fields list.

5. Select one or more fields and click the button labeled >. Access 2000 includes these fields in the resulting query data subset. If you want the query to extract all customer names and balances from a customer table, for example, select those two fields and click > to send them to the Selected Fields list. The Selected Fields list is the query's resulting structure, and holds a description of the data subset that the query eventually produces.

19

6. Optionally, select another table or query from the Tables/Queries drop-down list and add more fields to the Selected Fields list. If Access 2000 prompts you to create a relationship between the tables, click Yes to create the relationship. Access 2000 relates the tables automatically if you have created the relationship link elsewhere. You are now building a query that extracts data subsets from multiple sources. If you send the wrong field to the Selected Fields list, select the incorrect field and click < to remove it. To remove all your selected fields and begin again, click the button labeled <<.

7. Click Next to select either a detail or summary query. A detail query includes every field of every record; a summary query does not show duplicate selected records and includes summary statistics if you select them by clicking the Summary Options button.

8. Click Next and select a title for the query. Access 2000 bases the default name for the new query on the first selected table or existing query.

9. Click Finish to complete the query. Access 2000 builds the query and displays the selected records from the query in the Datasheet view. When you close the Datasheet view, you see the new query listed on the Queries page of the Database window. Again, you can often create a filter that produces the same extracted record subset as a query, but you can later re-extract queries by name instead of rebuilding them from scratch as you must do with filters.

FIGURE 19.3.

Use the Simple Query Wizard to generate your first query.

Take a moment or two to reflect on what you just did. For the first time, you have the power to extract records from multiple tables to create a new Datasheet view.

You can also create a new form (using one of the form wizards) to display the results of a query. When you created a new form in the previous hour, "Entering and Displaying Access 2000 Data," you knew only how to create forms from single tables. If multiple tables contain data you want to display in a form, however, create a query to extract from the two tables and base the form on that query.

> To synchronize a multiple-table query, all tables must have a common field (such as a customer number), or you must use advanced Access 2000 commands to relate the two tables in some way. Without a relationship, such as a common field, the query cannot combine the fields from the two tables.

Access 2000 does not save your query results. Therefore, if you want to see a data subset twice, you must open the Database window's Queries page, select the query, and click Open to generate the query extraction once again. Although the extraction requires a little time to generate (usually the speed is negligible unless the tables contain many records), the query is always fresh. If you change one value in any table and open the query again, your most recent table edit appears in the query.

Another advantage of generating the query every time you need to use the data subset is that Access 2000 does not have to store the data twice (once in the source tables and again in the query).

> If you edit data from the resulting query's Datasheet view (or from the query's Form view), Access 2000 updates the data in the original tables! Suppose that you want to edit the pay rate for every employee who works in your company's Northeast division; just create a query to extract only the Northeast division employees, make the edits, and close the query. Find and edit the Northeast employees' pay rates without the other employee records getting in the way.

19

Using the Query Design View

When you edit a query or create a query from scratch, you use the Query Design view (like the one shown in Figure 19.4).

Although the Query Design view looks somewhat strange at first, the view's design is logical. The top of the Query Design view contains the source tables and queries, and the bottom of the Query Design view displays the criteria (the query-selection commands).

You use the Query Design view when you must:

- Create an advanced query that the query wizards cannot create.
- Edit an existing query.

FIGURE 19.4.

The Query Design view enables you to create powerful queries.

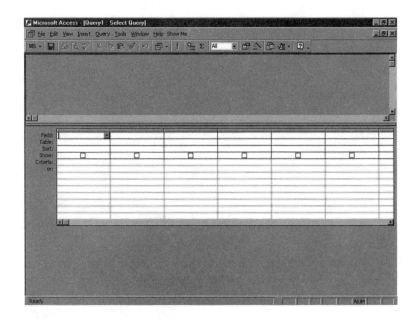

After you learn to create a query with the Query Design view, you will also understand how to use the Query Design view to edit existing queries.

Creating a Query

To use the Query Design view to create a query, follow these steps:

1. Display the Queries page in the Database window.

2. Click the New button to open the New Query dialog box.

3. Select Design View and click OK to open the Query Design view. Access 2000 displays the Show Table dialog box (shown in Figure 19.5).

FIGURE 19.5.

Select from your database's tables and queries for the new query.

4. Click the table or tables that you want to add to the query and click Add. As you add tables to the query, Access 2000 displays a new table in the Query Design view showing in the background. If you want to base your new query on another query, click the Queries tab to display a list of them from which you can choose,

and then add the selected query. If you want to add both tables and queries, click the Both tab to display all your database tables and queries, and then select the ones you need.

5. Click Close to close the Show Table dialog box.

You have yet to build the entire query, but you have selected tables, existing queries, or both, on which to base your new query. Next, enter the query's criteria so that Access 2000 knows which records and fields to select from your tables and existing queries.

Figure 19.6 shows the start of a new query. This query extracts from two tables, one named Customers and one named Orders. The line connecting the tables' common field, Customer ID, appears when you drag your mouse between the common field, as you do when you want to create a relationship. You recall from the preceding section that Access 2000 must base queries on related tables and queries, and the common field relates the two tables.

FIGURE 19.6.

This query can now extract from two related tables.

19

Think of the top half of the query's design window as starting the request, "Given these tables and queries..." and the lower half of the window as finishing that request, "...extract all data that meets these conditions." The Query Design view contains your instructions when you want Access 2000 to extract data from one or more tables or queries and display the result in a table subset.

Each column in the Query Design view's lower half contains the resulting query's fields. Therefore, if you want the resulting data subset to contain four fields, you fill in four of the Query Design view's lower columns. These columns contain the instructions that indicate to the query how to extract the data from the table, tables, query, queries, or combinations of tables and queries that you have specified for the query.

Working with Complex Queries

To complete the query, follow these steps:

1. Click the first column's row labeled Table and select the table that contains the resulting query's first field. If you want the query's data subset to start with a field from the Customers table, for example, you would select Customers from the drop-down list.

2. Click the first column's row labeled Field and select the field that you want to place first in the resulting data subset. You might select Customer ID from the list, for example.

3. If you want to sort the resulting query's subset based on the first field, select either Ascending or Descending from the row labeled Sort. You don't have to sort on the first field that you add to the query; you can sort on any field that you add. The query sorts all the resulting data based on the value of the field by which you sort. If you sort on two or more fields, Access 2000 sorts the data in the leftmost Sort column first.

4. Leave the Show option checked if you want the field to appear in the resulting query's data subset. Generally, you want the field to appear. If you want to sort the subset on a field but not send that sort field to the resulting extracted subset, uncheck the Show option for that field.

5. Click the first column's row labeled Criteria and enter a criterion. If you type a value, such as 101, Access 2000 extracts only those records with a field containing 101. You can continue adding criteria values beneath the first one. You can type the values 101, 102, 103, 104, and 105 for five rows of criteria (still in the first column). This is like asking Access 2000 to extract only those tenants whose Customer ID is 101, 102, 103, 104, and 105, for example. If the field is a text-data type, Access 2000 encloses the criteria in quotation marks (shown in Figure 19.7). Access 2000 encloses dates inside pound signs (#1/6/1898#, for example) if you enter dates in the criteria.

6. It gets fun here. Instead of selecting the field from the second column's drop-down list labeled Field, drag the field name from a table in the upper half of the Query Design view (such as the Order Date field in the Orders table). Access 2000 automatically fills in the table and field name in the second column of the query!

7. Enter the selection criteria for the new field. The criteria indicate exactly how you want to pull records from the table. If you want to extract all the records (all that fall within the criteria of the first field that you have entered), leave the second field's criteria blank. You can further limit the extraction by entering an additional criterion for the second field. Suppose that you not only want customers with the IDs listed in the first criteria, but also want to limit the selection to any of those five who have an order date of January 6, 1999. You enter #1/6/1999# for the criteria.

8. Continue adding fields that you want to appear in the resulting query. When you execute your query, these fields appear in the resulting table.

FIGURE 19.7.

This query must match several criteria values for Customer ID.

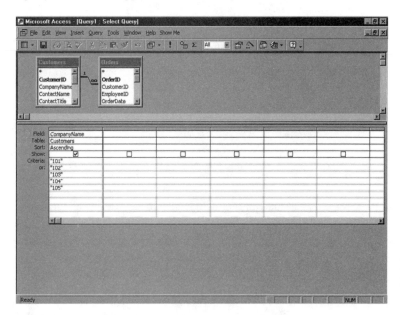

19

As you work with the query, you might want to add more tables. Add the tables in the Query Design view by selecting Query, Show Table. Add as many tables (or queries) as you like to the query from within the Query Design view, but remember that the tables and queries must relate somehow. Remove a table or query from the Query Design view by right-clicking the table name and selecting Remove Table.

You can use all the cut, copy, and paste methods that you learned earlier in the book for the query-extraction fields. You can move a field from one location to another by selecting, cutting, and pasting it, for example. You can also resize column widths by dragging the field column edges, and you can change any value by clicking that value in the Query Design view.

If you really want to get fancy, use the relational operators in Table 19.1 to add to your extraction power.

TABLE 19.1. ACCESS 2000'S RELATIONAL OPERATORS IMPROVE EXTRACTION POWER.

Operator	Description
>	Greater than
<	Less than
>=	Greater than or equal to
<=	Less than or equal to
<>	Not equal to
=	Equal to (not needed for simple matches)

Suppose that you want to include customer-order details in a query, but you only want to include orders with more than 19 units. Enter >19 for the Quantity field's criteria to limit the selection to those records that match the other criteria and that have order quantities of more than 19 units. The relational operators work with numbers, text values that fall within a range of words, and dates.

The Between keyword is useful when you want to extract values that fall between two other values. If you type Between #1/1/2000# And #1/31/2000# for a date criteria, for example, Access 2000 extracts only records whose date falls between 1/1/2000 and 1/31/2000 (including the days 1/1/2000 and 1/31/2000).

Access 2000 uses an implied Or when you specify multiple criteria. Instead of typing five separate Customer IDs such as 101, 102, 103, 104, and 105, for example, you could enter 101 Or 102 Or 103 Or 104 Or 105. (Of course, entering Between 101 And 105 would be even easier.)

Be sure to save your query when you finish with it. Click the Query Design view's Close Window button and name the query so that you are able to refer to it later. When you select the query and click Open from the Queries page of the Database window, Access 2000 runs the query, extracts the data, and displays the result in your Datasheet view.

Summary

This hour showed you how to narrow your data and form subsets. Often, a table contains many more fields and records than you want to work with at any one time. Access 2000's filter and query powers enable you to create subsets of data to make your work more manageable.

Filters provide quick subsets, but queries provide much more power. After you run a filter or query to create a subset of your data, you can make changes to the subset and still be changing the underlying tables. Although the Query Design view takes some getting used to, it enables you to specify powerful query extraction criteria so that Access 2000 searches for and finds the data with which you need to work.

Now that you can produce subsets of data, you need a way to report that data. The next hour, "Advanced Access 2000," explores some of the reporting capabilities. The Report Wizard makes quick work of report generation from your tables and queries.

Q&A

Q Should I use a filter or a query?

A When you quickly want to see a subset of a table, use a filter. You sometimes use the subset in another way (as input to a report, for example), so creating a query that you can name and execute makes more sense (except in the case of one-time extractions to a Datasheet view).

Q If I save a filter as a named query, what does the query's Query Design view look like?

A Filters are much less powerful than queries, but they are easier to designate. As you create more queries and get used to your data needs, you find that many of your queries are little more than filters. Instead of messing with the Query Design view to design the query, generate a simpler Filter by Form filter and save it as a query. If you then want to modify the filter-based query or add more complex criteria, open the query's Query Design view and you see that Access 2000 selected the proper source table and field names for you. You can then add to the criteria lines and request additional fields if you like.

Q Does the row on which I place criteria make a difference?

A Yes, although you are getting into some confusing logic. The way you specify criteria between two fields often indicates how you want the combined criteria to work. If you place one field's criteria on the same row as another field's, an

19

implied *and* relation takes place, and Access 2000 extracts only those records that contain a match for both criteria values. If you place one field's criteria on a different row from another field's, an implied *or* relation takes place between them.

Q How can I see my data in two ways, say, with the field names arranged alphabetically and with the fields arranged in the order of my table's design?

A Create a query that extracts all the fields from your table. The query's output, or data subset, will contain all data that the original table contains (the subset will be the same size as the table). Set up the query's output for ordering the fields alphabetically. Queries aren't just for creating smaller subsets of tables; you can create a query to report table data in an order that differs from a table's original design order.

HOUR 20

Advanced Access 2000

This hour shows you how to create custom reports. Access 2000 includes several reporting tools, both automatic and manual, that produce complex reports. You can create a simple report by clicking a toolbar button. If you spend a little time developing the report with a report wizard, you can create extremely professional-looking reports.

You do not have to master the Report Design view, an extensive and complex report-creating tool, to create most of your reports. Some people have never used the Report Design view to design an Access 2000 report from scratch because of the report wizards' power. The report wizards give you complete control over a report's design.

The highlights of this hour include the following:

- How to create report queries
- How AutoReport creates simple reports
- Which report wizards Access 2000 supports
- How to use the main Report Wizard to generate virtually any report you need by making a few selections

- When to request summary statistics
- Why you should preview reports

Introducing Access 2000 Reports

You often want printed listings of your data, and the Access 2000 reporting tools enable you to produce professional reports with ease. This hour explains how to use the report wizards and discusses the different reporting styles and options available. You learned how to produce printed listings in Hour 18, "Entering and Displaying Access 2000 Data"; in this hour you learn how to add flair to your reports.

Unlike forms, a report often displays multiple records in a view that resembles the Datasheet view. The difference between the Datasheet view and a printed report is that the report provides summary statistics, fancy headings, footers, page numbers, and styles that accent your data.

A *report* is not only a listing of multiple data values. Anytime you need to send Access 2000 data to paper, you must create a report. Therefore, a report might be a series of checks or mailing labels that you print.

Before you print any report, use the Print Preview to see the report on your screen. Often, you notice changes that you need to make, so previewing a report can save you time and paper. Your computer's print *spooler* is too difficult to stop quickly, so you usually end up printing the first few pages of a report even if you attempt to stop the printing.

 The *spooler* is the Windows memory area and disk file combination where Access 2000 sends your report before the report goes to paper. The spooler frees up your program while the printing continues.

When you are about to print a report, the Report sheet in the Database window enables you to preview any report by clicking the Preview button. Access 2000 can generate fancy reports (see Figure 20.1).

Rarely do you report all the data from a single table. Except for detailed reports, such as inventory listings and master customer listings, you almost always report part of a table or values from multiple tables.

Almost all reports that you generate, therefore, get their data from queries that you have created. If you need to report from part of a table's data or from multiple tables, create a query on which to base the report. Your queries can order the data the way you want to see it, and Access 2000 can then print your query's results.

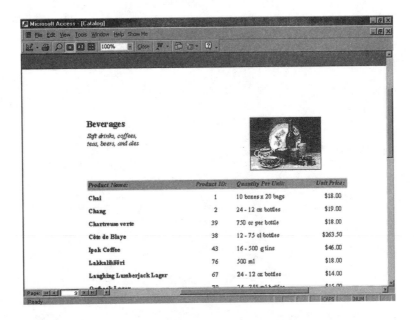

FIGURE 20.1.

The report preview shows how Access 2000 formats your report.

Generating Simple Reports Using AutoReports

Access 2000 includes an *AutoReport* feature, which quickly generates reports from your Datasheet views. As Figure 20.2 shows, the AutoReport feature is just a listing of field names and their corresponding field values.

NEW TERM *AutoReport* is Access 2000's automatic reporting tool that creates simple reports from your Datasheet views.

Unlike the printed listings you get when you select File, Print, AutoReport formats your data in a readable manner without squeezing too much information on a single page. If you need to run a quick report from a table, follow these steps to enable AutoReport to generate the report:

1. Display your data in a Datasheet view. If you want to report from a subset of data or from a collection of multiple tables, display the query's Datasheet view.

2. Click the down arrow next to the New Object:AutoForm button on the toolbar. Some toolbars already show the AutoReport button, depending on your last Access 2000 task.

3. Select AutoReport from the button's drop-down list. Access 2000 generates a report from the current Datasheet view and shows a preview of the report (shown in Figure 20.2).

20

FIGURE 20.2.

*AutoReprot generates
simple reports.*

4. If the preview shows what you want, click the preview's Print icon to print the report.

5. Click the Close button to close the AutoReport preview. Access 2000 displays the Report Design view (shown in Figure 20.3). The Report Design view can be difficult to understand when you first see it. For now, don't worry about the contents. AutoReport created the report's design and saved you from having to use the Report Design view.

6. Close the Report Design view and enter a report name if you want to save the AutoReport's design. If you think you will edit the AutoReport design later or generate the report often, save the report. Generally, you use AutoReport only to produce quick reports and use the report wizards (described next) to generate more standard reports.

AutoReport generates reports using Access 2000's report-designing tools. After you learn how to modify a Report Design view, you can use AutoReport to generate the foundation of a report, and then change the report to fit your exact needs.

If you like using AutoReport for quick reports, check out the AutoForm feature. AutoForm creates fast and simple forms from your Datasheet views.

FIGURE 20.3.

AutoReport enables you to avoid the Report Design view.

Generating Reports Using the Report Wizards

Access 2000 includes several report wizards that design reports for you. Select one of the report wizards by opening the Database window, clicking the Reports tab (which displays the database reports), and clicking New to create a new report. The New Report dialog box enables you to access the following reporting components:

- *Design View*. A blank Report Design view on which you can add a new report's headers, footers, detail, and *summary* requests. When you want to generate a report from scratch, use the Design View in the New Report dialog box.

NEW TERM A *summary* is a subtotal, total, average, minimum-value search, or maximum-value search that Access 2000 performs when printing your reports.

- *Report Wizard*. Walks you through the report-generation process by enabling you to select the source tables and queries as well as the fields that you want in the final report. You run Report Wizard the most often because it generates less specific reports than other reporting wizards. The next section, "Using the Report Wizard," explains how you use Report Wizard to create reports.

- *AutoReport: Columnar*. Generates a report that contains all the fields from the underlying table or query. The columnar report looks much like the AutoReport, except that the columnar report makes better use of your report's page space and designs a more routine report. As Figure 20.4 shows, a columnar report can include titles and special fonts, and can emphasize field data.

20

FIGURE 20.4.

*Columnar reports look
much better than
AutoReports.*

- *AutoReport: Tabular.* Generates a report that displays on a single line the record of each source table or query by adjusting the font size to fit your report page. The tabular report looks much better than a simple Datasheet view, and is often more useful than the generic AutoReport you learned about in the previous section. Figure 20.5 shows a sample of the wizard's tabular report. As You can see from the figure, Access is not always able to fit the complete field name at the top of a column of data. You can adjust the report's design to allow more room for the field name if you prefer.

- *Chart Wizard.* Produces graphs from your data. Access 2000 graphs resemble Excel 2000 graphs, and you can control the format and style as well as the table from which Access 2000 graphs.

- *Label Wizard.* A generic mailing-list report that produces mailing labels for all common labels. The mailing label industry has a standard numbering system (the *Avery numbering system*, after the company that is perhaps best known for computerized mailing labels). Most office-supply stores sell mailing labels with an official Avery number, so you can format a report for your labels.

NEW TERM   The *Avery numbering system* is an industry-standard, mailing-label numbering system. You can request an Access 2000 mailing-list report that works with your labels by matching the Avery numbers.

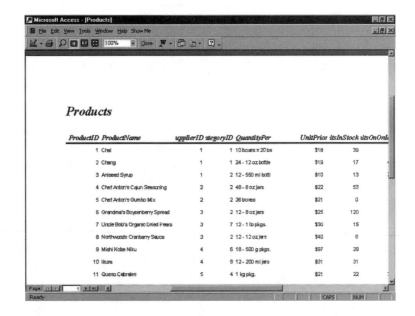

FIGURE 20.5.

Tabular reports produce well-organized listings of your data.

STEP-UP

You will be surprised at how little the report wizards in Access 2000 differ from those in Access 97. Except for some dialog box format changes, you will be familiar with every report wizard dialog box. If you have mastered the ins and outs of Access 97 reports, you may want to skip to the next hour's lesson, "Office 2000's Synergy."

Using the Report Wizard

The second New Report dialog box option, Report Wizard, is probably the most common selection you make when you generate customized reports. The Report Wizard walks you through a series of steps to create a custom report from your tables and queries, and it includes many common reporting styles and special features that you need.

20

You must create a named query before generating a report from any query.

To start the Report Wizard, follow these steps:

1. Display the Database window.
2. Click the Reports tab to display your Database reports.
3. Click the New button to display the New Report dialog box.
4. Select Report Wizard.
5. Open the New Report's drop-down box to select from a list of tables and queries that reside in your database. You are not limited to the data of a single table or query but can report from multiple tables and queries in the same report.
6. Click the OK button to display the Report Wizard's field-selection dialog box (shown in Figure 20.6).
7. Select the fields that you want in the final report by highlighting the field in the Available Fields list and clicking > to send the field to the Selected Fields list. As you can see when you open the Tables/Queries drop-down list box, you can select fields from several tables and queries in addition to the primary source you selected in step 5.
8. After you select the fields for the report, click Next.

FIGURE 20.6.

Select the fields you want for your report.

Grouping Report Summaries

Now that you have selected the report fields, you must indicate how the report is to be summarized. Rarely do you want to print a data listing without requesting a *report summary*. Depending on the type of fields you select for your report, the Report Wizard prompts you for subtotal and total summary information or *grouping* information. If your report contains numeric data, the Report Wizard shows its Summary dialog box (shown in Figure 20.7). Use this dialog box to indicate how you want Access 2000 to group your report. If Access 2000 does not display the summary dialog box, the Report Wizard prompts you for grouping information, and you can select the field on which you want your data grouped.

FIGURE 20.7.

*Indicate how Access
2000 is to produce the
subtotals and totals.*

NEW TERM   A *report summary* concludes a report by showing totals and averages from the
report detail.

NEW TERM   A *report group* is a collection of records whose designated group field contains
the same data values.

> Access 2000 can group the report on numeric fields, not text fields. The
> numeric fields enable the Report Wizard to produce subtotals and total
> summaries, whereas no such summaries are possible with text fields.

Select only those numeric fields that produce proper subtotals. If you report a division
number field and that field is numeric, for example, you wouldn't want Access 2000 to
subtotal and total the division number. If you print a report with customer past-due balances, however, you do want to print a subtotal for each customer and an overall grand
total of past-due balances.

The grouping field should be groups, such as customer IDs, for which you are printing a
detailed list. Although the same customer might appear on several report lines, you want
Access 2000 to subtotal only when the customer ID changes to the next customer in the
report. The grouping capability keeps multiple customer IDs from appearing down the
column when you print multiple records for the same customer.

As you click each field that you selected, the grouping dialog box displays a preview of
your report, showing how the grouping will fall out. Generally, the grouping options and
preview give you enough information to decide on a grouping scheme.

After you select your grouping preference. Access 2000 displays the grouping level dialog box.

20

If you want to group on multiple fields, the group order you select determines the priority that Access 2000 uses to group the data. The highest priority grouping level (if you select multiple groups) appears on the left of the report, the second grouping level appears to the right of the first one, and so on. Generally, multifield grouping gets confusing. If you want to add such grouping levels, click every group level from the series of fields that Access 2000 displays. The Report Wizard prioritizes the multifield groups in the order that you select the fields.

You can group by a maximum of four field-grouping levels. If you need to group by more than four fields, you have to edit the report design or create a report from scratch. Rarely do you need more than four groups.

If the Report Wizard has presented you with the grouping view dialog box rather than the subtotal and total summary dialog boxes described here, you need only click the field by which you want to group the report. If you are producing a customer balance report, for example, the Report Wizard might enable you to group by either the Customer ID field or the Customer Order Number field.

After you have set up the grouping levels that you need, click Next to select a sort and summary order for the report.

The Report's Sort and Summary Order

When you see the sorting and summary dialog box (see Figure 20.8), you are almost done creating your report. Select from one to four fields that you want Access 2000 to use for sorting your data. If you are reporting from a query that already contains sorted data, and if you generate the report so that the data groups in the order of those sorted fields, don't select any fields by which to sort. If you want to sort by one or more fields that do not enter the reporting system already sorted, however, select up to four fields and click the button labeled AZ to sort in ascending order.

The AZ button changes to ZA when you click it, so you can then select a descending sort.

FIGURE 20.8.

Select from one to four fields by which to sort.

Regardless of whether you select a sorting option, click the Summary Options button to display the Report Wizard's Summary Options dialog box. Each of your report's numeric fields appears in the box, so you can select any or all these summaries for that field:

- *Sum.* Requests a total for the field
- *Avg.* Requests an average for the field
- *Min.* Requests that Access 2000 highlight the minimum value in the field
- *Max.* Requests that Access 2000 highlight the maximum value in the field

> You cannot display summaries if your report has no numeric fields or if you are grouping by the numeric fields.

Choosing a Report Layout and Style

Click OK to close the Summary Options dialog box, and then click Next to choose a report layout. Click through the various layouts to select one that fits your needs. As you click layouts, Access 2000 displays thumbnail sketches of those layouts. If you click the Block style, for example, you see that Access 2000 displays boxes around your report fields.

After you select the layout, click Next to select from the Report Wizard's style dialog box (shown in Figure 20.9). From this dialog box, you can add the finishing touches to your report.

20

Click Next, enter a report title if you don't want to use the original source table or query name, and click Finish to generate the completed report. Sometimes Access 2000 takes several minutes to generate the report, especially if the source tables and queries contain several records and your report contains several grouping levels. When finished, Access 2000 prints a preview of your report so that you can look at your handiwork.

FIGURE 20.9.

The style dialog box determines the overall appearance of your report.

Summary

Access 2000 is certainly a powerful program. Despite its ease of use, it does take some getting used to before you fully master all its features. You will probably use the Access 2000 wizards more than any other wizard in any other Office 2000 product.

At this point, you are ready to begin generating sample databases and practicing with Access 2000. As you create more databases, you learn how to partition your data properly into tables and generate data-entry forms and reports.

The next hour begins the part of the book that explains how the Office 2000 programs work together to help you with your data-processing requirements. In addition, you learn more about using Office 2000 with the Internet.

Q&A

Q How does the toolbar's AutoReport differ from the AutoReport entries I see on the Report Wizard's opening dialog box?

A The AutoReport entries on the Report Wizard's opening dialog box create more finished reports than the AutoReport toolbar button. Use the AutoReport toolbar button to quickly generate a report from your Datasheet and Form views. Use the Report Wizard AutoReport entries to produce more complete reports without taking the time to set up summary and sorting features. Not all reports require summaries, and the two AutoReport wizards suffice for many reports that you will generate.

Q **What is the largest page size that I can produce in an Access 2000 report?**

A Access 2000 report pages can be as large as 22 inches wide by 22 inches long.

Q **Do I subtotal on numeric fields or fields that I want to group by, such as Customer ID numbers?**

A When you specify grouping instructions, the field that you group by is usually a nonnumeric field, such as a Customer ID field. Access 2000 collects all the customer ID records together and reports each customer's information in one group. When Access 2000 finishes reporting a customer's records (when the ID changes), Access 2000 subtotals the numeric fields in that group before starting the next group.

20

PART VII

Combining the Office 2000 Products and the Internet

Hour

HOUR **21**

Office 2000's Synergy

This hour explores how Office 2000 products work together and how you can enhance your documents. Office 2000 programs integrate so well that it is hard to know where to start describing the possibilities. Generally, if you need to work with two or more Office 2000 program documents together, you are able to load or embed one document within another even though the Office 2000 programs that created the two documents are completely different.

From inserting links in Word 2000 documents to combining an Access 2000 table and an Excel 2000 worksheet into a PowerPoint 2000 presentation, Office 2000 supplies the combining tools you need. You can also add your own graphics to your Office 2000 documents by using the supplied clip art or by drawing with the Office 2000 drawing tools.

The highlights of this hour include the following:

- Why drag-and-drop operations work so well between Office 2000 programs
- How to control a drag-and-drop operation to produce a copy, a move, a link, or a shortcut

- How to edit and break links between Office 2000 documents
- What requirements a Word 2000 document must meet to serve as a PowerPoint 2000 presentation
- Which steps you must take to import Access 2000 data into Word 2000
- How to write letters to Outlook 2000 contacts quickly
- How to add your own art (or sound or video) clip files to Office 2000's Clip Gallery
- When the AutoShapes toolbar comes in handy
- How to select WordArt styles when you want to add fancy text titles and banners to your Office 2000 documents

Sharing Data Among Applications

Office 2000's cornerstone is data sharing among its programs. Office 2000 offers several ways to share data among products. Almost all the Office 2000 products support the inclusion of other Office 2000 documents. Word 2000 includes the Insert Microsoft Excel Worksheet toolbar button that inserts any Excel 2000 worksheet in a Word 2000 document, for example.

Besides inserting full documents, you may want to insert part of a document in another Office 2000 application. The following sections explain the most common methods to embed part of one application's document inside another.

Drag and Drop

Suppose that you want to use part of an Excel 2000 worksheet inside a Word 2000 document. If you have both Excel 2000 (with the relevant data loaded) and Word 2000 running at the same time, perform these steps to drag the worksheet to the Word 2000 document:

1. Resize your Excel 2000 and Word 2000 program windows so that you can see both the *source document* (the Excel 2000 worksheet) and the *destination document* (the Word 2000 document).

 The *source document* is the document that holds an item that you want to drag to another location.

 The *destination document* is the document that receives the object that you drag from a source document.

2. In the Excel 2000 worksheet, select the cells that you want to copy and transfer to Word 2000.

3. Hold the Ctrl key and drag the edge of the highlighted cells to the location in your Word 2000 document where you want to place the table.

4. Release the mouse to anchor the table. (Figure 21.1 shows the result of such a copy.)

FIGURE 21.1.

Word's table came from Excel 2000.

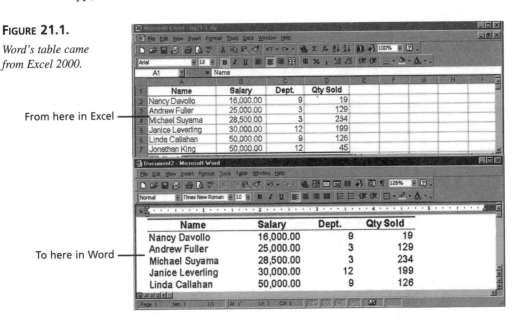

From here in Excel ——

To here in Word ——

 If you did not first press Ctrl before dragging the cells, Excel 2000 would have *moved* the table from the Excel 2000 worksheet to the Word 2000 document instead of copying the table.

 Depending on the size and style of your Word 2000 document, you might want to format the copied table differently from Excel 2000's format. Right-click the table and select Format Object to display the Format Object dialog box. You can apply colors, lines, shading, and other formatting attributes to the copied object from the Format Object dialog box.

21

Creating Links

Suppose that you create a monthly sales report using the same Word 2000 document and the same Excel 2000 worksheet every time. Only the details in the Excel 2000 worksheet change (obviously, you have created templates for these files long before now). You don't have to drag the updated Excel 2000 table to your Word 2000 document before printing the Word 2000 document each month. Instead of copying or moving the cells, you can create a *link* to the cells.

NEW TERM A *link* is a cross-reference to another file. Instead of copying or moving the contents of one file to another, the link maintains a live connection to the other file. Therefore, if the source file changes, the destination file always displays those changes. The destination file does not actually hold the source file's data, but displays the data as though it resided in the destination file.

As long as you have inserted a link to the Excel 2000 worksheet, you need only change the Excel 2000 worksheet each month, start Word 2000, load the report document, and print the document. You won't have to copy or move the actual Excel 2000 cells into the report. The report always points to the worksheet cells via the link that you inserted when you created the Word 2000 document.

To create a link, perform these steps:

1. Arrange and resize your two program windows so that you can see both the source document (the Excel 2000 worksheet) and the destination document (the Word 2000 document).

2. Select the cells in the Excel 2000 worksheet that you want to link and transfer to Word 2000.

3. With the right mouse button, drag the edge of the highlighted cells to the location in your Word 2000 document where you want to place the table.

4. Release the right mouse button. Word 2000 opens a pop-up menu with these options: Move Here, Copy Here, Insert Excel Object Here, and Create Shortcut Here.

5. Select Insert Excel Object Here to indicate to Word 2000 that you want to create an object link (as opposed to a move or a copy of the cells). Although the cells appear as though Office 2000 copied them into the Word 2000 document, the cells represent only the link that you created between the Excel 2000 source and Word 2000 destination document.

The destination document (in this case, the Word 2000 document) always reflects the most recent changes to the source document (in this case, the Excel 2000 worksheet). Therefore, if you must keep archives of old reports with the previous monthly values, you want to copy the cells instead of creating a link.

To see the interactive nature of the links, change a value in the source Excel 2000 worksheet. The Word 2000 document immediately reflects your change.

After inserting one or more links, select Edit, Links to produce the dialog box shown in Figure 21.2. The Links dialog box contains every link in your document and enables you to change, break, or lock any link. When you break a link, the data becomes embedded in the document and no longer updates when you update the source. When you lock a link, you temporarily prevent the link from being updated when its source is updated.

FIGURE 21.2.

Use the Links dialog box to manage your document links.

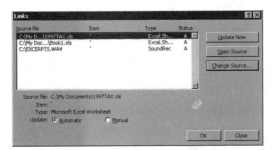

Creating Shortcuts

Instead of inserting a copy or a link, you can insert a *shortcut* in the destination document.

NEW TERM   A *shortcut* is an icon inserted in your document that you can double-click to access data from a document stored elsewhere.

You probably use shortcuts less often than links and embedded copies when producing reports because you usually want the reports to show actual data and not icons. If you often work with data from one program while in another program, however, the shortcuts are nice. The data does not get in your way until you are ready to work with it because you see only icons that represent the shortcut data.

21

If you create a shortcut from one Office 2000 program to another, Office 2000 actually displays the data and does not display a shortcut icon. If you double-click the data, Office 2000 opens the appropriate program and enables you to edit the original data using the source program that created the data. If you insert a shortcut into a non-Office 2000 program, however, Office 2000 inserts a shortcut icon that represents the data. If you double-click the icon from within the other program, the appropriate Office 2000 program begins, and you can edit the data.

Consider this scenario: You are working in Excel 2000, modifying weekly salary figures for a large worksheet that you maintain. Each week you must study the salary amounts and enter a 10-line explanation of the salaries. Instead of typing the definition each week or (worse) using Excel 2000 as a limited word processor and editing the text each week, you could embed a shortcut to a Word 2000 document that contains a template for the text. When you double-click the shortcut, Excel 2000 starts Word 2000, which automatically loads the template. You can create the final text in the template, copy the Word 2000 text into your salary worksheet (replacing the shortcut), and save the worksheet under a name that designates the current week's work.

To insert a shortcut, perform these steps:

1. Arrange and resize your program windows so that you can see both the source document (the Word 2000 template document) and the destination document (the Excel 2000 worksheet).

2. Select the Word 2000 template text that you want to use for the shortcut. (Press Ctrl+A if you want to select the entire Word 2000 template document.)

3. With the right mouse button, drag the edge of the highlighted template text to the location in your Excel 2000 worksheet where you want to place the shortcut.

4. Release the right mouse button.

5. Select Create Shortcut Here from the pop-up menu. Office 2000 creates the shortcut. As with a link, the shortcut data does not actually appear in the destination document. Unlike a link, you can drag the shortcut to your Windows desktop, to Explorer, or to another program to create additional copies of the shortcut.

Before inserting an Access 2000 table into another Office 2000 program, run a query to filter data that doesn't interest you. (Hour 19, "Retrieving Your Data," explains how to form data queries.) In most cases, you want to use Word 2000's special Access 2000 Database Insert feature to load Access 2000 data into a Word 2000 document. Later in this hour, the section titled "Using Word 2000 and Access 2000" describes how to insert Access 2000 data into a Word 2000 document.

Turning a Word Document into a Presentation

Word 2000 and PowerPoint 2000 share a special link that enables you to turn a set of notes into a presentation. Before creating your notes, be sure to use the Heading 1 through Heading 5 styles. PowerPoint 2000 uses the Heading 1 style for each slide's title and uses the Heading 2 through Heading 5 styles for the slide's subsequently indented text.

If your Word 2000 document contains other styles, PowerPoint 2000 ignores those paragraphs.

You can easily apply Heading 1 through Heading 5 styles to a Word 2000 document that you have already created by clicking a paragraph (or by moving the mouse pointer any-where within the paragraph), pressing Ctrl+Shift+S, and selecting Heading styles from the drop-down list box. You can also select the style by opening the Style drop-down list box and scrolling to the heading style that you want to select.

After you create the Word 2000 document, open it from PowerPoint 2000 or select the File, Send To, Microsoft PowerPoint option Word 2000 to create the presentation.

Using Word 2000 and Access 2000

A database can be extremely large with many tables. Often, you want to export a portion of an Access 2000 database to a Word 2000 document. The drag-and-drop method does not always offer exactly what you need to get the data you want into a Word 2000 document.

21

> If you want to use an Access 2000 table in a PowerPoint 2000 presentation, load the table into a Word 2000 document, and then convert the Word 2000 document to a PowerPoint 2000 presentation as described in the previous section.

To load Access 2000 data into a Word 2000 document, perform these steps:

1. Display the Database toolbar in Word 2000 (select View, Toolbars and click the Database option).

2. Click the Insert Database toolbar button. Word 2000 displays the Database dialog box.

3. Click the Get Data button and locate the database you want to import. Word 2000 does not import the data yet, but you must locate the database before specifying the data to be imported. To display Access 2000 databases, select MS Access Databases (*.mdb; *.mde) from the list box labeled Files of Type. Select the database you want to load. Word 2000 displays the dialog box shown in Figure 21.3, which contains a list of every table and query from the selected database.

FIGURE 21.3.

Indicate exactly which table Word 2000 is to use.

4. Select the table or query that you want to load into the Word 2000 document, and click OK to return to the Database dialog box.

5. Click the Query Options button if you want to limit the table's records or fields. (If you don't select the Query Options button, Word 2000 imports the entire table.) Word 2000 displays an Access 2000 query window, from which you can select records and fields using normal Access 2000 database-selection criteria. You can add tables if you want Word 2000 to import data from multiple tables.

6. Click the Insert Data button to insert your selected data.

7. You now can format the data and use it in your Word 2000 document as if you typed the data yourself.

Outlook 2000 Letters

Users often keep Outlook 2000 loaded throughout the day, making appointments, calling contacts, and planning meetings. Outlook 2000 includes a handy feature that enables you to write a letter to any contact quickly and easily. A wizard makes the connection between Outlook 2000 and Word 2000. The following steps explain how to access this often-overlooked feature from Outlook 2000:

1. Click to select any Outlook 2000 contact.
2. Select Actions, New Letter to Contact to start Word 2000 Letter Wizard shown in Figure 21.4.

FIGURE 21.4.

The Letter Wizard takes care of the letter's formatting and address details.

3. Select a page design and letter style from the dialog box.
4. Click the Recipient Info tab to display the letter's recipient information. The wizard will have already filled in the contact's name and address.
5. Click the Other Elements tab to define other aspects of the letter such as the reference line and subject if those items are to appear.
6. Click the Sender Info tab to enter information about you, the sender. You can put your return address information as well as a company name and closing, such as "Best Wishes."
7. Click Finish and Word 2000 builds the letter using the elements you selected. Your only job now is to fill in the details such as the body of the letter and to complete the elements such as the attention and subject lines.

21

Enhancing Your Office Documents

Office 2000 enables you to insert images and other objects into your documents. Graphics spruce up newsletters and other documents that require eye-catching images.

In Hour 13, "PowerPoint 2000's Advanced Features," you learned how to use the Clip Gallery to insert images, sounds, and videos into presentations. In addition to producing the Clip Gallery for clip art, the Insert, Picture option produces a menu that includes the following options:

- *From File*. Enables you to insert an image from any graphics file. Use this option when you don't want to confine your images to the ones supplied in the Clip Gallery.
- *AutoShapes*. Inserts one of Office 2000's *AutoShapes*, which you can manipulate.

NEW TERM *AutoShape* is a ready-made shape that you can use in a document. After you insert a shape, you can resize, rotate, flip, color, and combine that shape with other shapes. The Drawing toolbar contains an AutoShape section, which produces the AutoShapes floating toolbar. Use the AutoShapes floating toolbar to insert and edit AutoShapes.

- *WordArt*. Displays the WordArt Gallery of WordArt styles (shown in Figure 21.5).

    WordArt enables you to convert text into shapes. Despite its name, WordArt is available from all Office 2000 products, not just Word 2000.
- *From Scanner or Camera*. Enables you to scan an image into the Office 2000 document or receive a digital camera's image. You must have a TWAIN-compliant scanner or digital camera attached to pull such images into Office 2000. (Most scanners follow the PC scanner standard called TWAIN; your scanner's documentation should indicate whether your scanner is TWAIN-compliant.)
- *Organization Chart*. Starts an Office 2000 add-in application that creates organizational charts (available only in Excel 2000).
- *Chart*. Displays a small Excel 2000-like worksheet (called a datasheet) in which you can enter data. The datasheet offers a sample set of cells in which you can enter your own values or import data from Excel 2000. When you close the datasheet, the resulting bar chart appears in your document (available only in Word 2000).

FIGURE 21.5.

You can select a WordArt style from the WordArt Gallery.

The next three sections describe the most common graphics insertions you can make into your Office 2000 documents from the Insert, Picture menu.

Inserting Images from Files

To add an image (or sound or video) clip-art file to a document, select Insert, Picture, From File to display the Insert Picture dialog box. Locate the image on your disk (or on your network, or the Internet by selecting the source from the Look in list box) and click Insert to insert the image.

> **STEP-UP**
>
> Office 2000 products no longer anchor art over document text at a specific location but automatically float art over text so that you can drag inserted pictures anywhere you want them to go.

If you often insert the same image, sound, or video clip, consider adding the clip to your Office 2000 Clip Gallery. The Clip Gallery makes common clips easy for you to find, thus eliminating the need for you to search your disk drive every time you want to insert a clip file.

To add a clip file to your Clip Gallery, perform these steps:

1. Display the Clip Gallery by selecting Insert, Picture, Clip Art.
2. Click the Import Clips button.
3. Locate the clip-art file that you want to import. When you locate the file and press Enter, Office 2000 displays the Clip Properties dialog box (shown in Figure 21.6), which shows a thumbnail sketch of the image along with the image's details.

21

FIGURE 21.6.

*Add a description for
the image you want
to add to Office
2000's Clip Gallery.*

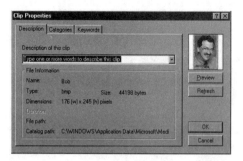

4. Select the category and add a keyword or two (to help with subsequent searches for the image).

5. Press Enter to add the image to the proper Clip Gallery category.

Using OfficeArt Tools

Office 2000 introduces a completely revamped set of *OfficeArt* tools. Instead of just upgrading previous Office drawing tools, Microsoft rewrote them for Office 2000 to improve performance.

NEW TERM   *OfficeArt* is the general term applied to the Office 2000 drawing tools such as AutoShape and WordArt.

OfficeArt provides a single drawing interface for all the Office 2000 programs. If you learn how to use AutoShape inside PowerPoint 2000, you also know how to use AutoShape in Excel 2000. Although you might expect such an integrated and consistent drawing system, Office 2000 is the first time Microsoft successfully integrated one consistent drawing interface into all the Office 2000 products.

> Unlike the other Office 2000 products, Outlook 2000 contains no OfficeArt tool support.

> OfficeArt's drawing tools work with all the applicable Office 2000 features. Therefore, you can spell check the text in an AutoShape drawing.

Not only did Microsoft help you learn the OfficeArt tools more quickly, but Office 2000 includes only one set of OfficeArt code. Therefore, whether you install only Word 2000 or the entire set of Office 2000 programs, Office 2000 installs a single shared copy of the

OfficeArt code. As a result, the drawing tools work quickly and efficiently, consuming much less disk space than if each program contained its own drawing code.

Inserting WordArt

WordArt displays text in several shapes, colors, and styles to add pizzazz to your documents. You can add an eye-catching title at the top of an Excel 2000 worksheet, for example, to grab the reader's attention.

To add a WordArt image, perform these steps:

1. Select Insert, Picture, WordArt to display the WordArt Gallery dialog box.

2. Select the WordArt style that you want to use by double-clicking the style. Office 2000 displays the Edit WordArt Text dialog box (shown in Figure 21.7).

FIGURE 21.7.

Provide text for WordArt to format.

3. Enter the text that you want to format as WordArt and select the proper font and point size. The WordArt style that you select follows your font and size request as closely as possible.

4. Click OK to insert the WordArt text. Office 2000 displays resizing handles around the WordArt image, which you can use to resize or move the image. In addition, the WordArt toolbar that appears provides several editing techniques that you can apply to the image, such as rotation and color.

Figure 21.8 shows a sample WordArt image inserted at the top of a small imported Excel worksheet.

21

FIGURE 21.8.

A sample of WordArt's appeal.

Inserting AutoShapes

The AutoShapes toolbar that appears when you insert an AutoShape provides numerous drawing tools for creating line drawings inside Word 2000, Excel 2000, or PowerPoint 2000. When you click one of the toolbar options described next, Office 2000 opens a set of drawing tools for that option. If you click the Basic Shapes tool, for example, Office 2000 displays a drop-down selection box of about 30 shapes. After you select a shape, you can continue drawing with that shape until you select a different shape or another AutoShape tool. To draw a shape, drag the mouse over the editing area.

The following list describes the AutoShape tools you find on the AutoShapes toolbar:

- *Lines.* Provides straight, curved, and freeform lines that you can draw with the mouse

- *Basic shapes.* Provides circles, ovals, rectangles, and other shapes that you can select and draw with

- *Block arrows (Word 2000 only).* Provides several connecting arrows that you can use for pointing parts of a drawing to each other

- *Flowchart.* Draws various flowcharting symbols

- *Stars and Banners.* Places stars and various banners on the editing area

- *Callouts.* Draws spoken and bubble-thought cartoon callouts so that the figures you draw can be made to speak

- *Connectors (Excel 2000 only).* Draws several kinds of lines that connect one AutoShape image to another

Figure 21.9 shows how you can have fun by combining AutoShape and OfficeArt images with WordArt to spruce up a Word 2000 document.

FIGURE 21.9.

Combine AutoShape and OfficeArt images to create doodles in Word 2000 documents.

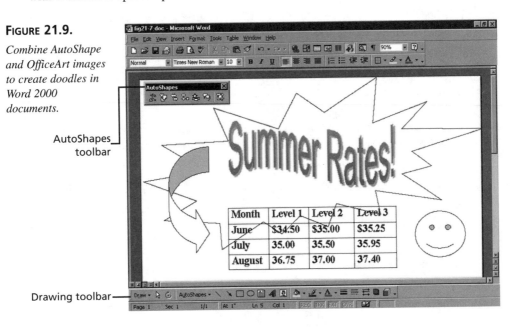

AutoShapes toolbar

Drawing toolbar

AutoShape offers two ways to add text to your image:

- *Placing text in a callout.* As soon as you add an AutoShape callout to your drawing, Office 2000 enables you to enter text for that callout.

- *Placing text anywhere on the AutoShape image.* Right-click anywhere over the AutoShape area and select Add Text from the pop-up menu to place text on any AutoShape image.

When you click any AutoShape image that you draw, resizing handles appear so that you can resize the image. In addition, you will see the image's yellow adjustment handle. Drag the adjustment handle to change the shape's most prominent feature, such as the smile on the happy face.

21

When you add an AutoShape to your document, Office 2000 displays the Drawing toolbar on your screen. Select from the Drawing toolbar to change the orientation of any
selected AutoShape image. You can vertically or horizontally flip an image, for example.
Any text you have placed on the image retains its original orientation.

Summary

This hour described how to integrate Office 2000 products by sharing data files among
the programs. One of the most elegant ways to copy or move data from one Office 2000
program to another is to use drag and drop. By holding your right mouse button, you can
control how the drag-and-drop operation sends the data from one document to another.

Word 2000 and PowerPoint 2000 share data files easily as long as you use the proper
heading styles. Presenters often use Word 2000 documents as a basis for a presentation,
and you will appreciate the automation Office 2000 provides. After you convert your
Word 2000 document to a PowerPoint 2000 presentation, you can adjust the presentation's format and add slides if you want.

When importing Access 2000 data into Word 2000, you must be selective. Databases are
often huge, and you usually want to import only a small part of the database into your
Word 2000 document. First, indicate to Word 2000 what data from what table you want
to import so that you get only the data you need.

This hour also explained how to use the graphics-related tools to insert art and draw pictures inside your Office 2000 documents. As you might expect, the Office 2000 tools are
easy to use and appear (along with their toolbars) when you request them, but stay out of
the way when you don't need to work with art.

The next hour, "Office 2000 and the Internet," introduces the Internet and shows you how
to access Web pages using the Internet Explorer Web browser included with Office 2000.

Q&A

**Q What format does my data take when I drag and drop something from one
Office 2000 product to another?**

A Office 2000 provides excellent intuitive conversions when you combine data from
more than one Office 2000 product. When you drag a worksheet from Excel 2000
to Word 2000, for example, the worksheet becomes a Word 2000 table. You then
can use all the standard table-editing tools in Word 2000 to modify the appearance
of the worksheet. Excel 2000 converts Word 2000 text to text-cell entries. Excel
2000 converts Access 2000 table data to worksheet cells, respecting the data types
when possible (so the numbers stay numbers and the dates stay dates).

Q What is the advantage of a shortcut over a link?

A If you are sticking with Office 2000 products only, you probably want to use links to embed live connections from one document to another. If you share Office 2000 documents with other programs, however, those programs probably recognize shortcuts and present your Office 2000 document as an icon. If you use a stand-alone email program (such as Eudora) to send a Word 2000 document, for example, the Word 2000 document appears in your email note as a Word 2000 icon. If you double-click that icon (or if your email recipient double-clicks the icon after receiving the email), Word 2000 starts (assuming Word 2000 resides on the system), and you (or the recipient) are able to edit the document.

Q Why would you ever want to copy data and not create a link to another document?

A When you copy data, it is copied into the destination document, so the data resides in both the destination document and the source document. If you were to take the destination document to another computer, the document could not access its original link (if you had used a link). In addition, you may not want the destination document's data being hooked "live" to the source data. If you are creating archive files of older data, for example, you want always to copy the data and not form a link or shortcut to the original source data.

Q Why would you not import a complete database into Word 2000?

A A complete database contains tables, queries, reports, forms, macros, and modules, and all those items make little sense in a Word 2000 document. If you need to report data using the entire Access 2000 database, use Access 2000 to generate reports. Word 2000 is useful for printing database subsets. If you want to include part of an Access 2000 database table in a Word 2000 report, you can easily send the table's data into Word 2000 using the tools described in this lesson.

Q What is the difference between AutoShape, WordArt, and OfficeArt?

A *AutoShape* is the general term applied to all the drawing tools provided when you insert an AutoShape picture into an Office 2000 document. The AutoShapes toolbar appears when you draw AutoShape graphics to help you with freeform drawings and to supply common shapes that you might need. *WordArt* is a system that manipulates and colors text to turn standard text into various eye-catching 3D colorful styles. The term *OfficeArt* is a general term applied to all the graphics and drawing tools you find in the Office 2000 suite of products, including AutoShape and WordArt.

Q What is the difference between an adjustment handle and a resizing handle?

A Adjustment handles change the form of shapes; resizing handles change the size of shapes.

21

Hour **22**

Office 2000 and the Internet

If you are new to Internet technology, this hour introduces you to a whole new world. The Internet is much more a part of computer users' lives than ever before. Microsoft recognizes this and includes Internet access capabilities in Office 2000. The individual Office 2000 products include Internet connections, and Office 2000 also includes Internet Explorer 5, an Internet browser that enables you to access the Internet from within Windows. Microsoft is committed to integrating Internet access more completely into future Office and Windows releases, and you see that commitment already in Office 2000.

If you have used the Internet before, you may want to skim this hour to see how the Office 2000 products and Internet Explorer 5 connect you to the Internet.

The highlights of this hour include the following:

- Why the Internet and the Web are so important
- How to start and use Internet Explorer

- How to surf the Internet to find and view multimedia information
- How to use search engines to locate the exact Internet information you need
- How to access the Internet from within an Office 2000 product
- How to view Office 2000 documents from within Internet Explorer
- How to include Web links in your Office documents

Introducing the Internet

The *Internet* began as a government- and university-linked system of computers that has since turned into a business and personal system that contains a seemingly infinite amount of information. The Internet is a worldwide system of interconnected computers. Whereas your desktop computer is a standalone machine, and a network of computers is linked together by wires, the Internet is a worldwide online network of computers connected to standalone computers through modems.

 The *Internet* is a worldwide network connection of computers that provides information and offers electronic mail services to the users who access the Internet from their own computers.

The Internet offers the most unique research and information-access tools ever invented. You can get up-to-date news, stock quotes, and sports scores. You can locate product information, purchase everything from cars to airline tickets, play games, listen to music, view videos, and chat with other Internet users around the world via your keyboard or microphone.

That vast amount and format of Internet data requires a standard so that all may share in the Internet's content. Users all over the world send electronic mail to each other, view each other's Internet material, send files back and forth, conduct business over the Internet, research from the Internet, keep up with the latest news, sports, entertainment, and business headlines, and chat with each other through the keyboard, voice, and video.

Introducing the Web

The *Web*, or *World Wide Web (WWW)*, is a collection of Internet pages of information. Web pages can contain text, graphics, sound, and video. Figure 22.1 shows a sample Web page. As you can see, the Web page's graphics and text organize information into a magazine-like readable and appealing format.

FIGURE 22.1.

Web pages provide Internet information in a standard format.

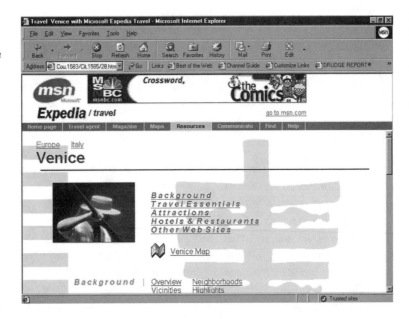

NEW TERM The term *Web*, or *World Wide Web (WWW)*, is given to the interconnected system of Internet information pages that you can access to read specific information. Many of the Web pages are connected with hypertext links that enable you to more easily traverse the pages that you view.

Generally, a Web site might contain more information than fits easily on a single Web page. Therefore, many Web pages contain links to several additional extended pages, as well as other linked Web pages that may be related to the original topic. The first page you view is called the home page, and from the home page you can view other pages of information.

The Internet has standardized Web page locations with a series of addresses called *URLs*, or *Uniform Resource Locators*, that are formatted like this: http://www.microsoft.com. You can view any Web page if you know its URL. If you do not know the URL, the Internet provides several search engines that find Web pages when you search for topics. You learn how to search the Internet later this hour in the "Searching for the Information You Need" section.

Using Internet Explorer

Internet Explorer is a *Web browser* (also called a *browser*) that brings Web data to your desktop. Microsoft's Web browsing program, Internet Explorer 5, comes with every version of Office 2000. Therefore, you already have the tools you need to access the Internet if you have Office 2000.

NEW TERM   A *Web browser*, or *browser*, is a program you use to access the Internet and display Web data.

If your company offers cabled Internet access, you need the interface card in your PC that can accept the cable. If you use the Internet from home, or from an office that does not provide cabled Internet access, you need to get Internet access through an *ISP*, an *Internet service provider*. One of the easiest ways to get access is through the Microsoft Network or America Online services, which have access programs that are available with all Windows 95 and Windows 98 installations. If you want Internet access through another ISP, such as a local Internet provider, your provider will tell you how to use Internet Explorer or another Web browser to access the ISP's Internet system. You will also need modem access (28.8Kbps is the minimum recommended speed these days) or another Internet connection that might be available in your area such as a cable modem, ISDN, or satellite access. Check your phone book for options that you can get locally.

NEW TERM   An *Internet service provider*, or *ISP*, is a company that provides you with a phone number that you can command Internet Explorer to dial for Internet access.

    Although Internet service is relatively inexpensive, it is not free. Most ISPs charge a flat rate, such as $19.95 a month, for unlimited Internet usage.

Starting Internet Explorer

Internet Explorer is easy to start. You literally can access the Internet with one or two clicks by running Internet Explorer. After you sign up with an ISP and get the Internet phone number to access the Web, you are ready to navigate the Internet.

To start Internet Explorer, double-click the Windows desktop icon labeled Internet Explorer. If you get an Internet Connection Wizard dialog box, you must contact your service provider to learn how to hook up Internet Explorer to the Internet. Internet Explorer prompts you for the username and password that you selected when you signed up for your Internet service.

22

Assuming that you have Internet access and have been set up with a provider, Internet Explorer dials your provider and displays the page set up to be your initial browser's *home page*. If you have high-speed, constant access, through a company connection or through cable modem service, you may not have to log on to the Internet to use it. Depending on the amount of information and graphics on the page, the display may take a few moments or may display right away.

NEW TERM — A *home page*, also called a *start page*, is the page you have requested Internet Explorer to show first when you sign on to the Internet.

The Home button on the Internet Explorer toolbar displays your home page. You can return to the home page by clicking the Home button. You can change your home page address by entering a new home page address within the Tools, Internet Options dialog box's General Tab. When you enter a new home page address, Internet Explorer returns to that page whenever you click the Home toolbar button or start Internet Explorer in a subsequent session.

Managing the Internet Explorer Screen

You can navigate Internet pages easily with Internet Explorer. If you are new to the Internet, study Figure 22.2 to learn the parts of the Internet Explorer screen. Internet Explorer displays your home page and lists the home page's address in the address area.

FIGURE 22.2.

Learn the Internet Explorer screen so that you can maximize the Internet Explorer browser.

Keeps track of favorite sites   Starts your email program

Returns you to previous Web page

Web page address

Web page viewing area

Hyperlinks to other sites

Use the following guidelines to familiarize yourself with the Internet Explorer screen:

- Some Web site addresses are lengthy. Drag the Address bar left or right (giving more or less room to the link buttons) to adjust the address display width.

- Click the down arrow at the right of the address entry to open a list of recently traversed site addresses. If this is the first time you or anyone has used your computer's Internet Explorer, you may not see sites other than the current home page sites.

- Use the scrollbar to see more of your home page. Most Web pages take more room than fit on one screen.

- Use the View menu to hide the toolbar and status bar so that you have more display room for the Web page. The Address list box can be hidden as well. You can still enter site addresses that you want to traverse from the File menu.

- Display the toolbar and status bar again by clicking the appropriate View menu options.

You will probably spend a lot of time on the Internet, so the better you understand Internet Explorer the more effective you will be online.

Surfing the Internet

Remember that the Internet's Web is a collection of interconnected Web pages. As you *surf* the Internet using Internet Explorer, you run across Web pages that contain *links* to other sites. These links (often called *hot spots* or *hypertext links*) may be underlined, appear in different colors from the surrounding text, or even be activated by clicking on an image or imagemap. After you click a link on a Web page, if you return to that Web page, the link appears in a different color to let you know that you have already gone there. You can locate these links by moving your mouse cursor over the underlined description. If the mouse cursor changes to a hand, you can click the hand to move to that page. After a brief pause, your Web browser displays the page.

NEW TERM To *surf* the Internet means to navigate the Internet by viewing Web pages that interest you.

NEW TERM A *link*, *hyperlink*, or *hot spot*, is nothing more than a URL to another Web site embedded on a Web page. The link often displays a description and not a technical URL. (As you move your mouse cursor over a link, your Web browser's status bar displays the actual URL to the link.) Therefore, you can traverse related Web pages without worrying about addresses; just click link descriptions to move to those sites.

22

Suppose that you view the home page of your financial broker to update an Excel 2000 investment worksheet that contains your stock portfolio. The page might include links to other related pages, such as stock quotation pages, company financial informational pages, and order-entry pages in which you can enter your own stock purchase requests.

One of the most useful features of Internet Explorer and every other Web browser is the browser's capability to return to sites you have visited both in the current session and in former sessions. The toolbar's Back button takes you back to a site you just visited, and you can keep clicking the Back button to return to pages you have visited in the current session. The Forward toolbar button returns you to pages from where you have backed up. Because this back-and-forth feature is so popular with Web browsers, Microsoft chose to add the Back and Forward buttons to all Windows 98 windows.

At any point, you can click the Address drop-down list box to see a list of URLs you have visited. You find addresses from the current as well as previous Internet Explorer Web sessions.

If you know the address of a Web site that you want to view, you can type the site's address directly in the Address text box and click Go. Internet Explorer takes you to that site and displays its Web page. In addition, you can select File, Open to display an Open dialog box in which you can enter an address. When you click OK, Internet Explorer displays the page associated with that address.

If you find a location you really like, save that location in Internet Explorer's Favorites list. If you run across a site that discusses your favorite television show and you want to return to that site again quickly, for example, click the Favorites toolbar button to add the site to your Favorites list. The Address history does not keep track of a lot of recently visited addresses; you can store your favorite sites in the Favorites folders, however, so that you can quickly access them during future Internet sessions.

As you familiarize yourself with the Internet, you will want to visit Web pages that interest you. After you visit a site, you can easily return to that site. Use the following steps to become comfortable surfing Web pages:

1. If you have not started Internet Explorer, start it and log on to the Internet.

2. Click the Address list box to select the URL of your home page.

3. Type the following Web page address: **www.mcp.com**. You see Macmillan Computer Publishing's home page appear, as shown in Figure 22.3. (Depending on the changes that have been made to the site recently, the site may not match Figure 22.3 exactly.)

FIGURE 22.3.

Practice surfing the Web to Macmillan Computer Publishing's home page.

Often, you see Web addresses prefaced with the text `http://`. This prefix indicates both for you and your browser that the address to the right of the second slash is a Web page's URL. This prefix is optional for today's Web browsers. If you type the prefix, be sure to type forward slashes and not the MS-DOS or Windows backslashes you may be used to typing for PC folder locations.

4. Click any link on the page. After a brief pause, you see the linked Web page.

5. Click the toolbar's Back button. Almost instantly, the first page appears.

6. After you are back at Macmillan Computer Publishing's home page, practice building a favorite site list by clicking the Favorites toolbar button.

7. Click the Add to Favorites option. Internet Explorer displays the Add to Favorites dialog box.

8. Enter a description for the page. Make the description something by which you can remember the page (such as **Macmillan Computer Publishing**).

9. Click OK.

10. Click the Favorites toolbar button again. You see the new entry. When you select the favorite entry, Internet Explorer looks up that entry's stored URL address and goes to that Web page.

If you add too many favorites, your favorites list might become unmanageable. As you add to your favorites list, you can create folders using the Create In button in the Add to Favorites dialog box. By setting up a series of folders named by subjects, you can group your favorite Web sites by subject so that they are easier to manage and find.

Some Web pages take a long time to display. Often, Web pages contain a lot of text and graphics, and that data takes time to arrive on your computer. Therefore, you might click to a favorite Web site but have to wait a minute or longer to see the entire site.

To speed things, Internet Explorer attempts to show as much of the page as possible, especially the text on the page, before downloading the graphic images. Internet Explorer puts placeholders where the graphic images are to appear. If you view the page for a few moments, the placeholders' images begin to appear until the final page, with all graphics, displays in its entirety.

Searching for the Information You Need

How can you expect to find any information on a vast network of networks such as the Internet? Web pages offer linked sites in an appealing format that enable you to comfortably view information and see related pages, but you must know the location of one of the site's pages before the links can help.

Fortunately, Internet Explorer offers a searching mechanism that helps you locate information on the Web. By clicking the Search toolbar button, you can access a search page, such as the one shown in Figure 22.4. As you can see, the search page consumes the left pane of your Internet screen. You can still see the Web page you were viewing while you perform a search. The resulting search page that you find will appear in the right pane when you make the search. You can easily return the browser to a single-pane Web view by clicking the × in the upper-right hand corner of the Search pane.

The Internet Explorer 5 search page offers the benefit of multiple search engines. The accuracy of the search depends on the words and phrases you enter, as well as the capability of the search engine. Some search engines you can choose from search only Web pages, for example, while others search *newsgroups*. To search with a different search engine, click the search pane's Customize toolbar button. The right pane displays a list of search engines that you can use for subsequent searching.

FIGURE 22.4.

Locate data on the Web.

Click to change search engine

Type search phrase here

NEW TERM A *search engine* is a Web program that enables you to enter words and phrases for which to search, and then scans the vast information on the Web to locate sites that contain the words or phrase.

NEW TERM *Newsgroups* are Internet discussion areas that hold files and messages related to topics. You can read messages and download files as well as post your own messages and files for others to see. Outlook Express, a program that comes with Internet Explorer 5, enables you to read newsgroups.

After the search engine locates its information, Internet Explorer displays from zero to several address links in the left pane that you can click to find specific Web-based information about your topic. (Figure 22.5 shows the result of one search.) By scrolling down the page (and by clicking the additional pages of links if your search turns up a lot of sites), you can read the descriptions of the pages. The descriptions often contain the first few lines of the located Web page text.

Each search engine locates information differently and each also has its own rules for the words and phrases you enter. Keep in mind that the more specific your search phrase is, the more accurately the search engine can find information that helps you.

FIGURE 22.5.

The results of a search might produce several pages of Web sites.

22

Search phrase —

List of found topics —

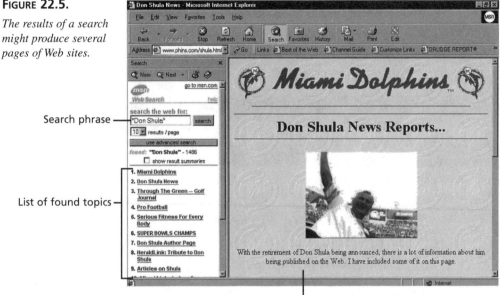

Result of clicking a topic

Generally, you can use these guidelines with most search engines:

- Enclose a multiple word phrase in quotation marks if you want the search engine to search for those words in the order in which they are listed. If you enter **West Virginia**, for example, the search engine searches for that specific name. If you enter **West Virginia** (without the quotation marks), however, most search engines locate every site that contains the word *West* and every site that contains the word *Virginia*, most of which would have nothing to do with the state you originally wanted to locate.

- Place a plus sign (+) before each word for which you want to search. Entering **+Tulsa +oil** would find only those sites that contain both the word *Tulsa* and the word *oil*.

Remember that these search criteria rules are only guidelines that usually work well with the most popular search engines. Some of the search engines follow slightly different rules, and you have to look up that search engine page's help references for specific information if the previous rules do not seem to work the way you expect.

Office 2000 Products and the Web

Office 2000 offers a complete set of tools that integrate the Office 2000 products and the Internet. From any Office 2000 product you can access files and Web pages on the Internet. The following sections describe how you can access the Web from Office 2000.

Viewing Web Pages Within Office Products

You don't have to start Internet Explorer to view a Web page from within an Office 2000 product. All you need to do is display the Web toolbar and type the address you want to see. While creating an Excel worksheet, for example, you may need to locate financial information from your company's Web site. Follow these steps to surf the Web from Excel:

1. Select View, Toolbars, Web to add a new Web-browsing toolbar to Excel.

2. Click the address area of the Web toolbar.

3. Enter the Web address that you want to see. (Alternatively, you can click the Favorites list on the Web toolbar to select the Web page that you want to view.) If you access the Internet from a modem, Excel dials your Internet Service Provider to get Internet access.

4. Excel's menus and toolbars change to match that of Internet Explorer and displays the Web site that you want to view. You can switch between the Web and Excel by pressing Alt+Tab. In addition, you can copy and paste information from Web pages to your Excel worksheet.

Viewing Documents in Internet Explorer

In addition to starting Internet Explorer from an Office 2000 product, you can view Office 2000 documents directly from within Internet Explorer. Whenever you are browsing the Internet, select File, Open and type the full path (or click Browse to locate the path) and filename you want to view from within Internet Explorer.

Internet Explorer opens the file and displays the file within the browser window. Not only does Internet Explorer display the file, but all Internet Explorer menus change to enable full editing capabilities for that Office 2000 document. If you open a Word 2000 document, for example, Internet Explorer menus change to Word 2000 menus; you can then insert a table or format the text as if you were using Word 2000. If you click the Internet Explorer Tools toolbar button while viewing the Office 2000 document, the Word 2000 toolbars appear beneath the Internet Explorer toolbar so that you have full Word 2000 toolbar capabilities from within Internet Explorer.

If you click the Back button, Internet Explorer displays the preceding Web page or whatever else you were viewing from Internet Explorer, and the menus change so that you can surf the Web normally.

> You might wonder why Excel 2000 seems to become Internet Explorer. Since Web pages do not actually appear inside the Excel 2000 worksheet window, it might seem like an anomaly. But when you use the Web toolbar to request the Web page, there it is. Excel 2000 cannot access the Web; for that, you need a Web browser. Nevertheless, the Web toolbar that you find in all the Office 2000 products does enable you to navigate between Office 2000 documents without changing programs, as you learn toward the end of this hour.
>
> Perhaps someday, the only program you will need is a Web browser! The browser menus and toolbars can change depending on the document with which you want to work. Internet Explorer 5 integrates with Windows itself so that the browser becomes part of your Windows environment. The Internet is so important to computing today that companies such as Microsoft are incorporating Web technology into all products as well as operating systems.

Creating Links in Office 2000

As you learned how to use Office 2000 products throughout the previous hours, you learned that you can type a Web address in an Office 2000 document to create a link to that address. When you type a Web address in a PowerPoint 2000 presentation, for example, that address becomes a link to an active Web site address. If you click that address, the Office 2000 product starts Internet Explorer, logs you on to the Internet if needed, and displays the Web page located at that address.

> You don't have to use Web addresses for hyperlinks in Office 2000 documents. You can enter path and filenames that reside on your own PC. When you or another user clicks the link, the Office 2000 product displays that link's file. Therefore, you can easily link documents together, even documents from different products within Office 2000.

Upgrading to Internet Explorer 5

Like most Office 2000 users, you probably had Internet Explorer 4 already installed on your PC. When you installed Office 2000, the installation routine offered to install Internet Explorer 5. To take advantage of all of Office 2000's Web-related features, and to use Internet Explorer's latest and greatest operations, you should upgrade to version 5. If you chose not to upgrade but stayed with version 4, you can still use most features in Office 2000. Unless you upgraded to 5, however, some of the remaining portions of this lesson will be different for you and your screens may not match exactly to the book's figures.

Use Internet Explorer 5 More Effectively

Now that you have gotten a taste for what Internet Explorer 5 can do (in this and the past two lessons), you are ready to take the browser to the next step so that you can utilize Internet Explorer 5, along with Office 2000, at their fullest potential.

Managing Favorites

You will add to your Favorites list as you find more Web sites that interest you. By adding Web sites that you visit frequently to your Favorites list, you receive these advantages:

- You can quickly return to these sites as you surf the Web, by clicking the Internet Explorer 5 Favorites button and selecting from the list.

- You can return to these sites even if you are not surfing the Web in Internet Explorer from one of the Office 2000 applications' Web toolbar or from the Start menu's Favorites option.

- You can manage your favorites list to keep your favorite sites organized for fast access and review.

To add a site to your Favorites list, select Favorites, Add to Favorites to display the Add Favorite dialog box shown in Figure 22.6. To add the current site to the Favorites list, you only need to click OK and Internet Explorer 5 adds the site to your list. You will almost certainly want to add your own name for the site (the default name is the site's title provided by the site authors) and store the site in a folder that exists or that you create to organize your favorite sites by subject. You might want to store a movie review site in a folder named Entertainment, for example.

FIGURE 22.6.

You can easily add and organize your Favorites list.

 When you click the Favorites button on the toolbar, a left pane opens with your Favorites list displayed. If you click the X in the Favorites list area, the Favorites list goes away, giving you more room to view the Web page content.

In addition to your Favorites list that you maintain, Internet Explorer 5 keeps track of your recently visited Web site addresses. If you click the History button on your toolbar, Internet Explorer 5 adds a History list in a left pane (where the Favorites list resided) so that you can select from a list of Web site addresses you have visited in the past few days.

Keeping Links

If you want your most important Web sites located even closer than the Favorites list, add the site to your Links bar. At the top of Internet Explorer, as well as on your Windows taskbar if you choose to display the Links toolbar, resides a series of links to Web sites. As Figure 22.7 shows, your links are always on your screen ready for your click to jump to that site.

To remove or change a link, right-click over the link and select the appropriate menu item from the pop-up menu. To add a link, drag its Web site icon from the Internet Explorer 5 Address text box to the Links bar. You can rearrange links by dragging them to a different location. To see the links that don't fit on the Links bar, click the arrow at the far-right of the Links bar.

FIGURE 22.7.

Your links are ready for one-click access.

Links

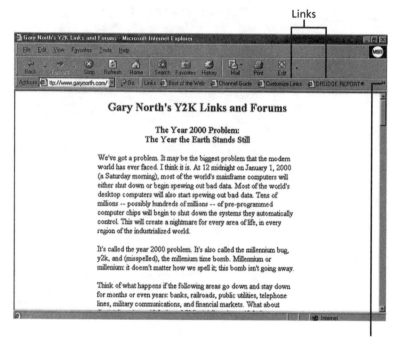

Click here to see more links

Internet Explorer 5 helps improve the way that you view Web pages with graphics. Some Web pages take several seconds, and possibly longer, to display. Although the text appears right away, the graphics take some time to load. Internet Explorer 5 puts a status bar at the bottom of the browser so that you know how much (by percentage) of the current page is loaded and how much is left. If you don't want to wait on a long load, you can load another page.

Using Shortcut Keys

Internet Explorer 5 supports these two shortcut keys that will save you time:

- *F4.* Opens the Web address's drop-down list box so that you can quickly jump to a site you have visited recently.
- *F5.* Places the text cursor in the Web address list box so you can type a Web address to display.

If a Web address meets this common format: `http://www.`*SiteAddress*`.com`, all you need to type is ***SiteAddress*** and Internet Explorer searches for the correct site using the fully formatted Web site address.

As Internet Explorer searches and locates Web sites, Internet Explorer produces sounds. A bell rings when a Web page you search for appears in the browser window, for example. The sounds are helpful when you work in multiple open program windows simultaneously. You can enter a Web address and press Alt+Tab to switch to Word 2000 and type more of a letter. When Internet Explorer locates and begins to display that site, you will hear the bell ring and know that it is time to return to Internet Explorer to view the Web page.

One final tip can provide multiple Web pages from one browser. Suppose you are viewing a Web page with links to another page. You want to read both pages, perhaps to compare notes in resized windows. You can open a second Internet Explorer browser window by right-clicking over the hyperlink and selecting Open in New Window from the pop-up menu that appears. A second Web browser window opens with that linked Web site there, but your original browser window will still be open displaying the Web site you started from. By judiciously opening new Web sites in additional windows, you can view several Web pages at the same time without having to browse between them each time you go back to one.

Summary

This hour introduced you to the Internet, the Web, Internet Explorer, and how Office 2000 and the Internet work together. The Internet is a vast collection of networked computers all around the world. You can access the Internet as long as you have access through an Internet service provider. Although Internet information appears in many forms, the most useful Internet information often appears on Web pages that contain text, graphics, sound, and video.

Internet Explorer includes searching tools as well as a history system that keeps track of recent Web pages. Not only can you view Web pages with Internet Explorer, but you can also view other kinds of files on your computer. As the Internet becomes more organized and Internet access gets faster and cheaper, the Web browser will become part of your daily computing routine. One day, you will find that you do most of your work from Web browsing software such as Internet Explorer.

The next hour continues the Internet discussion by explaining how to create Web pages from within the Office 2000 products.

Q&A

Q **I have clicked the Internet Explorer icon, but I don't see Web pages. What do I have to do to get on the Internet?**

A Do you have Internet access from Microsoft Network or from another Internet service provider? Generally, unless you work for a company that offers Internet access to its employees, you have to sign up for Internet access, get the access phone number, pay a monthly fee (most Internet service providers offer unlimited access for a flat monthly rate), and set up a browser, such as Internet Explorer, to access that provider.

Q **Does all Internet information appear on Web pages?**

A The Internet's information appears in many forms, sometimes in a form known as an FTP site or a newsgroup. The Web page standard, however, has become one of the most popular ways to organize and view Internet information. As more people used the Web-page standard, more modern technology enabled that standard to evolve into a uniform container of multimedia-based information. Therefore, with a Web browser, you can view all kinds of information over the Web.

HOUR 23

Creating Web Pages with Office 2000

You don't just have to be a user of Web pages. You can create them yourself with the tools available in Office 2000. By utilizing the Office 2000 wizards and design tools, you can quickly create Web pages that equal those from the pros. With Office 2000 you can hone text, graphics, and data tables and present that data to the world on the Web.

Most Office 2000 users use Word 2000 as their primary Web page development tool and import other Office 2000 product data into their Word 2000 Web pages. All the Office 2000 products are Internet-aware; they all enable you to convert their data to Web pages.

The highlights of this hour include the following:

- What you need to publish pages on the Internet
- How to save Word 2000 documents as Web pages
- When to use the various Office 2000 wizards to generate your initial Web pages

- How to export Excel 2000 and Access 2000 data to your Word 2000-based Web pages
- Why you should limit the amount of Access 2000 information that goes into your Web page
- How to save individual Access 2000 objects in a Data Access Page
- How to modify the way a PowerPoint 2000 presentation looks and behaves on the Internet

Preparing to Publish Web Pages

Before you can publish pages on the Web, you must have access to a *Web server*. Perhaps your company uses a Web server for its site; if so, you can store your Web pages on that computer. If you have access to an online service, such as CompuServe, it may offer an area for one or more Web pages that you can copy to the online site's Web server free or for a small charge.

NEW TERM   A *Web server* is a computer dedicated to presenting Web pages on the Internet.

If you want to publish a personal Web page for fun, you will enjoy telling the world your stories and sharing your family photos with others. If you want to start a business on the Internet, however, or offer timely information that you want others to visit often, you need to be aware that Web page *maintenance* is costly and time-consuming. You don't just create a Web page, load the page on the Web, and expect to keep people's interest if you don't keep the material up to date. In addition, performing *e-commerce* often requires the help of an outside agency such as a bank or credit card service so you may want to get help when you first go online with your organization.

NEW TERM   *Maintenance* is the process of modifying and updating Web page information.

NEW TERM   *E-commerce*, or *electronic commerce*, is business conducted over the Internet and includes transactions such as online banking and buying and selling transactions using credit cards.

Office 2000 and the Web

One of the reasons you should consider using Office 2000 to create Web pages is that you already have the Office 2000 tools. Office 2000 offers several wizards and templates that you can use to create your Web pages. Nevertheless, Office 2000 is not necessarily the best tool you can use to create Web pages. Office 2000 offers good tools with which you can create and maintain a Web page. If your Web page generates a lot of interest, however, you may want to use a more specific tool for Web page creation such as Microsoft FrontPage 2000 and Internet Explorer. FrontPage 2000 is to Web pages what Access 2000 is to databases; FrontPage 2000 offers specific Web page tools that create advanced Web pages with very little effort on your part. Hour 24, "Introducing FrontPage 2000," explains more about FrontPage 2000.

All the Web material in Office 2000 supports both the Internet and *intranets*. Therefore, if your company maintains an intranet, you can save Web pages to that intranet as easily (and sometimes more easily) as on the Internet.

NEW TERM An *intranet* is a local area network of computers whose users use Web pages and Internet technology to communicate with each other on the network. Instead of dialing up an Internet service provider and accessing a Web page from another location, you just access a Web page from a co-worker's PC.

Each of the following sections describe how you can use Word 2000, Excel 2000, PowerPoint 2000, and Access 2000 to generate Web-page information. If you connect to your Web server with a networked PC, you can offer live content on the Internet. In other words, as soon as you update your database, viewers of your Web site who access that database see the updated values. Once you see how these individual Office 2000 products support Web pages, you will be ready to learn more about FrontPage 2000 in the next chapter.

Most of your early Web page creations will probably take place in Word 2000 until you master a more full-featured Web-page creation program such as FrontPage 2000. Even if you embed an Access database on a Web page, you will probably do most of that Web page design in Word 2000. Therefore, most of this hour focuses on Word 2000's Web-editing tools. The final sections describe how to integrate the other Office 2000 products into your Word 2000 Web pages.

Word 2000 and Web Pages

Word 2000 offers two ways to create Web pages: You can save Word 2000 documents in a Web page format, or you can create a Web page using one of the Word 2000 wizards. The following two sections explain each method.

Saving Word 2000 Documents as Web Pages

One of the easiest ways to create a Web page from a Word 2000 document is to save the document in an *HTML format*. Suppose you create a company report that you want to publish on your Web server. All you have to do is select File, Save as Web page, and then click OK. Word 2000 then saves the file in an *HTML* Web page-compatible format that you then can transfer to the Web server.

 HTML, or *Hypertext Markup Language*, is the name of the language format used by Web pages. HTML pages contain formatting codes that define how the page looks from within a Web browser such as Internet Explorer or Netscape's Navigator.

After Word 2000 converts your document to HTML format, you can view your document from the Internet Explorer Web browser by selecting File, Web Page Preview. By viewing the document from the Web browser, you see how your Web page will appear to other Internet users. Notice that the format differs somewhat from the format of the Word 2000 document (especially italicized fonts).

When working with an HTML document in Word 2000, Word 2000 changes its toolbars to provide better tools for Web page editing. You can also choose to display the Web toolbar from the View menu. When formatting your Web page, keep your end user in mind and write for the largest audience possible. You can select a fancy font for your Web page text. If you stick with the standard fonts that come with Windows (such as Courier, Times New Roman, and Arial), however, you ensure that all viewers of your Web page will have those same fonts and the page will look the way you intend for it to look on their browsers.

Keep in mind that Web pages are often colorful. Color fonts can spruce up a Web page dramatically as long as you don't overdo the colors. Use the toolbar's Font Color button to select a new font color quickly.

 If you have written HTML code before, you can embed HTML commands in your Web page from within Word 2000. Format your HTML code with the HTML Markup style and Word 2000 embeds it as HTML code. The code does not appear on the Web page, but formats the page according to your instructions. All HTML markup text is hidden, but you can display the text by clicking the Show/Hide button on the Word 2000 toolbar. Actually, Word 2000 converts your Web page elements to HTML code as soon as you add something to a Web page. You can, at any time during the development of your Web page, select View, HTML Source to see the HTML code behind your Web page. Word 2000 starts a new environment known as the

Microsoft Development environment. Figure 23.1 shows HTML code for a
Web page being displayed for editing inside this Microsoft Development
environment. Inside the Microsoft Development environment, you can
return to the formatted Web page by selecting File, HTML. Although the
Microsoft Development environment's features are beyond the scope of this
book because they require skills the average newcomer to Office 2000 need
not master, the Microsoft Development environment provides a platform
from which you can develop and manage your own Web pages.

23

 The *Microsoft Development environment* is a program that enables users to manage HTML code from Web pages.

FIGURE 23.1.

*You can view the
HTML code for your
Web page.*

Using the Web Page Wizard

When you create a new document by selecting File, New, Word 2000 offers a dialog box
with a series of wizards and templates. If you click the Web Pages tab, you find Web
options such as the following:

- *Column with Contents.* A Web page designed for informational purposes with topics at the left and hyperlinked details from those topics in the right pane.

- *Frequently Asked Questions.* A Web page designed to ask a series of questions at
  the top of the page and include hyperlinked answers to those questions for the
  remaining portion of the page.

- *Left-Aligned Column.* As you can see from Figure 23.2's sample from the resulting template option, the left-aligned column includes a figure in the page's left pane and information flowing down the right pane. As with all the samples from the Web Page Wizard and templates, you can easily replace the figure and placeholder text in this sample.

FIGURE 23.2.

Word 2000 produces a clean sample you can work from.

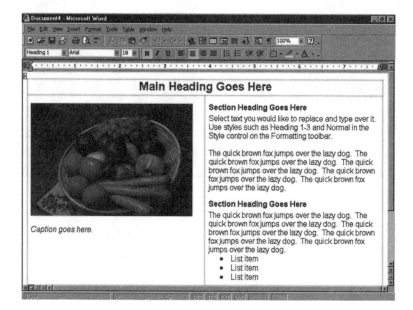

- *Personal Web Page.* A Web page that is simple and laid out well for personal, nonbusiness informational home pages that a family might use to provide news to other family members who live elsewhere.

- *Right-Aligned Column.* A Web page that is the mirror-image of the left-aligned column page with the figure in the page's right pane and information flowing down the left pane.

- *Simple Layout.* A Web page with its information down the middle column of the page.

- *Table of Contents.* A Web page with a table of contents section flowing down its middle.

- *Web Page Wizard.* The step-by-step wizard that creates a Web page according to your specifications.

The easiest way to create a Web page according to your specifications is to start the Web Page Wizard. (Figure 23.3 shows the opening screen.)

FIGURE 23.3.

Word 2000 builds a Web page as you respond to the wizard.

23

 Microsoft's Web site at www.microsoft.com includes several additional Web-specific Word 2000 templates that you can download.

As you follow the wizard, you see the underlying Word 2000 Web page take shape. The wizard prompts you for the style of the Web page. As you can see from the personal Web page outline built for Figure 23.4 by the Web Page Wizard, the pages can be fun.

FIGURE 23.4.

The Web Page Wizard generates many varieties of Web page styles.

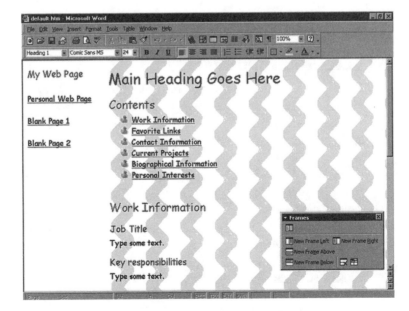

After the wizard does its job, you can edit the Web page and change the general text to the specific text you want on the page. As you edit, check out the Web tools toolbar that you can add from the View, Toolbars option as well as the Insert menu; when working with a Web page in Word 2000, the Insert menu and Web tools toolbar include several items you can insert in your Web page, including pictures, videos, text boxes, background sounds, scrolling text, and hyperlinks.

> If you want to add callout graphics to your Web page, Word 2000 offers all the drawing tools you learned about in Hour 21, "Office 2000's Synergy," including the AutoShape tools.

Now that you have seen how to use Word 2000 to create Web pages, you already know a lot about how the other Office 2000 products create Web pages. Many of the Web page features in the other Office 2000 products work the same way as in Word 2000. You can save an Excel 2000 worksheet as a Web page, for example. When saving Office 2000 documents as Web pages, most of the formatting and editing features you get with the products' native formats remain. In other words, an Excel 2000 worksheet that you save as a Web page contains all the same elements that the worksheet contains when you save that worksheet as an Excel 2000 file with the normal worksheet extension, .XLS. Revision markings do not appear in Web pages, but all other Office 2000 document elements do appear in the Web page.

The remaining sections build on your knowledge of using Word 2000 and the Web by showing you how Excel 2000, PowerPoint 2000, and Access 2000 also support the Web.

Excel 2000 and Web Pages

Excel 2000 supports most of the same Web features that Word 2000 does, including the capability to save worksheets in the HTML format. After you create the worksheet, select File, Save as Web page to save the worksheet in a format readable to any browser. In addition to the Web-based HTML format, Excel 2000 also supports the Web toolbar that you can display by selecting View, Toolbars, Web. From that toolbar, you can select other Office 2000 documents to display and edit from within Excel 2000 as well as enter an Internet Web site address to view. Because Office 2000 products all support the Web toolbar, and because you can display any document from Internet Explorer 5.0 (the browser engine used by all Office 2000 products when you work with Web-based objects and pages), all Office 2000 products enable you to view any of the other Office 2000 products' documents or any Web page just by typing that document or Web page address in the address text box of the Web toolbar.

If your company stores worksheets on the Internet or on an intranet, the File, Open option in Excel 2000 can open those worksheets. When you select File, Open and then enter the URL and filename, such as `http://www.mycompany.org/accts.xls`, Excel 2000 opens that worksheet. (Excel 2000 offers you the Internet Log On dialog box if you are not already logged on to the Internet.)

If you type a hyperlink Web address or a hyperlink to another Office 2000 document in an Excel 2000 cell, Excel 2000 takes you to that document and displays the Web toolbar automatically (if the toolbar is not already displayed). When you click the Web toolbar's Back button, Excel 2000 takes you to the preceding Web page.

23

Rarely does a Web page contain just an Excel 2000 worksheet. Web pages contain other text and graphics; that's why you probably want to create the general Web page in Word 2000 using the Web Page Wizard and then import (using the Windows Clipboard or Insert menu) your Excel 2000 data into the Web page. If you insert a link to your Excel 2000 data instead of inserting a copy of the worksheet, your published Web page always contains "live" worksheet data that changes as you update the worksheet.

If you use an online service to publish your Web page and not a local Web server networked to your PC, you have to update the Web page manually each time you want to update the worksheet data.

Access 2000 and Web Pages

Access 2000 supports hyperlinks in its database forms, reports, and fields in datasheets. Access 2000 supports Word 2000, PowerPoint 2000, Excel 2000, as well as Internet or intranet hyperlinks. In addition to other documents, the hyperlink can point to other Access 2000 tables, forms, and reports.

One reason you might want to store hyperlinks in a database field is to store Web pages for vendors, competitors, and customers in tables. When you view forms that display the hyperlink to those tables, you can click the hyperlink to see the Web site.

Obviously, a hyperlink is not active when it appears in a printed report or onscreen in Preview mode. If you import the report into a Word 2000 document, Excel 2000 worksheet, or an HTML page, however, the hyperlink is active.

The Hyperlink data type is one of the Access 2000 data types that you can designate as you create your table (shown in Figure 23.5).

FIGURE 23.5.

Access 2000 offers the data type when you design your tables.

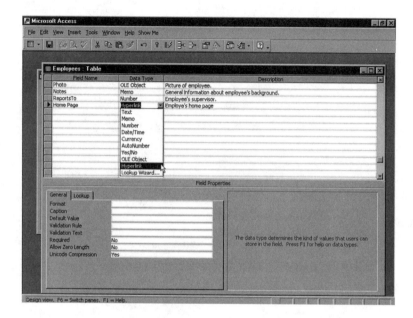

As you know, Access 2000 databases contain several objects, tables, forms, reports, and queries. A simple File, Save as Web page option cannot, without more information, determine exactly how you want to export the objects to the HTML document. You could use such an option for the other Office 2000 documents because they had fewer objects than an Access 2000 database. Therefore, to save a table or other object to its own Web page, select File, Save As and select *Data Access Page* for the type of file to save. Access 2000 stores the object as a Web page using the HTML format.

 A *Data Access Page*, new in Access 2000, is an HTML-based Web page bound directly to data in a database. These pages are like Access 2000 forms, except that Data Access Pages are to be navigated and edited over the Internet.

PowerPoint 2000 and Web Pages

When you save a PowerPoint 2000 presentation as a Web page, PowerPoint 2000 does not immediately save the file. Instead, it presents you with the Save As dialog box that contains a Publish button that, when you click the button, produces the dialog box shown in Figure 23.6. The dialog box determines how your presentation appears over the Internet when a remote site displays the presentation's Web page.

FIGURE 23.6.

The Publish as Web Page dialog box determines how your presentation will appear on the Internet.

23

Summary

This hour showed you how to use Office 2000 products to create Web pages. Word 2000 certainly offers the advantage in your initial Web page design, unless, of course, you want to put a PowerPoint 2000 presentation on the Web; in which case, the PowerPoint 2000 templates offer the best place to start your Web page design.

You can use Word 2000 as your primary Web page development tool and import other Office 2000 products as needed to add their elements to the Web page that you save from Word 2000. PowerPoint 2000 offers a unique Web page design wizard that designs Web-based presentations with the same look and feel as other Web pages.

Now that you have concluded your preliminary introduction to combining Office 2000 products and the Internet, you are ready to hone your Internet Explorer 5.0 skills in the next lesson so that you use the Internet more efficiently.

Q&A

Q Can I use my Windows 95 or Windows 98 PC as a Web server?

A You can, but you probably don't want to tie up your PC by using it as a Web server. Windows NT-based computers are better equipped to be Web servers. If you want to try, however, Windows 98 contains a special program you can install called Personal Web Server. This program provides the tools needed for your PC to operate as a Web server. If you use a slow PC and if you use a dial-up Internet connection, your PC offers slow Web page viewing. Therefore, no matter how effective your Web page content is and no matter how well you used the Office 2000 tools to develop an attention-getting Web page display, your Windows 98-based Web server is probably too slow to keep your viewers' interest.

Q Can I include Excel 2000 graphs on my Web pages?

A Certainly. You can copy the graph to your Windows Clipboard, and then paste the graph directly into your Word 2000 or PowerPoint 2000-based Web page. An Excel 2000 graph is no different from any other kind of data that you can copy and paste into a Web page from any of the Office 2000 products.

Windows supports *OLE (Object Linking and Embedding)* technology that enables you to insert virtually any object inside any other kind of document. If you want to insert an Excel 2000 graph or a video file with sound into a Web page, you can do so by using the Insert menu from the Office 2000 product's menu bar.

HOUR **24**

Introducing FrontPage 2000

Another new program called *FrontPage 2000* comes with Office 2000. With FrontPage 2000, you can create and edit your own Web pages as well as manage your entire Web site.

FrontPage 2000 works like a word processor and graphics controller for any Web pages you want to develop or edit. Not only can you create and edit your own Web pages, but you can edit Web pages of others that appear on the Internet (you won't be able to put the edited content back on another's Web site, however).

The highlights of this hour include the following:

- How FrontPage 2000 hides the job of HTML coding from your Web page designing job
- Where to store Web pages
- How to use FrontPage 2000's tools to edit Web pages

- When the FrontPage 2000 wizard can lessen your Web-page design workload
- What other products you can get to help you work with Web pages

Introduction to FrontPage 2000

FrontPage 2000 is a program that graphically enables you to edit Web pages. Behind all Web pages is the HTML language. HTML is a language that contains commands to format the text, graphics, video, sound, and applets that you place on your Web page. Listing 24.1 shows a partial HTML listing of a Web page. As you can see, the HTML language can get tricky.

LISTING 24.1. HTML COMMANDS CAN BE DIFFICULT TO DECIPHER.

```
<HTML>
<HEAD>
<META NAME="GENERATOR" Content="Microsoft Visual InterDev 1.0">
<META HTTP-EQUIV="Content-Type" content="text/html; charset=iso
-1">
<META http-equiv="PICS-Label" content='(PICS-1.1
"http://www.rsac.org/ratingsv01.html" l gen true comment
"RSACi" by "inet@microsoft.com" for "http://www.microsoft.com/"
 on "1997.0r (n 0 s 0 v 0 l 0))'>
<META NAME="KEYWORDS" CONTENT="products; headlines; downloads;
news; Web site; what's new; solutions; services; software;
contests;corporate news;">
<META NAME="DESCRIPTION" CONTENT="The entry page to Microsoft's
Web site. Find software, solutions and answers. Support, and
Microsoft news.">
<META NAME="MS.LOCALE" CONTENT="EN-US">
<META NAME="CATEGORY"CONTENT="home page">
<TITLE>Welcome to Microsoft's Homepage</TITLE>

<SCRIPT TYPE="text/javascript">

    if (navigator.userAgent.indexOf("MSIE") == -1 ||
navigator.appVersion.substring(0,1) < 4) {
            window.location.replace("/default.htm");
        }
        if (navigator.userAgent.indexOf("Mac") != -1) {
            sCSS = '<STYLE type="text/css">' +
            '.placeholder {color:red}' +
            'A:link    {color: #003399;}' +
            'A:visited        {color: #003399;}' +
            'A.bb:hover        {color:red;}' +
            'A.mw:visited     {color:white;}' +
            'A. mw:hover            {color:red;}' +
            'A.nodec {color:#000000;text-decoration:none;}' +
            'A.nodec:visited {color:#000000;text-decoration:
```

When an HTML page comes to your browser, your browser interprets the HTML formatting commands and displays the resulting Web page in a format useful for the person viewing the page. Figure 24.1 shows the resulting Web page from the full set of HTML commands contained in Listing 24.1. The Web page, once formatted, is easy to work with. The HTML is for the browser to interpret, not for the person viewing the Web page.

FIGURE 24.1.

Once your browser interprets all the HTML commands, the resulting Web page looks nice.

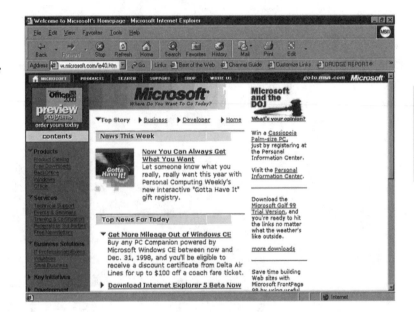

24

Before Web page editors such as FrontPage 2000, you'd have to master the HTML language before you could create or edit a Web page. Fortunately, FrontPage 2000 and other programs like it enable you to bypass HTML by putting a buffer between you and the underlying HTML code. If you want to draw a line or place a graphic image in a particular location on the Web page you're designing, you'll be able to drag that item onto the page with your mouse and with a little help from FrontPage 2000.

To start FrontPage 2000 and familiarize yourself with its interface, perform these steps:

1. Select the Start menu's Programs, Microsoft FrontPage menu option. FrontPage 2000 loads and displays a blank editing area.

2. Select File, Open and a dialog box appears that enables you to select a file from your disk or from the Internet.

3. Click the From Location option and type **www.mcp.com** in the text box to inform FrontPage 2000 that you want to edit that site's Web page.

In subsequent FrontPage 2000 sessions, the File menu keeps track of pages you've recently edited and displays the most-recent 4 Web pages at the bottom of the File menu for quick access. Therefore, you can then select File, 1; File, 2; File, 3; or File, 4 to open any of your four most recently edited Web pages. Although all Office 2000 products support this recently opened file shortcut, the shortcut is even more critical because FrontPage 2000's Web addresses can be so tricky to enter.

4. Click OK and FrontPage 2000 loads the Web page from the Internet. After a brief pause, depending on the speed of your Internet access, you'll see the Web page inside FrontPage 2000's editing area as shown in Figure 24.2. The three tabs at the bottom of the screen labeled Normal, HTML, and Preview, show three different views of the Web page. The Web page appears similar to the way it looks in your browser to simplify editing. Use the scroll bars to see more of the Web page if you need to adjust the display.

FIGURE 24.2.

FrontPage 2000 works graphically with Web page content.

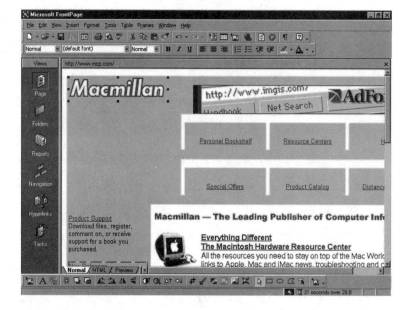

5. You can select File, Exit to close the Web page and leave FrontPage 2000 for now.

FrontPage 2000 enables you to edit Web pages located on your own PC or on the Web. The pages you view or edit don't have to reside on your PC as you saw here, but you can modify a Web site in place on the Internet. And unlike previous versions of FrontPage, with FrontPage 2000 you can work very easily with HTML and sophisticated features like frames, tables and imagemaps.

FrontPage 2000 does not actually edit Web pages in place; the changes you make can reside only on your own PC unless you have server access to the Web page you change.

Preparing for Web Page Publishing

Before you can publish pages on the Web, you must have access to a W*eb server*. Perhaps your company uses a Web server for its site; if so, you can store your Web pages on that computer. If you have access to an online service, such as America Online, it may offer an area for one or more Web pages that you can copy to the online site's Web server. Many Internet Service Providers also offer storage for Web pages.

If you want to publish a personal Web page for fun, you will enjoy telling the world your stories and sharing your family photos with others. If, however, you want to start a business on the Internet, or offer timely information that you want others to visit often, you need to be aware that Web page *maintenance* is time-consuming. You don't just create a Web page, load the page on the Web, and expect to keep people's interest if you don't keep the material up to date. Use FrontPage 2000's tools to maintain your Web pages and keep the viewers' interest.

FrontPage 2000 supports both the Internet and *intranets*. Intranets are networked computers that use Internet protocol, such as Web page technology, to communicate. Therefore, if your company maintains an intranet you are able to create, edit, and save Web pages to that intranet as easily (and sometimes more easily) than on the Internet.

Work with FrontPage 2000

A full hour is not enough time to master FrontPage 2000, but you can gain a quick understanding of the product in this section by learning some of the fundamental parts of the program.

When you want to create a Web page, you can select File, New. You then have the option of creating one of the following:

- A new Web page: A single Web page formatted according to one of several design wizards
- A new Web site: A complete collection of Web pages

24

Figure 24.3 shows the many wizards and design templates that appear when you want to begin to create a new Web page. Some of the Web pages you can create are:

- Normal Page: Creates a blank Web page
- Confirmation Form: Acknowledges the receipt of user input from an Internet source
- Form Page Wizard: Helps you create a Web page that collects information from the user
- Search Page: A Web page designed to help the user locate information
- User Registration: A Web page that enables the user to register products and services

FIGURE 24.3.

FrontPage 2000 offers several Web page templates and wizards.

All Web pages you create with FrontPage 2000 contain basic HTML editing tags that enable the Web page to operate in an Internet browser. You'll find the basic, HTML-based, blank Web page contents in Listing 24.2. As you can see, many HTML commands, called *tags*, are enclosed in angled brackets. Often, a command begins with an opening tag (such as <Head>) followed by a closing tag (such as </HEAD>) indicated with a forward slash before the closing tag.

LISTING 24.2. ALL WEB PAGES CONTAIN THESE FUNDAMENTAL HTML COMMANDS.

```
<html>

<head>
<meta name="GENERATOR" content="Microsoft FrontPage 4.0">
<meta name="ProgId" content="FrontPage.Editor.Document">
```

```
<title>New Page 1</title>
</head>

<body>

</body>

</html>
```

Although HTML is rather simple compared to major programming languages such as C++, HTML is cryptic and you can already see that working in a graphical environment such as FrontPage 2000 is much simpler than mastering HTML commands.

The initial tags shown in Listing 24.2 are only sufficient to define a blank Web page, and it's your job to fill in the page with text, graphics, and other elements. To get an idea of how FrontPage 2000 hides the underlying tags from you, the Normal view tab at the bottom of the screen shows that the FrontPage 2000 viewing area is blank (even though the tags from Listing 24.2, viewable by clicking the HTML tab at the bottom of the window, show the Web page does contain invisible HTML commands).

Select File, Properties and click the Title field to enter a title. Type **My Home Page** in the field and click OK. The title bar of FrontPage 2000's program window should show your new title. Select the HTML view tab to view the HTML window shown in Figure 24.4. FrontPage 2000 placed your title between two <TITLE> tags even though you entered the title using the Properties dialog box. Although you could have typed the HTML <TITLE> information, selecting from FrontPage 2000's menus was easier.

24

FIGURE 24.4.

Your title appears in the HTML window even though you did not type HTML code.

Your title ——

The title is not the only property that the Properties dialog box can help you manage. If you select File, Properties once again and click the tabs to see the other dialog box property sheets, you'll find these tabbed sheets that help you quickly place Web page elements on your page:

- Background: Select an image or colors to form your Web page's background
- Margins: Specify the top and left margins of your Web page
- Custom: Advanced Web-page designers can create variables that hold content that is placed in the variables when the Web page is displayed on the Internet

As you add to your Web page, watch your Status bar at the bottom of the FrontPage 2000 window. FrontPage 2000 estimates the amount of time required, in seconds, for your Web page to load on an Internet user's PC using a 28.8K modem connection. As you add elements to your Web page, the estimated download time will increase. You want your users to see your Web page as quickly as possible without sacrificing quality or attention-getting graphics and other Web page components.

FrontPage 2000's menus and toolbars go a long way towards helping you create and edit Web pages. Figure 24.5 shows one set of FrontPage 2000's toolbar options that appear when you click the Insert Component toolbar button. You can add such items as an Excel worksheet to the Web page you are creating or editing.

FIGURE 24.5.

Use the FrontPage 2000 toolbar to add special elements to your Web page.

To add one of the objects anywhere on your Web page, select the object and FrontPage 2000 places the object on the Web page. You then can drag the object to its proper location and size the control to the size you require. Unlike desktop-publishing programs and visual programming systems such as Visual Basic, FrontPage 2000 does not initially place the control in the center of the form, but places the controls side-by-side as you choose them. You then can drag and resize them as needed.

The Insert, Form menu option produces a large set of items you can include on your Web page. Here is a description of each item that you can include:

- Form: A rectangular form that acts as a separate table on your Web page
- One-line text box: An area where the Internet user can type and edit information on the Web page
- Scrolling text box: A multiline text box the user can scroll left, right, up, or down to read the full contents
- Check box: An option the user can click to add (select) or remove (deselect) a check mark
- Radio button: An option the user can click to select or deselect the option; only one radio option button can be selected in a single page frame, not unlike the old car radios that allowed for only one radio station button to be pressed in at any one time
- Drop-down menu: A menu that opens from its one-line station on the Web page
- Push button (sometimes called a command button): A button the user can click to trigger an action such as the playing of a sound clip
- Picture: A graphic image you want to place on the page.
- Label: A text box into which you can place and format text, such as a title or instruction header

 FrontPage 2000 requires that you master some programming skills to operate command buttons and respond to the option selections properly. This hour does not go into the advanced processing required for more complex Web pages that include interactive applets and multimedia segments.

Without programming in HTML, you can place tables, graphics, and hyperlinks (links to other Web pages that the user can click to select) by clicking the Insert Table, Insert Graphic, and Create or Edit Hyperlink toolbar buttons that appear on the toolbar beneath the menu. More advanced Web page components, such as animation and sound clips, still require that you master HTML.

24

To get some experience in creating a Web page, the next few steps walk you through the initial creation of a simple Web page using one of FrontPage 2000's Web page wizards.

1. Select File, New, Web to open the New dialog box.

2. Select Corporate Presence Wizard to start the wizard that creates a simple home page set. FrontPage 2000 displays the opening window shown in Figure 24.6.

FIGURE 24.6.

The wizard will walk you through your Web page creation.

3. Click Next and the wizard will offer a list of Web content choice that you can put on the site you are creating. Keep in mind that the wizard is creating a general Web page set, not just a single home page.

4. Click Next to determine the items you want on your home page.

5. Click Next to determine the items you want to appear on your remaining pages.

6. Keep clicking Next and answer the prompts. Eventually, the wizard prompts you for your company name, address, and other demographic information.

7. Not only does the wizard prompt you for content, but also for the overall theme of your site with the Chose Theme dialog box shown in Figure 24.7. The theme is a uniform appearance throughout all your site's Web pages. The tone can determine how users react to your Web site.

8. When you finish the wizard, FrontPage 2000 follows the wizard's instructions and produces the site's Web pages you specified. A table appears that summarizes each page in the site.

One of the most helpful views you can show for a multipage Web site is the Navigation view, obtained by clicking the Navigation button at the left of FrontPage 2000's screen. As Figure 24.8 shows, the Navigation view shows the hierarchical structure of your complete Web site beginning with the home page.

FIGURE 24.7.

The theme you select determines how users react to your site's pages.

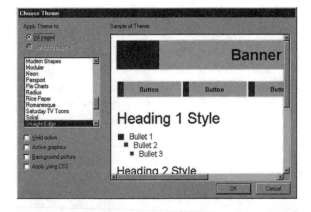

FIGURE 24.8.

The Navigation view shows the structure of your Web site pages.

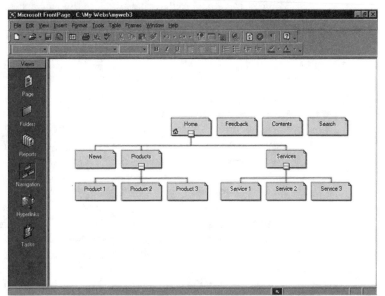

Scroll through your new home page to see the elements on it. You can add text boxes, check boxes, and options to the page, rearrange elements of the page, add graphics, and other elements. You can select HTML view tab to see the HTML code that you might want to edit as well.

Publishing Your Web Page

Once you finalize your Web page with FrontPage 2000, FrontPage 2000 can help you publish your page on the Web or on your local network server as an intranet using the

Web Publishing Wizard. The wizard translates your web page from the FrontPage 2000 format to HTML format to be compatible with Web browsers.

To start the wizard, select File, Publish Web. The wizard begins and collects information that your Internet provider needs about your web pages and sends that information, along with your Web pages, to your provider. (You'll need proper Internet access and a browser to use the wizard.) Once you complete the wizard, your Web page should be available for use.

> Although the Web Publishing Wizard helps gather information and makes publishing your Web page simpler than would otherwise be the case, you still may have to contact your Internet provider (the provider sponsoring your Web page) to determine some of the answers to the Web Publishing wizard's questions. For example, you'll need to tell the wizard the URL where your Web page will reside and the type of provider you use.

> In order to use some of the sophisticated Web management tools included with FrontPage 2000, you will need to install the proper Web server extensions and set up the Personal Web Server (PWS), included with Windows 98.
>
> Special FrontPage Server Extensions must also be running on the Web server that serves your Web site. In other words, your Internet Service Providerís Web server must be equipped with FrontPage extensions for you to take full advantage of FrontPage 2000ís Web management capabilities.
>
> To go into the setup and use of the PWS and FrontPage extensions is beyond the scope of this book; to learn more check out *Special Edition Using FrontPage 2000* (Que) or *FrontPage 2000 Unleashed* (Sams).

Summary

This hour explained how to use FrontPage 2000 to create and edit Web pages. Although FrontPage 2000 is rather simple to use, you can use FrontPage 2000's wizard to create common Web pages and then edit those pages to add your own graphics and other components to the page.

FrontPage 2000 makes it unnecessary to master HTML commands. The HTML language was the original formatting language of Web pages. Although all Web pages contain HTML code, programs such as FrontPage 2000 hide the underlying HTML code from you so that you can create Web pages from the graphical elements.

Q&A

Q How can users find my site?

A If you put a business on the Web, you certainly want to make it as easy as possible
for users to locate you site. One of the best ways to do that is to register your sites
with search engines such as *Yahoo!* (www.yahoo.com) or *Excite* (www.excite.com).
The search engines sites will include your site, indexed by keywords that you sug-
gest, for a modest fee. Each of the current search sites included with Internet
Explorer can be obtained by clicking the Search button and selecting Choose a
Search Engine. The search engine sites include contact information you can use to
find out more about registering your site with them.

24

Part **VIII**
Appendixes

Appendix

APPENDIX A

Small Business Tools

Office 2000 includes a group of tools designed to help small businesses get more out of the Office suite of applications. The tools are included in all editions of Office 2000, and they're not just useful for small businesses—large businesses, home offices, and individual users will all find something useful in one or more of the following Small Business Tools components:

- The Small Business Financial Manager
- The Business Planner
- The Direct Mail Planner
- The Small Business Customer Manager

To access these components click the Start button, and choose Programs. From the Programs list, select Microsoft Office Small Business Tools and then view the submenu and make your selection.

The Small Business Financial Manager

This small business tool adds a Financial Manager menu to your Excel menu bar, as shown in Figure A.1, although you can access it from the Programs list in the Start menu as well. The Financial Manager menu offers a series of wizards to help you create reports, charts, and tools to assist you in making business decisions based on your worksheet data.

FIGURE A.1.

If this menu doesn't show in your Excel window, choose Tools, Add-Ins, and click the Small Business Financial Manager check box.

Using the Import Wizard

The Import Wizard allows you to build a new database that is based on the data you've built using your accounting software. When you select Import Wizard from the Financial Manager menu, the wizard begins, as shown in Figure A.2.

FIGURE A.2.

Build a database for use in creating reports and to begin using your worksheets as true analysis tools.

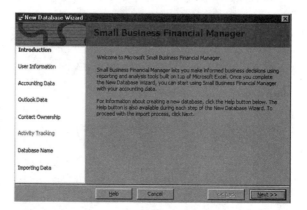

The New Database Wizard helps you extract data from your accounting software, such as QuickBooks or Microsoft Money. An Access database is created, although a knowledge of Access is not required to use the it.

After entering information about yourself (your name and an optional password of your choice), the Financial Manager searches your computer for accounting files. Once found, you choose which data to import, and your database is created. Figure A.3 shows an accounting database listing accounting categories.

FIGURE A.3.

Collate pertinent accounting information into one database.

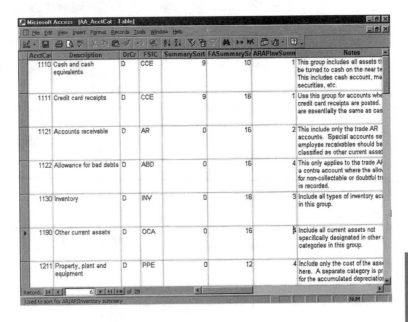

AcctCat	Description	DrCr	FSIC	SummarySort	FASummarySr	ARAPInvSumm	Notes
1110	Cash and cash equivalents	D	CCE	9	10	1	This group includes all assets th be turned to cash on the near te This includes cash account, ma securities, etc.
1111	Credit card receipts	D	CCE	9	16	1	Use this group for accounts whe credit card receipts are posted. are essentially the same as cas
1121	Accounts receivable	D	AR	0	16	2	This include only the trade AR accounts. Special accounts se employee receivables should be classified as other current asset
1122	Allowance for bad debts	D	ABD	0	16	4	This only applies to the trade AF a contra account where the allov for non-collectable or doubtful tr is recorded.
1130	Inventory	D	INV	0	16	3	Include all types of inventory ac in this group.
1190	Other current assets	D	OCA	0	16	4	Include all current assets not specifically designated in other categories in this group.
1211	Property, plant and equipment	D	PPE	0	12	4	Include only the cost of the asse here. A separate category is pr for the accumulated depreciatior

Record: 6 of 28

Used to sort for AR/AP/Inventory summary

A

If you don't have any accounting software on your computer, choose the option to not import any data. As a result, a generic database is created, with many database tables into which you can manually enter your own accounting information. The process of building this generic database requires additional steps during set up, but saves you the wasted time watching your computer search for accounting data that isn't there.

Working with the Report Wizard

The Report Wizard makes it easy to create a variety of standard accounting reports, such as income statements, balance sheets, and trial balances. To activate the Report Wizard, choose Financial Manager, Report Wizard from the Excel 2000 Menu bar. The Small Business Financial Manager Startup Screen opens, as shown in Figure A.4.

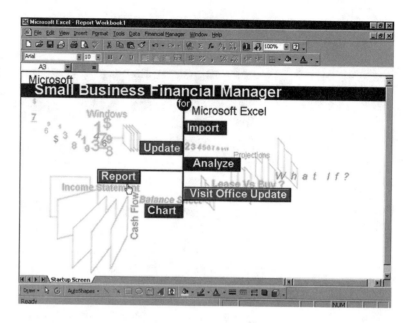

After selecting the Report link, the Create a Financial Report dialog box opens, as shown in Figure A.5.

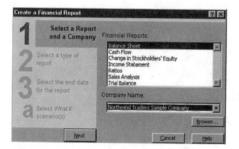

After choosing the type of report you want, the Financial Report Wizard asks you to specify which variation you want to use. Figure A.6 shows the two different types of Trial Balances you can create.

A series of dialog boxes follows, asking for further information. In the case of our sam-ple Trial Balance, the next step in the process requires choosing the date of the report, as shown in Figure A.7.

FIGURE A.6.

The number of report variations depends on the type of report you selected.

FIGURE A.7.

Make your date selection and click Finish to create the report.

The Report Wizard then completes the report, based on your data, drawn from your accounting software files. For the purposes of this appendix, we're using the Northwind Traders database that comes with Office 2000. Their Trial Balance with Comparisons is shown in Figure A.8.

FIGURE A.8.

The finished report contains your data in all the right places, along with text and numeric formatting to give the report a polished, professional look.

If you're not sure how you might use the Small Business Financial Manager tools, try running various reports with the Northwind Traders data—you'll have real data to look at, without spending time setting up your own information. The Sales Analysis and Cash Flow reports are two good choices for any small business—you'll see immediate uses for these reports in your own use of the Small Business Financial Manager.

Using the Chart Wizard

Don't confuse this Chart Wizard with Excel's Chart Wizard tool. This wizard offers only business-related charts and does the charting for you, based on data you added to your database through the Import Wizard. Again, we'll be using the Northwind Traders sample database.

To run the Small Business Financial Manager Chart Wizard, follow these steps:

1. Choose Financial Manager, Chart Wizard.

2. Choose the type of chart you want from the Create a Financial Chart dialog box, shown in Figure A.9.

FIGURE A.9.

Choose from four basic chart types.

3. Select the database you want to use from the Company Name dialog box and click Next.

4. Depending on the type of chart you selected, further questions and dialog box options appear in the next step. For this example, we're creating a Cash Flow chart and must choose the type of cash flow to include in the chart (see Figure A.10).

5. Click Next to choose a range of dates for the chart (see Figure A.11).

6. Click Finish to create the chart, which appears in Figure A.12.

FIGURE A.10.

How detailed should your chart be? Choose one or all of the options.

FIGURE A.11.

Your starting and ending dates dictate the time over which the cash flow trend is tracked.

FIGURE A.12.

The Chart Wizard selects the right kind of chart for the type of data being charted. A line chart is selected here to show trends in cash flow over time.

A

The Small Business Financial Manager charts are especially useful in that they are created for you and don't require you to use Excel's standard charting tools—tools that require a greater starting knowledge of charting concepts and terminology. The charts you create through the Small Business Financial Manager can be copied and pasted as graphic objects into PowerPoint slides, Word documents, or a Web page you create with Word, Publisher, or FrontPage.

Selecting an Analysis Tool

The Small Business Financial Manager offers a tool for making decisions such as choosing whether to buy or lease an item for your business. Like the other Small Business Financial Manager tools, the analysis tool asks you a series of questions in a series of dialog boxes. To access this Small Business Financial Manager feature, choose Financial Manager, Select Analysis Tool. The first dialog box is shown in Figure A.13.

FIGURE A.13.

Choose Buy Vs. Lease to ask the Small Business Financial Manager to help you make your decision.

After selecting the Buy Vs. Lease tool, you are asked to give the Small Business Financial Manager more information about your intended purchase (see Figure A.14).

FIGURE A.14.

Enter the name, price, and tax amount for the item you're considering.

Click Next to proceed to the dialog box shown in Figure A.15. Here, you can give the Buy vs. Lease tool your purchase options—paying cash, taking out a loan, signing a lease, or other financing options.

FIGURE A.15.

Document your purchase or lease options to help the Small Business Financial Manager analyze your alternatives.

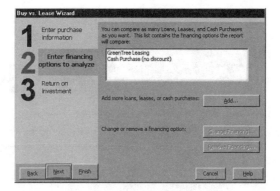

At this point, you can click Finish or Next. Clicking Next takes you to a final dialog box in which you can specify your tax bracket and any potential profit you'll make from the item (see Figure A.16).

FIGURE A.16.

If you don't know your tax rate or there is no potential profit, leave the options blank and click Finish.

The resulting analysis appears on a formatted worksheet as shown in Figure A.17. Scroll through the report to view the various calculations and use the information to make your decision.

The Business Planner

Not all businesses have an actual business plan, but documentation of a plan for your business can be very useful when you're starting out or when you're going through normal growth phases in the life of your business. The Small Business Tools package gives you a tool for building a business plan, eliminating your need to know how such a plan is traditionally structured. Enter the requested information and let the Business Planner do the rest.

To use the Business Planner, follow these steps:

1. From the Start menu, choose Programs, Microsoft Office Small Business Tools. From the resulting submenu, choose Microsoft Business Planner.

2. The Business Planner window opens, displaying the Personal Interviewer Step 1 (see Figure A.18). The instructions tell you to scroll through the displayed text and answer questions about yourself and your business.

3. Answer each of the questions. Some questions require you to choose one of several options; others require you to type in text boxes (see Figure A.19).

4. Answer the questions in Step 2 of 3, and click the arrow to proceed to the final step.

5. After answering the questions in Step 3 of 3, click the arrow again. The Business Planner displays a new window, as shown in Figure A.20.

6. Click the Business Plan Wizard hyperlink.

7. The Business Plan Wizard window contains a series of seven hyperlinks (see Figure A.21). Click the History and Position to Date link to start.

FIGURE A.18.

Although you have to wade through a lot of text, you'll find much of it to be helpful in understanding business plans.

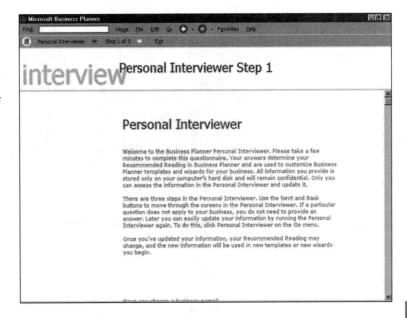

Click this arrow to move forward through the Personal Interviewer.

FIGURE A.19.

After you've entered your information, click the arrow to move to Step 2 of 3.

Click here to go back to a previous step.

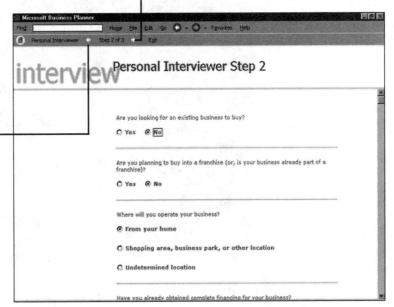

A

FIGURE A.20.

Follow each page of the Business Planner to answer questions and to get more information.

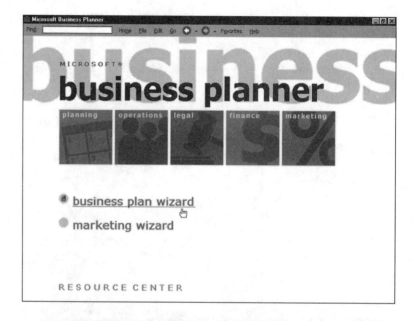

FIGURE A.21.

See the list of topic areas on which you'll read informative articles.

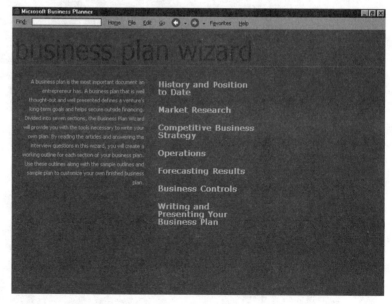

8. Read the first of 15 articles and click the right-pointing arrow to proceed (see Figure A.22). It's a good idea to read them all, clicking the arrow to move through the articles one by one.

FIGURE A.22.

Move through the articles by clicking the right-pointing arrow when you're ready to go to the next one.

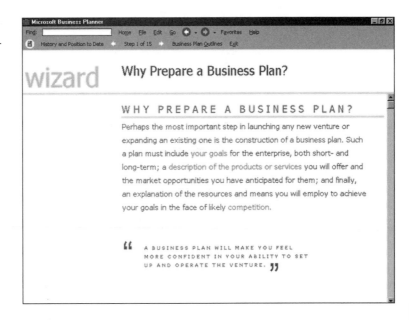

9. At Step 8 of 15, you are asked to name your business plan document in the dialog box shown in Figure A.23. Enter a name for your plan and click Save.

A

FIGURE A.23.

Give your business plan document a name and choose a folder in which to save it.

10. Step 8 of 15 continues by asking you to type answers to a series of questions (with intermittent option selections). After responding to all the questions, click the arrow to proceed.

11. At Step 10 of 15, questions regarding your Management Team are presented (see Figure A.24). Type your responses and click the arrow to move to Step 11 of 15.

FIGURE A.24.

Describe your management team. If you're a very small business, this might be just you.

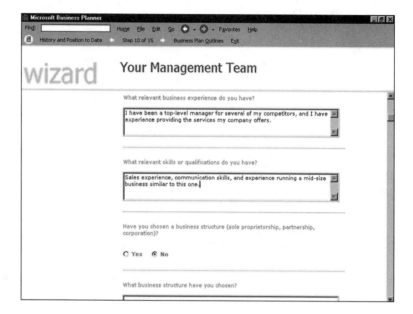

12. Articles appear in steps 11 through 15, at which point you are given a final set of questions regarding your Products and Services (see Figure A.25). Type your responses and click the arrow to proceed.

13. An Action Plan page appears, which includes links to more articles and some Web pages with information that may be helpful to you in growing your business (see Figure A.26). Click any links that interest you.

14. Click the Business Plan Outlines button and choose My Outline. An outline based on your entries to the questions posed throughout the previous steps appears (see Figure A.27).

FIGURE A.25.

Describe the products you sell and/or the services you provide.

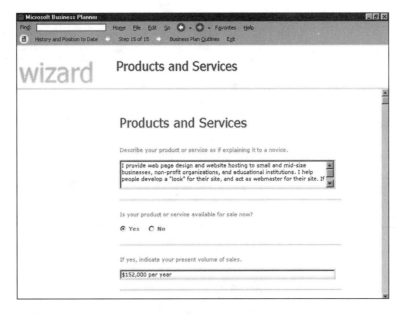

FIGURE A.26.

If you still want to know more about business plans, check these internal links and Web sites.

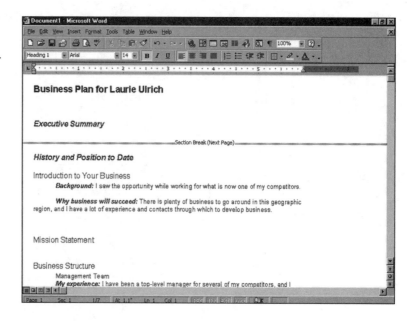

FIGURE A.27.

View the results of your Business Planner labors in the form of an outline.

15. Replace the instructional sample text in the outline with your own text. After completing and customizing the outline, you can save and print it as you would any Word document.

Your Business Plan can be used in a variety of ways—as part of a package you supply to the bank or investors or as a reference for yourself to keep things on track as you grow your business. As your business grows and changes, run through the Business Planner again and see how the resulting outline changes to reflect your new answers.

The Direct Mail Manager

If your business does a lot of direct mail, you may find this Small Business Tools component very useful. The Direct Mail Manager performs the following tasks:

- Imports your address list—If you've already built an address list in another program such as Outlook, Outlook Express, Excel, or Access, you can access it through the Direct Mail Manager.

- Verifies your addresses—The Direct Mail Manager checks for and inserts missing zip codes, checks spelling, and deletes duplicate addresses. The verification process saves your time and supplies by eliminating incorrect addresses and redundant mailings.

- Prints envelopes, labels, and postcards—U.S. Postal Service guidelines have been built-in to the Direct Mail Manager to make sure the output meets federal requirements.

- Saves the updated database—Don't risk forgetting to save the imported and corrected records for your next mailing.

The Direct Mail Manager performs these tasks through a wizard, as shown in Figure A.28.

FIGURE A.28.

Import, verify, print, and save your direct mail database with the Direct Mail Manager.

To access the wizard, start the Direct Mail Manager by following these steps:

1. From the Start button, choose Programs, Microsoft Office Small Business Tools, and then select Microsoft Direct Mail Manager.

2. After viewing the list of tasks the Direct Mail Manager will perform, click Next to get started.

3. Tell the Direct Mail Manager where to find your address list. Click the Browse button to navigate to the folder that contains the list and enter the path and filename into the File box. If your address list is stored in Outlook, click the Outlook Folder option and select the folder (see Figure A.29).

4. Click Next to proceed to the next step, wherein the Direct Mail Manager verifies the accuracy of your list and makes sure all your records are unique.

5. After verification, click Next to move on to the Print step. In the Print dialog box, choose the type of printed output you want for your mailing (see Figure A.30).

A

FIGURE A.29.

Select your Personal Folder, which contains the contacts you've entered through Outlook.

FIGURE A.30.

Print the envelopes, labels, or postcards you'll be using for your direct mailing.

6. Click Next and choose how to Save your database. Your options are shown in Figure A.31.

FIGURE A.31.

To save you from accidentally losing the changes made during the verification process, you are prompted to save your database.

7. Click Next to create a form letter using Word or Publisher, or you can opt to skip this step entirely (perhaps you already have the letter or you're mailing a flyer). Make your selection and click Next.

8. If you chose to create the form letter, the Direct Mail Manager asks you to name your document (see Figure A.32). Click the Create button to build the letter.

FIGURE A.32.

Build a form letter that will be merged with your database.

9. Choose the Letter Wizard from the Select a Mail Merge Template and follow the wizard's steps to create the letter.

After your letter is created, you can place the letters in your Direct Mail Manager-created envelopes and get the mailing out to your customers and prospects. The Direct Mail Manager can be run each time you do a mailing or just periodically as a means to verify the accuracy of your database.

For the Direct Mail Manager to verify your addresses, it must connect to the Internet and check phone and zip code databases there. If you would rather skip this step, click the Options button in the lower-left corner of the wizard dialog box and remove the check mark next to Run Address Verification. This step is skipped and you proceed to the Print stage.

The Small Business Customer Manager

You don't need to know how to use database software to query your list of contacts for specific records. If, for example, you need to see only your contacts in New Jersey, the Small Business Customer Manager helps you find them. In addition, the Small Business Customer Manager can be used to pull your contact information from popular accounting applications such as PeachTree, MYOB, and QuickBooks, or you can use your Outlook contacts folder.

To access and use the Small Business Customer Manager, follow these steps:

1. Open the Start menu and choose Programs, Microsoft Office Small Business Tools and then choose Microsoft Small Business Customer Manager from the submenu.

2. After starting the Small Business Customer Manager program, you are asked to select a database to use for your contacts (see Figure A.33). You can select one of the listed databases or click the Browse button to locate your file. For the purposes of this appendix, we'll be using the Northwind Traders sample database, provided by Microsoft.

FIGURE A.33.

Choose the database you want to view and edit through the Small Business Customer Manager.

3. Click OK to close the Microsoft Customer Manager dialog box and open the Small Business Customer Manager main program.

4. A dialog box opens asking for your personal information—name, company name, and so forth. Fill this out and click OK to proceed.

The Small Business Customer Manager opens, displaying the selected database (see Figure A.34). A full set of tools for selecting specific records from within the database is offered, in the form of a menu bar, toolbar, and list boxes designed for use with your particular database.

You can insert, edit, and delete records from within the database and save your changes before exiting. You can also save your database with a new filename, creating a new version of the database file. The database can be used for direct mailings and reports through any of the Office applications, such as Word and Excel.

Click the Find button to search for
a specific record based on key text.

FIGURE A.34.

*Click the Narrow Your
Choice and Action list
boxes to view only
those records that
match your criteria.*

Use the Ascending
and Descending Sort
buttons to change
the order of your
listed records.

APPENDIX B

Using PhotoDraw

Previous versions of Microsoft Office contained only the big basic programs—
a word processor, a spreadsheet application, software for creating presentations, a database management program, and communications software.
These programs supported the use of graphics (clip art, photographs, drawn
shapes and lines), but didn't give you very powerful tools for creating or
customizing the graphic content itself. With the release of Office 2000 and
its added PhotoDraw application, the Office user finally has a complete set
of tools for not just using, but building and fine-tuning clip art and photographs.

How does this affect you? Imagine not being bound by the clip art selection
that comes with Office or having to buy clip art on CD-ROM to round out
your collection of images. With PhotoDraw, you can customize your existing
clip art and create images of your own. You can retouch photographs from
scanned drawings or a digital camera, improving their appearance onscreen
and as printed. Create logos, icons, and backgrounds for use in documents,
worksheets, presentations, and on Web pages.

Getting Started with PhotoDraw

PhotoDraw works very similarly to PowerPoint in that you begin by choosing how your document will be created (see Figure B.1).

FIGURE B.1.

You can start from scratch with a blank image, or scan/capture an image digitally. You can also begin with an existing image.

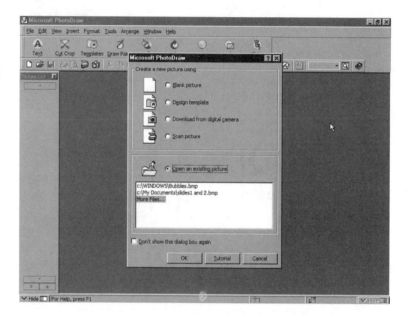

If you decide to create something from scratch, you then choose from a set of templates for common layouts. Instead of slide layouts, however, your choices include pictures, banners, envelopes, labels, and business cards, as shown in Figure B.2.

FIGURE B.2.

Choose a template on which to base your new PhotoDraw graphic.

After selecting the template, click OK, and the document appears, awaiting your drawing shapes, lines, and issuing commands for fine-tuning your creations. Figure B.3 shows a new blank picture window.

FIGURE B.3.

Choose to draw a shape, line, or arrow, or paint with freeform tools.

The Draw Paint menu

Draw Paint menu tools

You can access the familiar AutoShapes tools (found in your other Office applications' Drawing toolbar) by clicking the Rectangle or Oval tools. The AutoShapes toolbar appears, from which you can select a variety of lines, arrows, and geometric shapes to draw.

If you choose to begin by scanning an image or capturing one through a digital camera, PhotoDraw will display tools for using these peripheral devices. If you've already scanned or captured your image digitally and saved the image as a file, choose to open an existing image by choosing File, Visual Open.

Starting with an Existing Image

The first part of PhotoDraw's name indicates that it can be used for retouching photographs (and other existing images), not just for drawing things from scratch. Through

Word, PowerPoint, and now PhotoDraw, you can scan images or capture them with a digital camera, and save them as graphic files. These files can then be edited in PhotoDraw—removing blotches or scratches that scanned from the original, or editing out unwanted parts of the image. If you've scanned a drawing done by hand, you can clean it up for a better display onscreen or improve its printed appearance.

When PhotoDraw opens, you can choose to Open an existing picture, and then select that image from the Visual Open dialog box, as shown in Figure B.4.

If you've already opened PhotoDraw and have gone beyond the starting dialog box, choose File, Visual Open to access your existing graphics.

FIGURE B.4.

Navigate through your folders, and preview the thumbnails of your graphic images to find the one you want.

Choose a drive and a folder.

Thumbnail representations of images contained in the selected folder.

Once your image is opened, you'll see it listed in the Picture List on the left side of your screen. This list is useful when you have more than one image open at the same time, allowing you to switch back and forth between them as needed. To switch to another of your open images, click once on the thumbnail displayed in the Picture List (see Figure B.5).

FIGURE B.5.

Faster than using the Window menu, click to view one of your other open images.

> If you have similar images open, check to see which one is which by displaying a ScreenTip on the Picture List. Point to (don't click) one of the thumbnails in the list, and see the path and filename of the image.

Using Retouching Tools

After selecting the image (double-click the thumbnail image or click it once and then click the Open button), you can adjust it with any of the Touch Up menu tools described in the following list:

TABLE B.1. IMAGE RETOUCHING TOOLS

Tool	How It Works
Fix Red Eye	The floating Red Eye toolbar opens, with the Red Eye button active. Click on the red eye in your image, and click the Fix button.
Remove Dust and Spots	Using the floating Dust and Spots toolbar, click on the spots and marks you wish to remove.

continues

TABLE B.1. CONTINUED

Tool	How It Works
Despeckle	Drag the slider left (less despeckling) or right (more despeckling). You can also enter a number to indicate the amount of despeckling you wish to do.
Remove Scratch	Use the floating Scratch toolbar. Click at the start of the scratch and then again at the end of it. The scratch will disappear, replaced by the surrounding color.
Clone	Click on the part of your image you wish to clone, and then click elsewhere to deposit the cloned selection. You can choose the size and shape of the cloned selection by clicking the triangle on the Brush tool.
Smudge	Like rubbing your fingertip on a chalk drawing, the Smudge tool allows you to blur the edges between contiguous colors or textures. Drag your mouse across the image to smudge it.
Erase	Removes portions of the image. Drag your mouse as though painting, and the image in your path is erased.

As soon as you choose the Touch Up menu command, the TouchUp dialog box opens, as shown in Figure B.6.

FIGURE B.6.

Scroll through the Touchup options and view the setting for the individual tools.

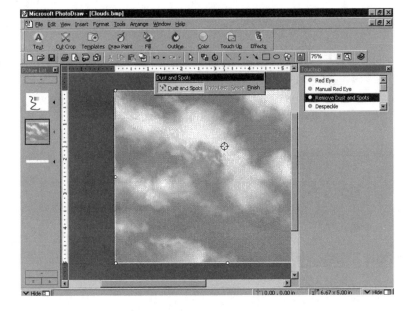

The Clone, Smudge, and Erase tools open a slightly different version of the Touchup dialog box, as shown in Figure B.7.

FIGURE B.7.

Choose your Touchup tool from the list box, and view the accompanying floating toolbar.

Applying Special Effects

The Effects button on the toolbar displays a list of effects that can be applied to any drawn shape or line. Choose from the text effects described in Table B.2.

TABLE B.2. SPECIAL TEXT EFFECTS

Effect	How It Works
Shadow	Choose the direction that the shadow will fall (suggesting a light source on the opposite side)
Transparency	Drag the slider left (to decrease transparency) or right (to increase transparency)
Fade Out	Fade Out offers a gradient transparency—choose the starting and ending points (drag the sliders) and the shape, angle, and center of the gradient to apply.
Blur and Sharpen	Like adjusting the contrast on your TV, the Blur and Sharpen tool gives you the ability to make your picture more grainy (sharper) or softer (blurred).

continues

B

TABLE B.2. CONTINUED

Effect	How It Works
Distort	Choose from 15 (16 if you include None) distortion effects. Double-click the thumbnail sample for the effect you wish to apply to your image. You can also choose to Distort by painting, allowing you to use your mouse to drag a distortion effect through selected areas of the image.
3-D	Click on a shape or line, and then choose 3-D from the Effects menu. Choose from a series of 3-D samples by double-clicking the one you want to apply to the selected shape. You can fine-tune your 3-D effects by choosing and resetting the Fill, Rotate and Fill, Beveling and Extrusion, Lighting, and Size and Position options.
Designer Effects	Choose from preset effects such as Angled Scribbles or Burlap Impression. Double-click the thumbnail for the effect you want, and it will be applied to the selected image.

These tools give you the ability to not just improve an image by cleaning it up or editing its content, but to create your own interpretation of the image, enhancing it beyond the capabilities of the tools used to create or capture it in the first place.

Using Additional PhotoDraw Editing Tools

Photodraw gives you the ability to add content to your new or existing images through its picture menu buttons (see Figure B.8).

FIGURE B.8.

Add text, crop your image, or change the fill and outline colors of your selected image.

Table B.3 describes each menu and how its commands/tools can be used.

TABLE B.3. ADDITIONAL EDITING TOOLS

Menu Name	Available Commands and Tools
Text	Choose to Insert Text, Format Text, or Bend Text. You can also apply 3-D and Designer effects to your existing text. As you choose a command, a dialog box appears to allow you to choose exactly how the effect will be applied to your text.
Cut Crop	Cut shapes through your image, or Crop away the edges of an image. You can also Erase with your mouse by dragging.
Fill	Choose from Solid Color, Texture, Designer Gradient, Two-color Gradient, or Picture fills for your selected shape. Each command opens a dialog box for choosing exactly how the fill effect will be applied.
Outline	Select an outline style—Soft Edges, Plain, Artistic Brushes, or Photo Brushes. These choices give you the ability to edit the edges of your selected shape, affecting how it appears in relation to adjacent objects or the background.
Color	Rather than selecting a color (you do that through the Fill menu), choose from a series of tools that allow you to change the way your colors are shown onscreen and/or appear when printed. Adjust your Brightness and Contrast, Tint, Hue and Saturation, Color Balance, and Grayscale. You can also Colorize or change your image to a Negative, reversing your colors for their color-wheel opposites.

B

Using PhotoDraw Creations

After your image has been created or customized, save it just as you would any other Office 2000 document—choose File, Save. You can choose from a variety of graphic file formats, such as GIF, JPG, TIF, and PNG (see Figure B.9). Your intended use for the graphic will dictate which one you choose.

If your image is bound for the Web, choose GIF or a compressed format such as JPG for compatibility with most web browsers and to achieve a smaller file size. Smaller files load faster, making it easier for people to view the site that contains your graphic image.

Figure B.9.

*PhotoDraw format is
the default, but you
can choose from a list
of other graphic for-
mats for your saved
image.*

Figure B.9.

*PhotoDraw format is
the default, but you
can choose from a list
of other graphic for-
mats for your saved
image.*

Your saved PhotoDraw image can be used in many ways—to enhance a Word document,
Excel worksheet, PowerPoint slide, or even an Access database report. In addition, web
pages designed with Word, FrontPage, or Publisher can be improved by adding your
original artwork created in PhotoDraw, or through the use of images you enhance with
PhotoDraw's tools. To add a PhotoDraw image to your file, choose Insert, Picture, From
File, and navigate to the drive and folder on which you've stored your image. The item
can then be formatted to determine how surrounding text will wrap to accommodate the
image (Format, Object), and you can use the Drawing and Picture toolbars in the current
application to make further changes to the size, rotation, and position of your graphic.

In addition to the standard use of graphics in your business documents, consider some of
these less obvious uses for your PhotoDraw images:

- *Hyperlinks*. Whether pointing to another file or a web page, using a graphic as your
  hyperlink is much more interesting than text. Design button images or appropriate
  representational clip art using PhotoDraw.

- *Buttons*. Using PhotoDraw's templates, create a button image for use on a web
  page (as a hyperlink or merely for decoration) or as a large graphic "bullet" in a
  Word document or PowerPoint presentation.

- *Logos*. Design a logo for your company, department, or for a specific event. Use
  that logo in your documents and presentations.

- *Business stationery.* Use PhotoDraw's templates to create flyers, bulletins, and certificates. Announce your seminar with a flyer and then hand out the diplomas afterward, using PhotoDraw to create both documents.

- *Cover pages.* Dress up your employee manual or other multi-page documents with a cover page that includes an image you created with PhotoDraw. Design an interesting background for the entire cover, and use text and drawn shapes to create a truly original cover for your book.

B

APPENDIX C

Reviewing Windows Fundamentals

If the Office 2000 Windows environment is new to you, this hour briefly covers some of the fundamentals you need to use Office 2000 effectively. This appendix does not give you an in-depth Windows tutorial. Instead, it reviews the tasks and features that directly relate to Office 2000.

Although the Windows interface has been around for a while, many companies are slow to upgrade from older Windows interfaces (such as Windows for Workgroups 3.11) to Windows 95, Windows 98, or Windows NT (the required Office 2000 operating environments). Therefore, even if you have used previous versions of Windows, you might need this hour's refresher so that you can hit the ground running with Office 2000.

The highlights of this appendix include the following:

- What the Windows interface provides
- What improvements Office 2000 brings to the Windows interface
- How to access the Start menu

- Why the Open dialog box is so crucial to your Office 2000 work
- Where to find ToolTips
- How to use dialog box tabs
- How to preview your documents before printing to save time and paper
- Why you should master Windows terminology while learning Office 2000 with *Sams Teach Yourself Microsoft Office 2000 in 24 Hours*
- How Windows and the Internet combine to give you worldwide data access

Basic Windows Elements

Although this book does not assume you are a Windows guru and teaches Office 2000 from the ground up, it does assume you possess those basic Windows skills that you can pick up in less than an hour with the Windows Tour (available from the Start menu's Help option). Therefore, you won't find any instructions for using the mouse except where the mouse specifically works in a unique way with Office 2000.

Just to keep terminology straight throughout the book, take a moment to study the call-outs in Figure C.1. When this book mentions the Control menu or the window's Close button, you'll know exactly what is meant.

FIGURE C.1.

Common window element descriptions.

When you maximize a window's size by clicking the Maximize window button, that button changes to the Resize window button.

You might save time by skimming through this material if you're already familiar with many of this hour's topics, such as ToolTips. By presenting all the required Windows interface elements in one hour, the remaining hours are devoted to Office 2000 without Windows reviews. You'll be better able to concentrate on the differences and improvements in Office 2000.

The Windows Interface

If you use Windows NT, Windows 95, or Windows 98, the interface that your Windows version uses is called the *Windows 95 interface* because it has been around since the first version of Windows 95. The most prominent features of the Windows 95 interface are the *Start button* and the *Start menu* (see Figure C.2).

FIGURE C.2.

Click the Start button to see the Windows 95 Start menu.

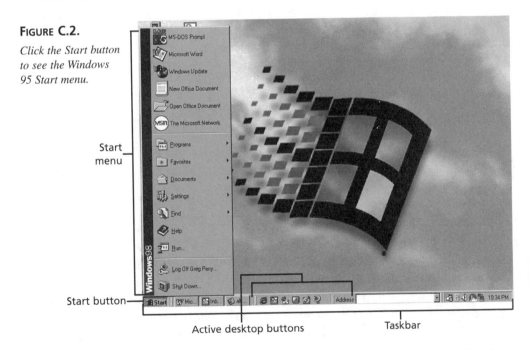

Start menu

Start button

Active desktop buttons

Taskbar

NEW TERM The *Windows 95 interface* is the user interface all versions of Microsoft operating systems have used since Windows 95 was released. The interface makes Windows simple to learn and use.

NEW TERM The *Start button* is the button labeled Start from which you display the Windows Start menu. The *Start menu* is the menu from which you can start any Windows program or shut down your PC.

Your Windows screen might differ slightly from Figure C.2 because of the programs and icons you have installed on your computer. In addition, the *wallpaper*—the screen's background picture—might differ from the figure's. Two things should be similar: You should see the Start menu when you click the Start button, and you should see two commands, New Office Document and Open Office Document, at the top of your Start menu.

NEW TERM *Wallpaper* is the graphic background on your Windows 95 interface.

The Start menu provides access to all your computer's programs. If you want to start any program, click the Start button, select Programs, and follow the Start menu path to the program. You can start more than one program if you want to share work between two or more programs, such as between Word 2000 and Access 2000. As you start and run programs, the Windows *taskbar* displays all the program icons on task buttons. Click the task buttons to switch between running programs just as you click the remote control to switch between television programs.

NEW TERM The *taskbar* at the bottom of your screen displays all programs currently running.

Office 2000 provides you with a shortcut to all the Office 2000 programs. Select New

You can also switch between running programs by pressing Alt+Tab.

Office Document if you want to create a new Office 2000 *document* (as you'll recall from Hour 1, "Getting Acquainted with Office 2000," an Office 2000 document is any data file you create or edit with Office 2000) by using any of the Office 2000 programs. Select Open Office Document if you want to work on an existing Office 2000 document. To *open* a document means that you want to work with the document somehow, just as when you open a file cabinet drawer you want to work with a file from the cabinet.

NEW TERM To *open* a document is to load it into your program workspace so that you can work with it.

When you open an Office 2000 document, a window such as the one in Figure C.3 appears.

Figure C.3.

The Office 2000 Open dialog box.

 The Open dialog boxes in Office 2000 differ somewhat from other Open dialog boxes you'll find in Windows. The Office 2000 Open dialog boxes are customized to give you quicker access to Office 2000 documents.

 As you use Office 2000 more, you learn which *icons* (pictures that represent items on your screen) go with which Office 2000 products. When you display the Open dialog box, the icons indicate which Office 2000 program created the document listed. For example, the flying W icon represents documents created by Word 2000.

New Term   *Icons* are small colorful pictures that represent items on your Windows screen.

The Open dialog box can be simple or complex, depending on what you need to do with it. Most of the time, you see the Office 2000 document that you want to open and you simply double-click the document's name to load it. The Open dialog box is smart enough to know which Office 2000 product created the document; therefore, if you click a PowerPoint 2000 document, the Open dialog box starts PowerPoint 2000 and loads the selected document into PowerPoint 2000 for you.

Each time a new Office 2000 product is introduced in an hour in this book, that hour introduces the program's initial screens and describes how you can begin to create documents from within that product. For now, concentrate on getting an overall feel for the Windows interface.

C

Following is a summary of other common tasks you can perform from the Open dialog box:

- If you want to open a document located in a folder or disk drive other than the one showing, or even on a different computer on a network across the Internet, click the Look in drop-down list box and select the location.

- You can limit the files shown to specific Office 2000 programs by selecting from the drop-down list box labeled Files of Type. For example, the Open dialog box displays only web pages if you select Web Pages.

- The toolbar buttons across the top of the Open dialog box display the files in a different format, giving you more or less detail about the documents that appear. (Rest your mouse pointer on each toolbar button to see what that tool does.)

ToolTips

As you work with the Office 2000 products and dialog boxes, such as the Open dialog box, you'll need to use the toolbar buttons across the top (and sometimes the bottom and sides) of your screen. Office 2000 fully supports Screentips (also called *ToolTips*). Figure C.4 shows an Excel 2000 *ToolTip* describing the button to which it is pointing.

FIGURE C.4.

ToolTips indicate what the buttons do.

ToolTip

ToolTips are floating toolbar button descriptions that appear when you rest your mouse pointer over any toolbar button.

As you read this book, you won't find long boring tables that describe every toolbar button. Let the ToolTips guide you! Although many of the buttons are obvious, you might need to use ToolTips to locate a particular button.

Dialog Boxes

You've probably worked with dialog boxes before. Earlier in this appendix, you saw the Open dialog box. Dialog boxes give you access to a set of related *controls* and selection options that not only let you issue commands, select items, and set options, but also display information.

 Windows contains *controls* such as buttons, labels, and scrollbars that display data values, prompt you for information, and enable you to enter new information and manage the windows.

Starting with Windows 95, many dialog boxes took on an added dimension. Instead of containing a single set of controls, such as command buttons and text boxes, *tabbed dialog boxes* contain several sets of controls. Each set appears on a tabbed page in the dialog box. Figure C.5 shows one such dialog box. Notice the tabs across the top of the dialog box.

Click a tab to see a different dialog box page.

FIGURE C.5.

Windows dialog boxes often contain several pages.

When you click one of the tabs, you display a different page that contains an additional set of dialog box controls within the dialog box. The use of the tabbed pages in dialog boxes gives you access to much more information from a single menu command.

 Tabbed dialog boxes contain pages that hold a set of controls and are common in Office 2000 and other Windows programs.

Printing from Office 2000

Because it is a Windows program, Office 2000 uses the Windows printer subsystem for printing, so you'll always see the same print options throughout the Office 2000 suite of products. Windows controls all printing from Windows programs. Therefore, no matter what kind of printer you connect to Windows, Office 2000 requires only that you inform Office 2000 of the print type or location of the printer.

Windows lets you direct printed output to any printer device, including fax/modems that you might have connected to your computer. Windows always defaults to your system's primary printer, but you can override the default printer by selecting a different target printer.

The most common way to initiate the print process is to select File, Print. Office 2000 opens the Print dialog box shown in Figure C.6.

FIGURE C.6.

The Print dialog box controls all Office 2000 printing.

Your Print dialog box might look different depending on your printer hardware.

With the exception of FrontPage 2000, the Office 2000 products always contain a Print toolbar button that you can use to print, but the Print toolbar button does not display the Print dialog box. Therefore, if you want to select a printer that differs from your usual Windows default printer, or if you want to select different print options, you'll need to use the Office 2000 File, Print menu command to display the Print dialog box before you print.

From the Print dialog box you can change several options, including

- The number of copies
- The range you want to print, such as selected pages or only a portion of text from a single page
- The collation selection of output papers
- The target printer

Before printing, you'll almost always want to preview your printed output on the screen. Although Office 2000 products are generally *WYSIWYG*-based (What You See [on the screen] Is What You Get [on the page]), you rarely see an entire page at once unless you use an extremely high-resolution monitor and graphics adapter. Therefore, when you click the Preview button in the Print dialog box (or select File, Print Preview from the menu bar), Office 2000 displays the printed page on your screen, as shown in Figure C.7. If your output looks correct, you can send it to paper.

 NEW TERM *WYSIWYG* (pronounced *wizzy-wig*) is an acronym for *What You See Is What You Get*, and refers to the concept that your screen shows your output as it will look when printed on paper.

C

When previewing any Office 2000 document, your mouse pointer changes to a magnifying glass. If you click the glass over any portion of the preview, Office 2000 magnifies the preview to make the text more readable (at the expense of displaying less of the preview). Click the magnifying cursor once again, and the preview reverts back to its original full-page state.

FIGURE C.7.

Preview your output before printing it.

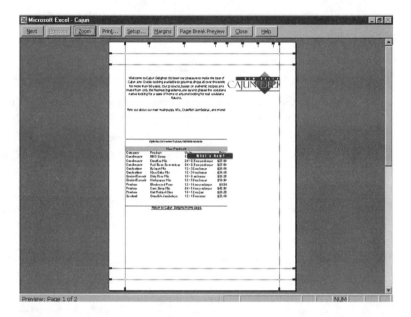

A Word on Shortcut Keys

Often, a menu option or toolbar button has an associated *shortcut key* (sometimes called an *accelerator key*) that you can press to trigger the same operation. For example, if you display Word 2000's File menu, you see that Ctrl+S is an equivalent shortcut key for the File, Save option. The Office 2000 suite of applications uses a consistent shortcut key interface across all programs. Therefore, Ctrl+S saves a document in every Office 2000 program. When you learn one Office 2000 program's shortcut key, you know the other programs' equivalent keys as well.

 A *shortcut key* is a keystroke, often combined with the Ctrl key, that enables you to access a menu option without having to use the menu. *Accelerator key* is another name for shortcut key.

The primary goal of this book is to acquaint you with Office 2000 as quickly as possible, showing you the basics as well as useful shortcuts and tricks to make your Office 2000 life simple. Generally, Office 2000 offers several ways to accomplish the same task. This book does not discuss a lot of the shortcut key equivalents. You see shortcut key equivalents when selecting from Office 2000 menus, and you learn those shortcut keys as you use Office 2000.

If a shortcut key seems obvious (for example, Ctrl+S for the Save operation) and generally easier to use (as opposed to an equivalent menu option or toolbar button), this book teaches you the shortcut key for the task. If, however, the shortcut key is not the best way to trigger a task, this book does not waste your time with the shortcut key description.

As you use Office 2000, you'll discover the shortcut keystrokes that you prefer. Everybody has different preferences.

Windows and the Internet

Microsoft is moving toward integrating between Windows and the Internet. The Internet's slow speed (for dial-up modem-based users) is keeping the Internet from truly integrating into your Windows desktop, but the day is not far off when quick Internet access will be available. Microsoft is preparing for that day by making the Windows operating system as well as products such as Office 2000 as compliant and compatible with the Internet as possible.

If you are a PC user who has not yet worked on the Internet, this book discusses the Internet throughout these 24 hours. You never have to access the Internet to use Office 2000 because Office 2000 is standalone software designed to be used on a PC whether or not that PC is connected to the Internet. Nevertheless, the presence of the Internet runs throughout Office 2000; you don't have to use the Internet features, but if you want them, you'll be surprised at how easily Office 2000 helps bridge the Internet-to-PC connection.

With every copy of Windows sold today, as well as with Office 2000, Microsoft gives you a free Internet *browser* called Internet Explorer. In addition, you'll probably run across a competitor to Internet Explorer named Netscape Navigator. After you locate a provider for Internet access, you'll be able to *surf* the web like a pro.

NEW TERM A *browser* is a program that lets you traverse the Internet and view graphical and textual content that you find.

NEW TERM To *surf* the Internet means to view Web pages that you find while you use the Internet. Browse is another word for surf in Internet terminology.

C

Hours 22, "Office 2000 and the Internet," and 23, "Creating Web Pages with Office 2000," explore some of the ways you can use Office 2000 along with the Internet to accomplish your job. Hour 24, "Introducing FrontPage 2000," examines Microsoft's Internet authoring tool that comes with Office 2000.

If you want to learn more about Windows, check out *Sams Teach Yourself Windows 95 in 24 Hours, Second Edition*; *Sams Teach Yourself Windows 98 in 24 Hours*; *Using Windows 98, Second Edition*; and *Easy Windows 98*.

INDEX

Symbols

3-D special effect (PhotoDraw), 444
35mm slides (PowerPoint), 199

A

Abs() function (Excel), 166
absolute cell addressing (Excel), 160-161
Access, 8
  commands
    Exit (File menu), 302
    Filter (Records menu), 320
    Filter, Filter Excluding Selection (Records menu), 321

    Print (File menu), 311
    Print Preview (File menu), 311
    Show Table (Query menu), 331
    Spelling (Tools menu), 307
  databases, 285-286, 305, 319, 360
    AutoShapes, adding, 360, 364-366
    creating, 292-302
    database management systems, 286
    Datasheet view, 299-301
    entering data, 299-301, 306-316
    exporting to Word documents, 357-358
    fields, 288-291, 295-297

    file images, inserting, 361-362
    filters, 320-323
    keys, setting, 296-297
    objects, 292-293
    queries, 323-332
    quitting, 302
    records, 288-290
    scope, 286
    tables, 287-288, 294-299
    window, 292
    WordArt, inserting, 363
  dialog boxes
    Form Wizard, 312
    New Form, 312
    New Query, 325
    New Report, 339
    New Table, 294
  features, 14-15
  Form Wizard Layout dialog box, 313